THE QUICK-REFERENCE GUIDE TO
BIBLICAL COUNSELING

The Quick-Reference Guide to

BIBLICAL COUNSELING

Personal and Emotional Issues

DR. TIM CLINTON
DR. RON HAWKINS

BakerBooks

a division of Baker Publishing Group
Grand Rapids, Michigan

© 2009 by Tim Clinton

Published in 2009 by Baker Books
a division of Baker Publishing Group
P.O. Box 6287, Grand Rapids, MI 49516-6287
www.bakerbooks.com

Previously published in 2007 under the title *Biblical Counseling Quick Reference Guide: Personal and Emotional Issues* by AACC Press

Printed in the United States of America

Library of Congress Cataloging-in-Publication Data
Clinton, Timothy E., 1960–
    The quick-reference guide to biblical counseling / Tim Clinton and Ron Hawkins.
       p.   cm.
    Includes bibliographical references (p.   ).
    ISBN 978-0-8010-7225-3 (pbk.)
    1. Counseling—Religious aspects—Christianity—Handbooks, manuals, etc. 2. Bible—Psychology—Handbooks, manuals, etc. 3. Pastoral counseling—Handbooks, manuals, etc. 4. Bible—Use—Handbooks, manuals, etc. I. Hawkins, Ronald E. II. Title.
    BR115.C69C48 2009
    253.5—dc22   2009025632

      21   22   23   24   16   15   14   13   12

Contents

Introduction

Since the early days of the American Association of Christian Counselors (AACC), we have been consistently asked to catalog and provide "quick reference" materials that could be easily accessed for the variety of issues faced by pastors and counselors. This first volume on personal and emotional issues—and the volumes to follow—is our response to that legitimate call. Topics for the quick-reference guides are:

Personal and emotional issues

Marriage and family issues

Issues in human sexuality

Teenager issues

Women's issues

Singles issues

Money issues

We are delighted to deliver to you *The Quick-Reference Guide to Biblical Counseling* and trust that God will use it to bring His hope and life to millions of believers throughout America and the world to whom the continually growing membership in the AACC minister.

Everywhere we look in this new millennium, we find people who desperately need God's touch, who cry out constantly for His gracious care. The mind-boggling advances in every professional and scientific field have stoked, along with a multibillion-dollar advertising blitz, the false expectation that we can "have it all, and have it all now." This only reinforces the aching "hole in the soul" that so many suffer in the midst of our material abundance, and intensifies the stress that we all live under in our 24/7 socio-cultural landscape. Does an authentic remedy really exist?

Since you are reading the introduction to this book, you have likely been called to counseling ministry, to a work of authentic caregiving. You have been called and are likely trained to some degree to deliver care and consolation to the many broken-down and brokenhearted souls living in your church and community. You will find this book and this entire series most helpful if you have been called to remind others that "the LORD is close to the brokenhearted; he rescues those whose spirits are crushed" (Ps. 34:18 NLT). He has chosen you as a vessel for delivery of His special grace; you have both the privilege and the responsibility to deliver that care in the most excellent and ethical way possible.

There are a number of critical attributes that you need to exhibit toward others if you are called to intervene in someone's most needy of times—if you are called to "bear one another's burdens" in a way that will "fulfill the law of Christ" (Gal. 6:2). The first characteristic is something you have as a result of God's Spirit working in you and transforming your heart and mind—something that this book cannot give you but can only enhance if you already have it. This is a spirit of authentic kindness—the kindness that draws others to you automatically because they sense that you really do care.

This also reveals a compassionate empathy that can deeply relate to others because you too have walked a path of suffering and pain and yet have not turned bitter or cynical. Instead, you have learned to trust God in everything—especially in those things of life that you would not choose to suffer. You have found God to be faithful to you and yours, and you know Him (which is distinct from *merely knowing about Him*) to be loving and wise and strong and kind. You have truly come to know that "God is our merciful Father and the source of all comfort. He comforts us in all our troubles so that we can comfort others. When they are troubled, we will be able to give them the same comfort God has given us" (2 Cor. 1:3–4 NLT). And if you consistently deliver this comfort and care with integrity, you are a trustworthy servant in whom God delights and blesses in all that you do.

Added to the twin characteristics of authenticity and empathy are the twin requirements of knowledge and skill—something this book can help deliver to you more directly. The knowledge base of biblical and theological studies, combined with the behavioral and social sciences, is advancing far faster than anyone can keep up with in the twenty-first century. Therefore, we have culled from this burgeoning data the most critical and relevant facts and contextual clues that you should know for each of the forty topics that make up the content of this and all the books to follow. Finally, the eight-step outline we follow in every chapter will shape your thinking and mold your process so as to increase your skill as a counselor, in whatever role you do such work.

THE THREE LEGS OF HELPING MINISTRY

We have written these books to apply to every leg of our three-legged stool metaphor. We advance the idea that the helping ministry of the church is made up of *pastors*, who serve in a central case-managing role, as the client nearly always returns to the role of parishioner; of *professional Christian counselors*, often who serve many churches in a given geographic area; and of *lay helpers*, who have been trained and serve in the church in individual or group leadership roles.

People serving at all three levels must develop both the character and servant qualities that reflect the grace and truth of Christ Himself. God has also distributed His gifts liberally throughout the church to perform the various ministry tasks that are central to any healthy church operation. For no matter how skilled or intelligent or caring we are, unless we directly rely on the Spirit of God to work in us to do the ministry of God, it will not bear kingdom fruit. He will bring to us the people He wants us to help, and we must learn to depend on Him to touch others in a supernatural way—so that people exclaim, "God showed up (and miracles happened) in that counseling session today!"

Pastor or Church Staff

If you are a pastor or church staff member, virtually everyone sitting in your pews today has been (or soon will be) touched by addiction, divorce, violence, depression, grief, confusion, loneliness, and a thousand other evidences of living as broken people in a fallen world. This guidebook will help you:

- deliver effective counseling and short-term help to those who will come to you with their issues
- teach others and construct sermons about the leading issues of the day with which people struggle
- provide essential resources and materials for staff and lay leaders in your church to advance their helping and teaching ministries

Professional Clinician

If you are a professional clinician, licensed or certified in one of the six major clinical disciplines, you are likely already familiar with most of the topics in this book. It will assist you best to:

- review the definitions and assessment questions to use in your initial session with a new client
- understand and incorporate a biblical view of the client's problem
- shape your treatment plans with the best principles and resources available from the AACC
- deliver information to your clients that best helps them get unstuck and move forward more resolutely with the right thinking and focused action of this treatment process

Lay Leader or Minister

If you are a lay leader or minister, this book will help you plan and deliver the best care you can from beginning to end. We recommend that you read through the entire book, highlighting the material most useful to you in either individual or group formats. This guide will best help you to:

- understand and accurately assess the person's problem
- guide discussions and deliver helpful suggestions without assuming too much control or yielding too little influence
- remember key principles in the process of moving from problem to resolution more effectively
- remember the limits of lay ministry and make constructive referral to others who have more training

USING *THE QUICK-REFERENCE GUIDE TO BIBLICAL COUNSELING*

You will notice that we have divided each topic into an outlined format that follows the logic of the counseling process. The goal and purpose of each of the eight parts is as follows:

1. **Portraits.** Each topic begins with three or four vignettes that tell common stories about people struggling with the issue at hand. We have tried to deliver stories that you will most often encounter with the people you serve.

2. **Definitions and Key Thoughts.** This section begins with a clear definition of the issue in nontechnical language. Then we add a variety of ideas and data points to help you gain a fuller understanding of the issue and how it lives in and harms the people who struggle with it.

3. **Assessment.** This usually begins by suggesting a framework by which to approach assessment and is followed by a series of specific questions to ask to gain a more complete understanding of the client's problem. There may a section of "rule-out questions" that will help you determine whether referral to a physician or other professional is needed.

4. **Wise Counsel.** This section usually presents one or more key ideas that should serve as an overarching guide to your intervention—wise counsel will help you frame your interventions in a better way. These key insights may be cast in either clinical or pastoral form but they are useful to all three types of helpers we have noted above and will give you an edge in understanding and working with the person(s) in front of you.

5. **Action Steps.** This section—along with wise counsel—will guide you in what to do in your counseling interventions. It allows you to construct a logical map that can guide you and your client from problem identification to resolution in a few measured steps—always client action steps (with specific instructions to counselors noted in italics). For without a good action plan, it is too easy to leave clients confused and drifting rather than moving in a determined fashion toward some concrete change goals.

6. **Biblical Insights.** Here we provide relevant Bible passages and commentary to assist you in your counseling work from beginning to end. Embedding the entire process in a biblical framework and calling on the Lord's power to do many things we cannot do solely in our own strength are essential to doing authentic Christian counseling. You may choose to give your clients these verses as homework for study or memorization or as a guide to spiritual direction, or you may want to use them as guides for the intervention process.

7. **Prayer Starter.** While not appropriate with every client, many Christians want—and even expect—prayer to be an integral part of your helping intervention. You should ask each client for his or her consent to prayer interventions, and every client can and should be prayed for, even if he or she does not join you and you must pray silently, or in pre- or post-session reflection. Prayer is usually the most common spiritual intervention used in Christian counseling, and we prompt a few lines of good prayer that can serve, in whole or part, as

effective introductions to taking counseling vertically and inviting God directly into the relationship.

8. **Recommended Resources.** We list here some of the most well-known Christian resources and the best secular resources for additional reading and study. By no means an exhaustive list, it will tune you to other resources that will in turn reference further works that will allow you to go as deep as you want in the study of an issue.

ADDITIONAL RESOURCES

The AACC is a ministry and professional organization of nearly fifty thousand members in the United States and around the world. We are dedicated to providing and delivering the finest resources available to pastors, professional counselors, and lay helpers in whatever role or setting such services are delivered. With our award-winning magazine, *Christian Counseling Today*, we also deliver a comprehensive range of education, training, ethical direction, consulting, books, and conference events to enhance the ministry of Christian counseling worldwide. Visit www .aacc.net.

The AACC provides additional books, curricula, training, and conferences to equip you fully for the work of helping ministry in whatever form you do it. While some of these are noted in section 8 in every chapter of this book, some additional resources for your growth might also include:

The Bible for Hope: Caring for People God's Way by Tim Clinton and many other leading contributors (Thomas Nelson Publishers, 2006).

Competent Christian Counseling: Foundations and Practice of Compassionate Soul Care by Tim Clinton, George Ohlschlager, and many leading contributors (Water-Brook Press, 2002).

Caring for People God's Way (and *Marriage and Family Counseling* and *Healthy Sexuality*—upcoming books in the same series) by Tim Clinton, Arch Hart, and George Ohlschlager (Thomas Nelson Publishers, 2005).

Light University also provides various church and home-based training courses on:

Caring for People God's Way

Breaking Free

Marriage Works

Healthy Sexuality

Extraordinary Women

Caring for Kids God's Way

Caring for Teens God's Way

Please come online at either aacc.net or at ecounseling.com to consider other resources and services delivered by AACC for the growth and betterment of the church.

Abortion

PORTRAITS

- Kate is in trouble—big time. She's got a scholarship waiting at her chosen college, a great boyfriend, a leadership role in her church youth group, and an at-home pregnancy test that just turned positive. She can't give up her dreams for this one mistake. Besides, it's such a simple procedure, and no one needs to know . . .

- *I have been forgiven, I know it, but why can't I get over this?* Nancy kept repeating the words to herself as she glanced down the pew at church where her two little daughters squirmed beside her, waiting for the chance to be released to go to children's church. She tried to concentrate on the sermon but the Right to Life announcement in the bulletin claimed all of her attention. *I didn't realize what I was doing.*

DEFINITIONS AND KEY THOUGHTS

- The term *abortion* actually refers to any premature expulsion of a human fetus, whether naturally spontaneous, as in a miscarriage, or artificially induced, as in a surgical or chemical abortion. Today the most common usage of the term *abortion* applies to *artificially induced abortion.*

- A young woman with an unplanned pregnancy will need to understand that the *"quick and easy" choice is neither quick nor easy* but will carry repercussions for the rest of her life.

- Often a woman chooses to keep the abortion a secret, especially if she is part of a Christian community that she perceives might be judgmental or condemning. Her own family members might not know. Therefore the *grief and loss* surrounding an abortion may remain unprocessed for years.

- An abortion is *not only experienced as a loss but also often as a trauma.* Some of the possible side effects are both a tendency to reexperience the trauma, such as distressing dreams or flashbacks, and a tendency toward denial and the attempt to avoid all thoughts or feelings associated with the abortion.

- Possible other *side effects* from the trauma of an abortion are emotional numbing, sleep disorders, difficulty concentrating, hypervigilance, depression, guilt, and an inability to forgive oneself.

> Nearly half of pregnancies among American women are unintended, and four in ten of these are terminated by abortion.[1]

- Coping alone with the reality of an abortion is isolating and may reinforce a woman's *sense of shame*. Self-destructive behaviors, such as substance abuse, may also be present.
- If someone confides in you that she has had an abortion, realize that in sharing this experience, she has decided to trust you. *Be careful with any verbal or nonverbal behaviors* that might complicate her guilt and shame.

Myths about Abortion

Twenty-two percent of all pregnancies (excluding miscarriages) end in abortion.[2]

Myth 1: "It's a simple procedure; life will resume on Monday."

Myth 2: "It's not a baby; it's a blob of tissue."

Myth 3: "It's okay; abortion is legal."

Myth 4: "My life will be ruined if I have this baby."

Myth 5: "It's *my* choice, *my* responsibility, *my* decision."

Myth 6: "It's okay to have an abortion if there's something wrong with the baby."

Myth 7: "I am alone; no one cares about me."

Myth 8: "I don't deserve forgiveness; I knew it was wrong."

Myth 9: "I got what I deserved; I did it more than once."

Myth 10: "This won't hurt; the pain will subside."

Myth 11: "It is my only option; he doesn't want the baby."

Myth 12: "It's okay in cases of rape or incest."

From *A Time to Speak: A Healing Journal for Post-Abortive Women*
by Yvonne Florczak-Seeman

3 ASSESSMENT INTERVIEW

For the Woman Contemplating Abortion

1. How do you know that you are pregnant? Have you had a medical examination? (*These gentle questions about the pregnancy will help the counselee feel comfortable and take responsibility.*)
2. How far along are you in your pregnancy?
3. What are your current life circumstances?
4. What do you expect will be your family's response to your pregnancy?
5. Do you have adequate social support?
6. Who is the baby's father? What kind of relationship do you have with him?
7. Have you considered any other options besides abortion? Have you thought about carrying the baby to term?
8. What do you see happening in your life if you have an abortion? What do you see happening if you make a different choice? (*Often abortion is chosen because no other option looks even possible. Sometimes the decision to have an abortion is made quickly to "solve the problem." Communicate with your*

counselee that she has some time to make her decision. Help her see that her life will not be "ruined" if she carries her baby to term.)

9. Do you have any questions about pregnancy and abortion? (*Do not assume that she is fully informed about either.*)

For the Woman Who Had an Abortion in the Past

1. What is currently causing distress in your life?
2. Take me back and tell me what happened. (*Listen for any signs of post-traumatic stress, such as disturbing dreams or triggers that bring back the event. By choosing to begin to tell you her story, she is breaking her silence, which is the beginning of the healing process but also potentially disturbing, as denial of the event is no longer possible.*)
3. What were the main reasons at the time for your making the choice that you did?
4. Do you feel depressed, down, or sad most of the time?
5. Do you have difficulty eating or sleeping?
6. Do you have suicidal thoughts? (*If suicidal tendencies are evident, see the section on Suicide and get other help immediately.*)
7. Are you using drugs or alcohol to deal with the pain?
8. How are you managing life now? What triggers your pain?
9. Do you feel that you have been forgiven by God? Why or why not?
10. Do you feel that you can forgive yourself? Why or why not?

> In 2005, 1.21 million abortions were performed, down from 1.31 million in 2000. From 1973 through 2005, more than 45 million legal abortions occurred.[3]

WISE COUNSEL 4

Be sure to provide the woman contemplating abortion with *adequate practical support* to encourage her to carry her baby to term. Have on hand information about agencies that provide medical care and a home to stay in for pregnant women. Emphasize to her that she is making a decision for both her life and her baby's life. Encourage her to see the longer perspective rather than going to college next semester or keeping her place on a sports team. Address any *behaviors that endanger your counselee's safety*, such as suicidal behavior or substance abuse.

1. Ask God for forgiveness.
2. Accept God's forgiveness.
3. Forgive yourself.
4. Seek professional and pastoral care.
5. Visualize God holding your baby.
6. When God gives grace, serve in some capacity to help pregnant young women.

5 ACTION STEPS

For the Woman Contemplating Abortion

1. Consider Options

- You may feel that your only option is an abortion. This simply isn't so. Throughout the United States, there are nearly three thousand Crisis Pregnancy Centers (CPC) staffed by volunteers who want to give true alternatives and who will lovingly help you.
- Find the nearest CPC in your community. Look in the Yellow Pages under the heading "Abortion Alternatives" or call 1-800-848-LOVE.

2. Communicate

- You will need to communicate with other family members about the situation.
- *Assess how to do that (depending on what you know of the family members). You may need to be involved as a third party in such a conversation.*

3. Get Help

- *Encourage the young woman and her parents to contact the Crisis Pregnancy Center together.*

4. Follow Up

- *Be sure to follow up with her by setting another appointment.*
- Although you may regret your pregnancy, you can begin immediately to make some wise choices regarding the future of your baby.

For the Woman Who Had an Abortion in the Past

1. Tell Your Story

- Continue to tell your story through future counseling sessions and journaling.

2. Get Help

- Several organizations and materials exist to facilitate the healing from abortion. *Know which ones exist in your area for a referral. Some possible organizations are A Time To Speak, Project Rachael, and Victims of Choice.*

3. Find Support

- *If there is a confidential grief support group in your area, encourage your counselee to attend.*

4. Be Reassured

- *Be sure to communicate both verbally and nonverbally your acceptance of her and God's forgiveness to her.*

Each year about 2 percent of women aged fifteen to forty-four have an abortion; 47 percent of them have had at least one previous abortion.[4]

Healing from an abortion is a process and certainly cannot be accomplished in one session; however, healing is possible. Reassure your counselee that forgiveness, including an ability to accept God's forgiveness and to forgive herself, are possible through God's grace.

Abortion is not the unforgivable sin.

BIBLICAL INSIGHTS 6

If men fight, and hurt a woman with child, so that she gives birth prematurely, yet no harm follows, he shall surely be punished accordingly as the woman's husband imposes on him; and he shall pay as the judges determine.

Exodus 21:22

This verse shows God's protection of the most defenseless people on the planet—children in the womb. Even causing a premature but otherwise healthy birth was a punishable offense.

God is the champion of life and has always protected women, children, and the weakest members of society.

A baby's heart begins to beat around twenty-two days after conception.[5]

Your eyes saw my substance, being yet unformed. And in Your book they all were written, the days fashioned for me, when as yet there were none of them.

Psalm 139:16

God knows each person from the moment of conception. His eyes see the unformed body in the mother's womb.

Many claim that a child in the womb is no more than a mass of tissue, but the Bible makes it clear that God sees the tiny embryo as a new life with a future already prepared.

To abort a child is to end a human life unjustly.

Before I formed you in the womb I knew you; before you were born I sanctified you; I ordained you a prophet to the nations.

Jeremiah 1:5

God is well acquainted with every individual from the time each person is conceived. He has plans for each one.

God knows everything, so He knows that some young lives will end all too soon.

Then Herod, when he saw that he was deceived by the wise men, was exceedingly angry; and he sent forth and put to death all the male children who were in Bethlehem and in all its districts, from two years old and under, according to the time which he had determined from the wise men.

Matthew 2:16

> The highest percentages of reported abortions were for women unmarried (82 percent), white (55 percent), and aged less than twenty-five years (52 percent).[6]

Although the arguments over abortion almost always use the language of agonizing choices between two lives, the practice of abortion almost always comes down to the choice between a life and convenience or between a life and other plans or between a life and a lifestyle.

The thinking that makes an unborn child disposable doesn't have to change much before people consider the elimination of unwanted living children.

The defenders of the "right of choice" believe they can make any choice they want and that a choice is right because they made it. Choice may be a human right, but every choice isn't a right one.

There is an absolute standard in the character and revelation of God. All choices we make will be measured against this standard and we will be accountable for them.

Focus on heaven and God's care of the child for eternity (see 2 Sam. 12:22–23).

7 PRAYER STARTER

Lord, we pray for Your grace and wisdom to overflow into this woman's life. She is worried, scared, and needs a touch from you . . .

8 RECOMMENDED RESOURCES

Florczak-Seeman, Yvonne. *A Time to Speak: A Healing Journal for Post-Abortive Women.* Love From Above, 2005. Books can be purchased at www.lovefromaboveinc.com.

Focus on the Family. *Post-Abortion Kit: Resources for Those Suffering from the Aftermath of Abortion*, n.d.

Freed, Luci, and Penny Yvonne Salazar. *A Season to Heal: Help and Hope for Those Working through Post-Abortion Stress.* Cumberland House Publishing, 1996.

Reardon, David. *Aborted Women—Silent No More.* Acorn Books, 2002.

Websites
Ecounseling (www.ecounseling.com)

Focus on the Family (www.family.org)

Justice for All (www.jfaweb.org)

Addictions

- Rachel was very active in the church, along with her family. Although she was not always reliable, she was eager to help. She attended church regularly—even the midweek services. One Sunday evening Rachel came in late. She was loud and obviously drunk. Her children were in tow and very embarrassed.
- Tim never seemed to have money for all his bills. He was also sick a lot with a constant stuffy nose. Then a congregation member saw him on a street corner in the city playing the cello and begging for money.
- Dawn loved the bingo games. No one thought much about it until a neighbor discovered her young children home alone one night while Dawn was playing the cards at the bingo parlor.
- Reggie had always been famous for how many beers he could drink without feeling any effects. But something had changed. He'd been drunk several times recently, according to friends. You're called in when he's arrested for a DUI.

> Fifty percent of child abuse and neglect cases are connected with the alcohol or drug use of a guardian.[1]

DEFINITIONS AND KEY THOUGHTS : 2

- An addiction is *a dependence on a substance* (alcohol, prescription medicine, marijuana, or street drugs) *or activity* (gambling, shopping).
- An addiction is *a physical* (as in alcohol or most other drugs) *or psychological* (as in gambling or shopping) *compulsion* to use a substance or activity *to cope with everyday life.* For example, without alcohol, the alcoholic does not feel "normal" and cannot function well.
- Addiction is a behavior that is *habitual and difficult or seemingly impossible to control.* It leads to activity that is designed solely to *obtain the substance or cover up its use*—the housewife hiding bottles all over the house, the drug addict shoplifting to support the habit, the gambler embezzling to pay off debts.
- Characterized by the *defense mechanism of denial*, the addict blames his or her problems on someone else—the boss is too difficult, the spouse isn't affectionate enough, the kids are disobedient, or the friends are too persuasive. The addict refuses to take responsibility.

> In 2001 there were 1.4 million arrests for driving under the influence of alcohol or narcotics. That is 1 out of every 137 drivers.[2]

- *Drug addiction is the biochemical dependence* on a substance—over time the body needs the substance in ever-increasing amounts to stave off the symptoms of withdrawal.
- *Non-drug addictions* include compulsive overeating, gambling, sexual addiction, such as that to pornography (see the section on Pornography), compulsive spending, and smoking.

Causes of Addiction

- *Emotional:* Addicts are emotionally wounded. One study of sex addicts found 81 percent to be sexually abused, 74 percent physically abused, and 97 percent emotionally abused (from *Don't Call It Love* by Patrick Carnes, Mark Laaser, and Debra Laaser).
- *Relational:* Addictive behaviors are positively related to troublesome early life relationships. For adults, addiction causes stress in interpersonal relationships and leads to social difficulties.
- *Physical:* Addicts become physically dependent on their substances of abuse, experiencing withdrawal without them.
- *Cognitive and Behavioral:* Addicts often have illogical or irrational thoughts that cause them to forget their identity as children of God. Unrealistic expectations about themselves and others are also common.
- *Spiritual:* Addiction at its core is rebellion against God. In addition, whether it is drugs, alcohol, or sex, the addiction becomes a false idol to the addict.

Character of Addiction

- *Unmanageability:* For addicts, their dependency on the addiction is out of their control.
- *Neurochemical Tolerance:* God designed our bodies to adapt to what is presented. Therefore, addicts experience tolerance—their bodies need increasing amounts of a chemical/behavior to procure the same effect.
- *Progression:* Many addicts begin by simply experimenting—trying out a drug, going to a casino, taking a puff on a cigarette. However, because more is needed to achieve an effect, the addict will increase addictive actions in strength or frequency.
- *Feeling Avoidance:* The addiction is used to improve the addict's emotional/psychological state—it is a way of avoiding feelings, such as loneliness, anxiety, anger, and sorrow.
- *Consequences:* Estrangement from God, the manifestation of habitual sin, health issues, and social and interpersonal problems are all consequences common to addiction.

ASSESSMENT INTERVIEW 3

Remember that *a key characteristic of addiction is denial*. The substance use is rarely an issue for the user. Breaking down this denial is part of your job in assessment (if it already seems clear that dependency exists).

When interviewing the user, *focus on asking concrete questions* about circumstances, events, and symptoms. If asked in a nonthreatening and nonjudgmental fashion, the counselee should respond fairly honestly. If speaking with a family member, reframe these questions and ask them about the user.

Rule Outs

1. Has your use of this substance increased or decreased over the years? (*Tolerance, or the need for increasing amounts of the substance, is a key distinguishing factor between a substance abuse problem and dependency. Answering yes to the following questions about alcohol use indicates dependency as well.*)

2. (*If alcohol is the substance*) Have you ever experienced a time when you did not remember what you did while drinking (you had a blackout)? Have you ever experienced anxiety, panic attacks, shakes, or hallucinations after not drinking for a while?

General Questions

1. Has anyone ever suggested that your use of _____ is a problem? If so, why do you think the person said that?
2. Have you ever been concerned about your use of _____? If so, why?
3. How often do you use this substance and how much at each use?
4. Do you ever try to hide your use from family members or friends?
5. At what age did you first use _____?
6. Have you ever done anything while under the influence of _____ that you later regretted? Have you ever had a conviction or ticket for driving under the influence?
7. Did anyone in your family of origin use a substance in excess while you were growing up? Who?
8. Has your use of _____ ever affected your job or your family? What happened?
9. Have you ever quit using the substance? What happened when you did? How did you feel?
10. Do you want to quit for good?
11. How do you see your life improving if you can quit using _____?

Approximately 40 percent of all crimes are committed under the influence of alcohol; 40 percent of people convicted of rape or sexual assault state that they were drinking at the time of the offense; 72 percent of rapes on college campuses occur while victims are intoxicated.[3]

In 2007, there were 12,998 fatalities in crashes involving an *alcohol-impaired* driver (BAC of .08 or higher)—32 percent of total traffic fatalities for the year.[4]

4 WISE COUNSEL

Safety is always the key issue. Try to find out if the user has been driving under the influence or has small children at home who might be endangered. If so, take immediate steps to protect the user and others.

Try to speak with other family members, who are old enough to understand, about how to handle the user's behaviors, in particular driving under the influence. Family members must be taught to say no to rides with the user or to call for help if the user is unable to supervise younger children.

If physical or sexual abuse occurs when the user is under the influence, encourage *family members to leave the home immediately,* going to a relative's home or a shelter for victims of domestic violence and reporting the behavior to appropriate authorities.

If *verbal abuse* is an issue when the user is under the influence, encourage family members to seek counseling, especially counseling or group sessions for family members of addicts.

> Traffic fatalities in alcohol-impaired driving crashes decreased nearly 4 percent from 13,491 in 2006 to 12,998 in 2007.[5]

5 ACTION STEPS

1. Sign a Contract of Accountability

- *The user must sign a contract with you that he or she will stop use and get immediate help for the addiction.*

2. Do Not Drive

- *Get rid of the user's car the first time he or she drives under the influence—this sets a clear boundary regarding substance abuse.*
- *To protect family members, the user, and innocent bystanders, you need to convince this person to stop driving or doing anything while under the influence.*
- *The Club and other antitheft devices prohibit driving; sophisticated electronic devices can prevent driving unless a breathalyzer test is first passed.*
- *Point out that this is for the good of the user and others and that continued usage will cause repercussions in the rest of his or her life, such as not being able to drive to work or other places.*

> For the drunkard and the glutton will come to poverty.
> *Proverbs 23:21*

3. Get a Thorough Medical Checkup

- A medical exam will rule out any medical problems caused by use of the substance.
- With an addiction such as alcoholism, treatment from a doctor is certainly recommended.

4. Get Professional Help

- Allow a professional in chemical dependency to assess whether your substance use is an addiction. Such assessments are available at community mental health agencies, some hospitals, and community substance abuse centers (common in urban and suburban areas and through county governments in many rural areas).

5. Encourage Family Members to Seek Support

- Your community may have support groups such as Al-Anon, Families Anonymous, or a Christ-centered 12-step recovery program. *You may need to do some research to direct the family to a good program. These programs are based on the Twelve Steps of Alcoholism, the most successful program in the world for treating addiction.*

BIBLICAL INSIGHTS 6

Woe to those who rise early in the morning, that they may follow intoxicating drink; who continue until night, till wine inflames them!

Isaiah 5:11

Many alcoholics are so dependent on alcohol that they begin early in the morning and continue drinking until late at night.

The tragedy of addiction is that it controls and dominates the desires and choices of the addicted.

The even greater tragedy is that addicted people reject the Lord's work in their lives. God alone can provide the lasting comfort, joy, and relief that people mistakenly seek in alcohol.

And I said to her, "You shall stay with me many days; you shall not play the harlot, nor shall you have a man—so, too, will I be toward you."

Hosea 3:3

Addictions are powerful enemies to our relationship with God. Whether the addiction is to alcohol, drugs, sex, gambling, web-surfing, shopping, or whatever, addicted people can attest to their seeming inability to control their desires.

Addictions usually begin very subtly—an experience, substance, or individual that brings pleasure begins to become an obsession. Eventually, the obsession takes control. Rarely can a person escape the addiction without some form of intervention.

Addicts must determine to change, replace the addictive substance/behavior with something more wholesome.

In fatal crashes in 2007 the highest percentage of drivers with a BAC level of .08 or higher was for drivers ages 21 to 24 (35 percent), followed by ages 25 to 34 (29 percent) and 35 to 44 (25 percent).[6]

The 12,998 fatalities in alcohol-impaired-driving crashes during 2007 represent an average of one alcohol-impaired-driving fatality every 40 minutes.[7]

In 2005, a total of 33,541 persons died of drug-induced causes in the United States.[8]

Addictions destroy individuals, families, friendships, reputations, and careers. Addictions make people victims of their own desires. Despite all this, God offers hope to the addict. God wants to free His people from anything that takes His rightful place in their lives. He wants to show them that He can meet all their needs. With God's help and the compassionate accountability of other believers, addicts can be set free—bought back. Jesus has already paid the price.

All things are lawful for me, but all things are not helpful. All things are lawful for me, but I will not be brought under the power of any.

1 Corinthians 6:12

God gave people "richly all things to enjoy" (1 Tim. 6:17), but Satan works tirelessly to take God's blessings and twist them into evil.

Believers are allowed to enjoy many things as long as they are not forbidden by Scripture. But they must never allow themselves to be controlled or "brought under the power of any."

In 2005, a total of 21,634 persons died of alcohol-induced causes in the United States.[9]

Therefore put to death your members which are on the earth: fornication, uncleanness, passion, evil desire, and covetousness, which is idolatry. Because of these things the wrath of God is coming upon the sons of disobedience.

Colossians 3:5–6

These verses describe some of those sinful desires that believers should "put to death." Sexual sins, evil desires, and covetousness (a form of idolatry) should have no place in a believer's heart.

It takes a conscious daily decision to say no to these sinful temptations and rely on the Holy Spirit's power to overcome them.

7 PRAYER STARTER

Dear Lord, thank You that _____ has come here today to seek help for an addiction. Please help him [her] be open to considering that this might be a true addiction for which he [she] needs to get practical assistance. Lead us by Your Holy Spirit to the resources that will be most helpful and thank You for Your willingness to forgive even addiction . . .

8 RECOMMENDED RESOURCES

Anderson, Neil T., and Mike and Julia Quarles. *Freedom from Addiction: Breaking the Bondage of Addiction and Finding Freedom in Christ.* Gospel Light, 1996.

Arterburn, Stephen. *Healing Is a Choice: 10 Decisions That Will Transform Your Life and 10 Lies That Can Prevent You from Making Them.* Thomas Nelson Publishers, 2007.

Clinton, Tim. *Turn Your Life Around: Breaking Free from Your Past to a New and Better You.* Faith Words, 2006.

Hart, Archibald D. *Healing Life's Hidden Addictions: Overcoming the Closet Compulsions That Waste Your Time and Control Your Life.* Vine Books, 1991.

Laaser, Mark. *Healing the Wounds of Sexual Addiction.* Zondervan, 2004.

Websites

American Association of Christian Counselors (www.aacc.net)

Ecounseling (www.ecounseling.com)

From 2001 to 2005, there were approximately 79,000 deaths annually attributable to either excessive or hazardous drinking—making alcohol the third actual leading cause of death.[10]

Adultery

1 PORTRAITS

- Carol wanted to trust Don. She continually reminded herself that Don was a good father and husband. She would push out of her mind the thoughts that there might be someone else. Then one morning, as she was cleaning up his den, she found a credit card statement that detailed hotels and restaurant charges in New York. She had not heard Don talk about traveling there.
- Barb enjoyed working with her boss, Carl. Their conversations were stimulating and she always came away feeling affirmed. She was thankful that she had such a good relationship with him . . . until it became more than that. Her eyes filled with tears as she began to recount their affair. "I can't remember exactly when we started having more feelings for each other," Barb recounted. "I never imagined it would lead to this!"

2 DEFINITIONS AND KEY THOUGHTS

- Adultery occurs when someone has a sexual relationship with *someone other than one's spouse*. This relationship may or may not include an emotional connection.
- Adultery may also involve an emotional affair. Less understood, an *emotional affair can be even more threatening* to a marriage than physical adultery. It occurs when the husband or wife turns to someone outside the marriage for primary emotional support. For example, when a couple is experiencing conflict, hostility, or distancing, and the husband or wife turns to a friend of the opposite sex for companionship, support, and sharing of personal information, an emotional affair has begun.
- Tragically, infidelity in marriage is becoming *increasingly common*. Christians are just as likely to be tempted to marital unfaithfulness as non-Christians. Women are as likely to have an affair as men.
- *Poor communication, unresolved conflict, and/or unrealistic expectations* leading to marital dissatisfaction are common reasons for extramarital affairs. Any perceived need that goes unfulfilled in marriage will seek its expression elsewhere.
- Spouses may become involved in affairs because they are exposed to situations for which they are *unprepared* or *have not set wise boundaries*.

He heals the brokenhearted and binds up their wounds.
Psalm 147:3

- Many affairs begin so gradually as *well-meaning friendships* that the people involved are unaware of how the relationship is changing until significant behavior occurs.

- Infidelity can also stem from emotional deprivation in childhood when a person had a *constant hunger for approval and attention.* If the spouse cannot fulfill these needs, the person will feel cheated and let down and will seek the attention of others outside the marriage relationship.

- Many adulterers think they are looking for love when in fact they are seeking to *feel better about themselves.*

- A person may be unfaithful as an act of *retaliation and anger* against his or her spouse.

- For some, as money and positions of power increase, so does an increasing *sense of entitlement* to life's pleasures. It is therefore not surprising that this can extend to the sexual realm as well.

- Ultimately, adultery is a *self-centered choice,* intentionally ignoring the needs of one's spouse and family and the commandments of God to satisfy one's own selfish desires.

- At its root, adultery is about a *lifestyle of deception.*

> The best way to ensure your marriage is to maintain your friendship. A lot of times, what men miss most is the time they spend just hanging out with their wives. That's why so many affairs begin as friendships—it's that intimacy a man is looking for.
>
> *Scott Stanley*

ASSESSMENT INTERVIEW 3

For the Faithful Spouse

1. How did you find out about the infidelity?
2. How long have you known?
3. What do you feel you need right now in light of this information?
4. What feelings has this stirred up for you? (*It is not uncommon for the person to feel a variety of emotions from resentment to sadness.*)
5. What do you want to do about your relationship with your spouse?
6. Are you willing to work with a professional counselor to explore the wounds that have been created?

For the Unfaithful Spouse

1. Have you told your spouse?
2. What prompts you to want to discuss this now?
3. Do you want to restore your marriage? (*It is not uncommon for the offending spouse to feel confused as to what he or she wants to do, especially if the affair was longstanding and/or involved a deep emotional commitment.*)

> You shall not commit adultery.
>
> *Exodus 20:14*

If the Unfaithful Spouse Wants to Restore the Marriage

1. Are you willing to completely cut off all ties to the third party? (*This is the most significant question. You will be able to tell a lot by how the person replies. Is there hesitation? Does he or she avoid eye contact?*)

2. Do you desire to explore the reasons that perpetuated the affair?

3. Are you aware of what needs you were seeking to have met from this relationship?

4. What do you see are the effects on your spouse as a result of your having an affair?

5. Are you willing to take full responsibility for your actions without placing any blame on your spouse?

6. Are you committed to being accountable for your time and relationships on a daily basis?

7. Are you willing to pursue professional counseling?

4 WISE COUNSEL

Healing is possible after infidelity. Increasing numbers of couples are braving the path of forgiveness and the restoration of their marriages. To begin the healing process, both spouses will need to:

- *understand what caused the infidelity in the marriage.* This will require a long, thoughtful look at the marital pattern that has developed, as well as what each person has contributed to the marital breakdown. Difficult though it is, each spouse should focus on his or her own issues as opposed to criticizing and blaming the other person for the problem of infidelity.

- *rebuild trust in each other* by telling each other the truth and by being accountable to each other. It is vital for each person to keep his or her word. If one spouse promises to do something, he or she needs to follow through and do it. Finally, trust can be rebuilt by using gestures of affection and nonsexual touch to express caring and affirmation.

- *take time for restoring and enriching the marriage.* The restoration process involves identifying and reestablishing what was good about the marriage before the adultery. The enriching process involves learning and implementing new skills and behaviors to strengthen the relationship.

> By the most conservative estimate . . . in the United States, 1 in every 2.7 couples—some 20 million—is touched by infidelity. That number equals almost 4 out of 10 husbands and 2 out of 10 wives.
>
> *Janis Abrahams Spring*

If the Counselee Is the Faithful Spouse

There is a normal process of grieving that occurs when someone has been deeply wounded. (See Elisabeth Kübler-Ross and David Kessler, *On Grief and Grieving: Finding the Meaning of Grief through the Five Stages of Loss.* Scribner, 2007.)

- *Shock and Denial.* The "No, not me" stage is when the wounded spouse is unwilling to accept the reality of the spouse's unfaithfulness. He or she may blatantly deny facts presented about the spouse's activities.
- *Anger.* The "Why me?" stage is when the person is aware of being violated and hurt and may express deep resentment and/or rage toward the unfaithful spouse.
- *Bargaining.* In the "If I do this, you'll do that" stage, the person wants to see changes in behavior as an avenue to avoid further pain. For example, he or she says, "If you stay, I'll change," rather than addressing the deeper implications of the infidelity.
- *Depression.* The "It really happened" stage is when the person realizes the full impact of the infidelity on the marriage and mourns the loss of what the relationship once was. The wounded spouse realizes he or she will need to make a decision as to the future of the relationship.
- *Acceptance.* The "This is what happened" stage is when the person has come to terms with all of the implications of the unfaithful spouse's actions and is willing to move forward.

These stages can be experienced rapidly within a few hours, or across days or months, depending on the individual. You need to *evaluate which stage the person is currently experiencing* and be sensitive to gently encouraging him or her to work through that stage. *Note*: The stages of grieving may be experienced out of order, several at once, and a person may repeat these stages many times.

Encourage the person to *avoid immediately making any long-term decisions*. It is not uncommon for a hurt spouse to have feelings of wanting to end the marriage because the task of rebuilding the relationship seems as though it would take too much energy.

Separation, especially if the affair has been going on for a long time, *may allow both parties time and emotional space to process feelings* and clarify the situation. The goal of separation is to *begin to build a friendship between the person you're counseling and the unfaithful spouse* and to reestablish trust between them.

Strongly encourage the person to require the unfaithful spouse to have *no further contact* with the third person and to ask the unfaithful spouse to *expose the details of the relationship* so there is no further secrecy.

If the Counselee Is the Unfaithful Spouse

- *Require full disclosure of the steps leading up to the affair*, the details of the relationship, and any information that was kept hidden.
- Remind the person that there will be *a "withdrawal" factor* as he or she breaks off any connection with the third party.
- Inform the person that he or she needs to *reengage emotionally with his or her spouse* by spending as much time as possible with him or her.
- The person will need to begin a lifestyle of *accounting for all of his or her time* to begin to rebuild trust.

Representative, scientific surveys indicate that extramarital relations are less prevalent than pop and pseudo-scientific accounts contend. The best estimates are that about 3–4% of currently married people have a sexual partner besides their spouse in a given year and about 15–18% of ever-married people have had a sexual partner other than their spouse while married.[1]

- Inform the person that healing *will take time*. Developing new patterns and a commitment to learn about oneself and one's spouse on a deeper level will be involved in the healing process.
- Inform the person that *seeking forgiveness* also involves restoration and a deeper commitment to love and honor his or her spouse than has been previously given.

5 ACTION STEPS

1. Pray

Both spouses: Seek daily time before God in prayer, reading the Scriptures, and asking God for the ability to grow in Christlike attitudes and actions.

2. Have No Contact

The unfaithful spouse: You must have no contact whatsoever with the third party. Like an addiction, the way out is to go cold turkey.

3. Make a Commitment

The unfaithful spouse: You must be willing to make a radical commitment to regain the trust that has been broken.

4. Begin a New Lifestyle

The unfaithful spouse: Commit to a lifestyle of transparency and honesty. Remember, there is no area that is off-limits for inquiry.

5. Forgive

The faithful spouse: Commit to the process of forgiveness. Forgiveness is an "act" and a multilayered journey. You will often need to make daily decisions to release the hurt.

6. Work at Reconciliation

Both spouses: Remember that forgiveness is required but reconciliation is conditional. It is based on true remorse and repentance. While the Bible permits divorce for sexual infidelity, and many couples do stay together and heal, some may never be able to work through the brokenness.

Whoever commits adultery with a woman lacks understanding; he who does so destroys his own soul.
Proverbs 6:32

7. Get Wise Counsel

Both spouses: You will need to commit to working with a counselor who can help you evaluate the communication patterns that may have contributed to the affair.

BIBLICAL INSIGHTS 6

Drink water from your own cistern, and running water from your own well.

Proverbs 5:15

This beautiful metaphor describes the joy of marital fidelity. To "drink water from your own cistern" pictures the marriage partners belonging only to each other, enraptured with each other's love.

By contrast, to become enraptured by another, to turn to adultery, may feel exciting at first, but will end up being "bitter as wormwood, sharp as a two-edged sword" (Prov. 5:4).

God's Word clearly teaches that married people should keep their vows and remain committed to each other.

Adultery is embracing a false love—it will hurt everyone involved.

Let your fountain be blessed, and rejoice with the wife of your youth. As a loving deer and a graceful doe, let her breasts satisfy you at all times; and always be enraptured with her love.

Proverbs 5:18–19

The Bible does not speak against sexual fulfillment—in fact, sexual delight and marital love are exalted in the Song of Solomon. Sexual fulfillment is always depicted in the Bible as within the boundaries of marriage.

Adultery is a great tragedy, for it has severe consequences. People risk all that they have built over a lifetime—marriage, family, ministry, respect, honor—when they commit adultery. Sexual sin can be very appealing, almost an overwhelming temptation.

The way out is to rejoice in one's marriage and to be satisfied with the love of one's spouse. To violate this commitment will lead to pain, grief, and self-destruction.

"When I passed by you again and looked upon you, indeed your time was the time of love; so I spread My wing over you and covered your nakedness. Yes, I swore an oath to you and entered into a covenant with you, and you became Mine," says the Lord God.

Ezekiel 16:8

We can find great comfort in the fact that our heavenly Father can empathize with the pain of someone who has been betrayed by a loved one. Knowing that He understands can help us trust Him in our own hurt and pain.

There is little direct and reliable trend information on extra-marital relations before 1988. Since then, levels have not changed much. Prior to then there is indirect evidence that extra-marital relations may have increased across recent generations. The figure of ever having extra-marital relations rises from 13% among those 18–29 to 20% among those 40–49. It then falls to 9.5% among those 70 and older.[2]

You have heard that it was said to those of old, "You shall not commit adultery."

Matthew 5:27

Quoting from Exodus 20:14, Jesus reminded His listeners of the commandment against adultery. Then He said that looking at another person lustfully is committing adultery in one's heart. Jesus explained that thinking about an act is the same as doing it, because actions begin with thoughts and desires.

Since lust and adultery are first embraced in the mind and heart, believers should try to avoid situations that cause temptation.

7 PRAYER STARTER

Dear Lord, there is much pain here today. Hurt and betrayal are affecting this marriage. You have promised, Lord, that You are close to the brokenhearted and will bind up their wounds. You are the Healer, the Restorer. We ask for Your guidance in this painful situation . . .

8 RECOMMENDED RESOURCES

Abrahams Spring, Janice. *After the Affair: Healing the Pain and Rebuilding Trust When a Partner Has Been Unfaithful.* Harper Books, 1997.*

Carder, Dave. *Torn Asunder: Recovering from an Extramarital Affair.* Moody, 2008.

Dobson, James. *Love Must Be Tough: New Hope for Marriages in Crisis.* Tyndale, 2007.

Snyder, Douglas K., Donald H. Baucom, and Kristina Coop Gordon. *Getting Past the Affair: A Program to Help You Cope, Heal, and Move On—Together or Apart.* The Guilford Press, 2007.*

Websites

American Association of Christian Counselors (www.aacc.net)

Ecounseling (www.ecounseling.com)

Note: These are not written from a Christian perspective but offer relevant and helpful material.

Aging

- Will and Marilyn had married late and had kids even later. With their kids entering adolescence, they were confronted with the possibility of becoming caregivers for Marilyn's widowed mother after she fell, breaking her hip.
- Sarah served as a frequent volunteer for years, ever since retiring from the school district. But her health has been failing recently and she's not sure how much longer she can live alone.
- Edward is a widower and has cancer that has spread to his liver. A church member has expressed concern over his living conditions, believing that he has not been caring for himself properly.

DEFINITIONS AND KEY THOUGHTS **2**

- Aging is a natural process. The rate at which people age varies widely according to many factors, such as family history, emotional attitude, chronic medical conditions, and lifestyle.
- Although the risk of disability and illness increases with age, poor health is not an inevitable consequence of aging. Persons with healthy lifestyles that include regular exercise, balanced diet, and no tobacco use have half the risk for disability as those with less than healthy lifestyles.
- Caring for aging parents can be gratifying, but that depends on a lot of complex issues, such as your own health, whether you are still raising children, your financial resources, and your emotional resilience. Even though being a caregiver is laudable, it is not necessarily the wisest decision if there are other options.
- The "sandwich years" refers to the period of middle age when people are often still raising children and are also caring for their parents. They are "sandwiched" between these two generations, and it can feel like either a vice grip or a well-coordinated dance.
- As people age, their *idiosyncrasies tend to become more pronounced.* Easygoing people may continue to be laid back, but those who were uptight at a younger age may become more anxious or paranoid as they age.
- Persons entering their later years *experience many transitions and endure many losses,* such as retirement; moving from parenthood to grandparent-

hood; lessened physical abilities, strength, and energy; the deaths of friends and peers; lowered social status; a tighter financial budget; and the loss of a spouse.

3 ASSESSMENT INTERVIEW

As you talk to the aging person or the family member, remember that *aging and caregiving take many forms.* Try not to project your own values on the person. The older person may value independence far more than you would think is healthy, or the family member might be convinced that anyone older than sixty-five can't be independent. *Listen first,* then gently offer a different opinion if necessary.

Rule Outs

1. If the elderly person is confused, has he or she been ill? Is there a chance of depression, dehydration, other medical problems, or poor nutrition? (*Several medical conditions and depression can mimic the symptoms of dementia, so always be sure that medical problems and depression have been ruled out by professionals before making any assumptions about a person's ability to live independently.*)
2. Is the older person lonely? (*Simple loneliness can prompt a person to reach out for help, sometimes acting needier than he or she truly is.*)

General Questions

1. What level of care do you think you [your loved one] need?
2. What are your [your loved one's] financial resources?
3. What medical issues are there? Are these issues terminal, chronic, permanent but not debilitating, degenerative and progressive? (*Clearly, if a medical condition is temporary, the future plans will be very different than if it is terminal, progressive, or chronic.*)
4. How do you feel emotionally about the possibility of needing to get more care [give care to a loved one]?
5. What family members are available to help?
6. Is the aging person in danger? Dangerous conditions would include:

   – memory loss that leads to accidental fires, wandering, or destructive behavior
   – medical conditions that require constant supervision or that contribute to sudden loss of stability or consciousness
   – a residence that is deteriorated, unhealthy, or structurally too demanding (for example, too many stairs)
   – an emotional state that could lead to extreme despondency or psychosis ("crazy" thinking such as paranoia)

In God's view, aging is merely the final phase of an upward climb from earth to heaven.

David Seamands

WISE COUNSEL : 4

When counseling a caregiver, impress on the person the complexity of issues related to aging and the wealth of resources for caregivers and for the elderly.

Encourage the person to *gather all the facts* (from doctors, if possible, other family members, neighbors, and others). The goal is to find out how the aging person has been doing and whether there are critical concerns.

Assess whether there is any possibility of *physical or financial elder abuse or neglect.*

- *Financial abuse* occurs when friends or family members take financial resources from an older person for their own benefit. This is a particular risk when the older person is confused and no longer controlling his or her own finances.
- *Elder neglect* occurs when a spouse or live-in family member deliberately neglects the needs of the older person for food, clothing, shelter, a clean environment, and protection from extremes of temperature. Sometimes this occurs inadvertently when a previously healthy spouse becomes confused or sick and is no longer able to provide a safe environment for a vulnerable spouse.
- *Elder abuse* is physical violence directed at an older person. This could be a form of domestic violence that has been ongoing for years but the victim is now over sixty-five. Or it could be abuse of an older person by a caregiver who is a family member or a stranger.

> The silver-haired head is a crown of glory, if it is found in the way of righteousness.
> *Proverbs 16:31*

ACTION STEPS : 5

For the Older Person

Poor health and the loss of independence are not the inevitable consequences of growing older. To preserve health and independence, older persons should consider the following strategies:

1. Have Medical Screenings

- Screening to detect diseases early, when they are most treatable, saves many lives. *Older adults should be encouraged to participate in the recommended screenings.*

2. Lead a Healthy Lifestyle

- A healthy lifestyle is more influential than one's genes in helping older people avoid the decline traditionally associated with aging.

3. Get Immunizations

- Flu shots, pneumonia vaccines, and other important immunizations will reduce your risk for hospitalization and death from illness.

4. Take Steps to Prevent Injury

- Falling is the most common cause of injury with older adults. More than one-third of adults sixty-five and over fall each year, and of those 20–30 percent suffer moderate to severe injuries that reduce mobility and independence, says the CDC. Remove tripping hazards in your home and install grab bars in key areas, like bathrooms. These simple measures will significantly reduce your chances of falling.

5. Attend Programs That Teach Self-Management

- *Consider finding programs to teach older Americans self-management techniques. These programs help older adults cope with and manage the transitions of their later years.*

For Caregivers

1. Rank the Need

- With your elderly loved one rank needs in order of importance. Begin to brainstorm how these needs can be met with minimal upheaval. Most of the time, the choice is not between living alone or moving to a nursing home. There are dozens of options in between, including:

  - *nonmedical home care* for cleaning, meals, or home maintenance
  - *Meals on Wheels* and similar programs for delivery of meals
  - *help at home* during key hours for things like bathing and dressing
  - *adult daycare* during daytime hours for those who have family members with them at other times
  - *seniors housing complexes* (apartment complexes with some extra supports available that are offered at a lower price for needy older folk)
  - *shared housing* with a younger person (who is not a family member)
  - *retirement home living* (which often relieves an older person of loneliness or the need to make meals, maintain a home, and so on)
  - *catered/sheltered care or assisted living* (situations that provide meals, some medication reminders, transportation to stores, and other support services)
  - *care in a private group home* (where two to six older people might be cared for by a couple who make caregiving their full-time job)
  - *skilled nursing care*

2. Consider the Effects

- Consider the effect of any changes in lifestyle on all family members, not just the older one. A change in location, for example, will not just affect the older person but also any family members who are going to be involved.
- Attempt to keep upheaval to a minimum, especially if your family life is already tense or demanding. (*Adding a family member requiring twenty-four-hour care to a household with teenagers or a special-needs child, for example, might not be the best idea.*)

Even though our outward man is perishing, yet the inward man is being renewed day by day.

2 Corinthians 4:16

In 2005, life expectancy was at 77.8 years. The difference between male and female life expectancy remained at 5.2 years more for females.[1]

3. Consider All Options

- Enumerate all the options and then give all of them much prayerful consideration.
- Enlist several people—both in and outside the family—to pray about the possibilities.

BIBLICAL INSIGHTS : 6

You shall rise before the gray headed and honor the presence of an old man, and fear your God: I am the LORD.

Leviticus 19:32

God's laws include prohibitions against disrespecting the elderly. The "gray headed" and the "old man" are to be treated with honor and respect.

The Bible commands respect for one's elders, who have much to teach from their vast experience.

Moses was one hundred and twenty years old when he died. His eyes were not dim nor his natural vigor diminished.

Deuteronomy 34:7

Our generation tends to emphasize the importance of youth, but God uses servants of all ages.

Age does not limit God's ability to work through people. As long as we have breath, we should be serving God.

And now, behold, the LORD has kept me alive, as He said, these forty-five years, ever since the LORD spoke this word to Moses while Israel wandered in the wilderness; and now, here I am this day, eighty-five years old.

Joshua 14:10

The Bible identifies the key to Caleb's lifelong health, vitality, and special favor with God. He "wholly followed the LORD" (Josh. 14:8).

Caleb is a wonderful model for the proposition that a faithful life—one that perseveres through every trial and hardship—is rewarded with blessings in old age.

> Persons reaching age 65 have an average life expectancy of an additional 18.2 years (19.5 years for females and 16.6 years for males).[2]

LORD, make me to know my end, and what is the measure of my days, that I may know how frail I am. Indeed, You have made my days as handbreadths, and my age is as nothing before You; certainly every man at his best state is but vapor.

Psalm 39:4–5

People's lifetimes are but a small measure in the hand of God; it is "as nothing" to Him, like a raindrop in the ocean.

Half of older women age 75+ live alone.[3]

One of the great challenges of aging is to understand that, while time is passing, God is working through us to make a difference in the world.

No matter what our age, we must use our time wisely, fully, actively, and selflessly, giving thanks for each new day and seeking how God would have us serve Him.

Do not cast me off in the time of old age; do not forsake me when my strength fails.

Psalm 71:9

Older people often feel that because they lack their youthful vigor, they cannot effectively serve God. God says, however, that His people "shall still bear fruit in old age" (Ps. 92:14).

Older believers have a lifetime of wisdom and experience that is valuable to younger people. Believers can and should continue to grow spiritually even in their twilight time. They can continue to make a difference for God, helping build His kingdom.

Young people must not dismiss older people; instead, they should look to their elders for the godly wisdom they have gained from years of knowing Christ.

7 PRAYER STARTER

Dear Lord, thank you for the life of _____ and for my life to this point. Please reveal to me/us through Your Holy Spirit what I/we should do next to meet the needs of _____. Give us wisdom and kindness. Help us to see all the options, and lead us in the direction we should go that will be best for all involved . . .

8 RECOMMENDED RESOURCES

Focus on the Family. *Caring for Aging Loved Ones* (FOTF Complete Guide), 2002.
Morley, Patrick. *Second Wind for the Second Half: Twenty Ideas to Help You Reinvent Yourself for the Rest of the Journey.* Zondervan, 1999.

Websites
American Association of Christian Counselors (www.aacc.net)
Ecounseling (www.ecounseling.com)

Anger

PORTRAITS 1

- David and his wife fight constantly. Last week David got so angry that he took a glass vase and smashed it against the wall.
- At sixteen Sarah feels she is just a burden to her busy mom. So Sarah locks herself in her bedroom with the stereo at maximum volume.
- Brian's new supervisor has been pushing him all day. Wanting to turn off the world, he goes home and drinks himself into a stupor.
- Only five years old, Timothy hardly understands how he feels, besides pain from the bruises on his back. While other kids draw peacefully, he can't focus. Scribbling in burgundy crayon, he tears a hole straight through his paper.

DEFINITIONS AND KEY THOUGHTS 2

- Anger is a *God-given powerful emotion* (see Eph. 4:26) with intensity that ranges from being frustrated to severe fury. It can last from a few seconds to a lifetime. Anger itself is not a sin. What we *do* in our anger determines whether we sin.
- Anger is best understood as a *state of readiness*. It is a natural response to a real or perceived injustice, and it inspires a powerful alertness that allows us to defend good or attack evil. Even Jesus showed anger (see Mark 3:5).
- Anger is *mentioned more than five hundred times in Scripture*; the only emotion in the Bible more common than anger is love. Anger first appears in Genesis 4:5 and last appears in Revelation 19:15.
- Anger can lead to *healthy or unhealthy/sinful behavior. Careful assertiveness* is a healthy response to anger that involves problem-solving and compassion. *Aggression* is an unhealthy/sinful response to anger that involves hurting or controlling others, revenge, or hatred.
- Anger, when it is an automatic response to a situation, is considered a *primary emotion*. Anger can also be a secondary emotion, meaning it is felt in reaction to another feeling, such as fear, hurt, or sadness.

> Men in rage strike those that wish them best.
>
> *Shakespeare*

Expressions of Anger

Anger always finds an *expression*. It is often revealed as:

- *a response* to a person, situation, or event; to an imaginary or anticipated event; or to memories of traumatic or enraging situations
- *a response* to a real or perceived injustice or hurt—in the form of frustration, betrayal, deprivation, injustice, exploitation, manipulation, criticism, violence, disapproval, humiliation, intimidation, threats, and so on
- *a response* when a boundary in their life has been crossed

People handle anger by:

> How much more grievous are the consequences of anger than the causes of it.
>
> *Marcus Aurelius*

Internalization

Sometimes people *repress* the anger, meaning they deny anger's presence. This is unhealthy because even though it may not be observable, the anger is still present— turned inward on the person. Repressed anger can lead to numerous emotional and physical problems including depression, anxiety, hypertension, and ulcers.

Or people may *suppress* their anger, meaning they acknowledge anger and then stuff it. With this approach to coping, they redirect anger-driven energy into unrelated activity. This can be effective, though it neglects addressing the root causes of anger. One risk is that people who suppress may become cynical or passive-aggressive—an indirect form of revenge manifesting as sarcasm, lack of cooperation, gossip, and so on.

Ventilation

Healthy expression of anger entails nonaggressive, gently assertive actions that promote the respect of self and others. This addresses problems in a constructive manner.

Unhealthy/sinful expression involves acting in an aggressive way that hurts others. Whether one yells, uses violence, or withdraws, the motivation involves revenge or "payback." Persons expressing anger this way might say, "At least you know where I'm coming from!" However, they refuse to acknowledge the destructive force of their expression.

Physical symptoms

Physical symptoms of anger include headaches, ulcers, stomach cramps, high blood pressure, colitis, and heart conditions.

Emotional symptoms

Emotional symptoms include criticism, sarcasm, gossip, meanness, impatience, being demanding, withholding love, and refusing to forgive.

Levels of Anger

Irritation—a feeling of discomfort

Indignation—a feeling that something must be answered; something wrong must be corrected

Wrath—a strong desire for revenge

Fury—the partial loss of emotional control

Rage—a loss of control involving aggression or an act of violence

Hostility—a persistent form of anger; enmity toward others that becomes rooted in one's personality, which affects one's entire outlook on the world and life

Causes of Anger

External Causes

Anger can be a response to the harm someone has inflicted (a physical attack, insult, abandonment) or to a circumstance where there is no person at fault (100-degree days, physical illness, highway traffic).

Internal Causes

Anger is sometimes caused exclusively by an individual's misperceptions of reality or destructive thinking about normal life issues ("I should not have to pay taxes!"). Also memories of traumatic past events can be an internal impetus of anger, as can biologically rooted causes from medication, caffeine, or other stimulants; and health issues, such as diabetes or dialysis treatments.

> Men are like steel: when they lose their temper, they lose their worth.
> *Chuck Norris*

ASSESSMENT INTERVIEW 3

When people seek help for anger, *the problem is often already out of control.* Also such persons may be experiencing shame and perhaps even fear because they do not yet understand how to identify and control their angry feelings. At the onset of counseling, *resist the urge to give advice.* Instead, *calmly hear the client's story.* It is important to *ask the rule-out questions* below to see if the problem is rooted in something other than anger. Then choose appropriate questions from the remaining general questions.

Rule Outs

Depression has often been described as "anger turned inward." Both men and women can express their anger as depression.

1. If 10 is extreme depression, and 1 is no depression, where are you today on a scale of 1 to 10?

Substance abuse is often an accompanying issue.

,

2. Are you ever under the influence of alcohol or drugs when you experience anger? Do you use alcohol or drugs to avoid feelings of anger?

If you suspect that either depression or substance abuse is present, you should first deal with that underlying problem. Refer to the sections on Depression or Addictions in this manual. Other underlying issues include ADD/ADHD, brain trauma, personality disorders, attachment issues, and physical or sexual abuse.

Anyone can become angry. That is easy. But to be angry with the right person, to the right degree, at the right time, for the right purpose and in the right way—that is not easy.

Aristotle

General Questions

1. What makes you angry?
2. How do you express your anger? Is the way you are expressing your anger working?
3. What is your first memory of feeling out of control when you got angry?
4. Do you ever take any action to redirect your anger to a nonrelated activity?
5. Are you ever able to calm your anger? If so, how?
6. Has anger created any health issues?
7. How did you see anger expressed during childhood?
8. Could there be anger from your past that is affecting you now?
9. What was it like to be on the receiving end of someone else's anger?
10. How is the way you express your anger harming you in your relationships?
11. How often do fights get physical?
12. When you get angry, how safe do you feel? How safe do those around you feel?
13. Do others see anger in you that you do not?
14. Do you have anyone with whom to talk about your anger?
15. Will you consider forgiving the people with whom you are angry?
16. Do you pray to God about your anger?
17. Do you ever allow your anger to escalate?
18. Do you deal with your anger "before the sun goes down" (see Eph. 4:26)?

4 WISE COUNSEL

Share some information about anger with the counselee. In your own words, be sure to convey that being angry is not sinning and that anger needs to be expressed and dealt with in constructive ways.

Offer encouragement since the counselee is willing to address the problem, and stress the importance of beginning immediately to do so given the possible destructive ways that anger can be expressed. The Bible says that we should be "looking carefully lest anyone fall short of the grace of God; lest any root of bitterness springing up cause trouble, and by this many become defiled" (Heb. 12:15).

Explain the importance of following the action steps because those who repress their anger are often depressed, anxious, hostile, or have other psychological and biological problems. Those who express their anger in unhelpful ways will devastate their relationships with others. Anger leads to resentment (resentment is anger with a history), which then turns to bitterness or hostility.

Evaluate the history of anger expressed in the client's life. It is possible that the anger the client feels today is not due to a "trigger" but is instead rooted in anger from his or her past. For example, a client who is angry at his boss for being demanding might be thinking, "This man is heartless—the same as my father was." Such anger is misdirected at the boss, who is not heartless.

ACTION STEPS 5

The goal is not to be "anger free." Instead, it is to teach the counselee how to control his or her response to the present anger—both the emotional and biological arousals that anger may cause.

1. See It

- Focus on the source of the anger. List the triggers (in session and as homework). *Until the client can control the anger, he or she should avoid the triggers as much as possible.*
- Learn to identify anger before it is out of control. How do you feel physically when experiencing anger? Do the following:

    – Identify angry feelings while they are still minor. State out loud, "I'm feeling angry right now."
    – Be aware of the first warning signs of anger, which may be physical changes. Anger promotes a sympathetic nervous system response (a physical state of readiness) and the following biological changes: rising heart rate and blood pressure, amplified alertness, tensed muscles, dilated pupils, GI tract disturbances, clenched fists, flared nostrils, and bulging veins.

> Consider how much more you often suffer from your anger and grief than from those very things for which you are angry and grieved.
> *Marcus Antonius*

2. Delay It—Proverbs 16:32; 29:11

- *Brainstorm ways to delay the expression of anger:*

    – Take a "time out"; temporarily disengage from the situation if possible (twenty-minute minimum).
    – Perform light exercise until the intensity of anger is manageable.
    – "Write, don't fight"; jot down troubling thoughts. This exercise is personal and writings should be kept private, possibly destroyed, not sent.
- Talk with a trusted friend who is unrelated to the anger-provoking situation. Don't just vent; ask for constructive advice.
- Pray about the anger, asking God to give you insight.

- Learn the value of calming. (*A person in a state of fury is not equipped to deal healthily with an anger-provoking situation. Calming will help him or her let some of his angry feelings subside before expressing anger in a healthy way. Note: Ruminating is the opposite of calming, and makes anger worse by repeating destructive thoughts about an anger-producing event.*)

3. Control It

A fool gives full vent to his anger, but a wise man keeps himself under control.

Proverbs 29:11 NIV

- *Brainstorm some ways for the client to express his or her anger in a healthy way:*

  – *Respond* (rational action); don't react (emotional retort).
  – *Maintain a healthy distance* until you can speak constructively (see James 1:19).
  – *Confront* to restore, not to destroy.
  – *Empathize* (yelling is a failure to empathize). Speak slowly and quietly (makes yelling difficult).
  – *Surrender* the right for revenge (see Rom. 12:19).

- If anger begins to escalate to wrath or fury, it is not the time to engage in interactions with others. Instead, temporarily redirect your energy to solo activities, or reestablish calm before confronting others.

4. Settle It

- A plan should be made for follow-up, perhaps:

  – finding an accountability partner
  – individual counseling
  – joining an anger-management group
  – considering medication

- You should actively continue spiritual growth if you are going to effectively manage anger. The Bible says, "The fruit of the Spirit is love, joy, peace, longsuffering, kindness, goodness, faithfulness, gentleness, self-control" (Gal. 5:22–23).

- Remember to:

  – *surrender*—to the Holy Spirit (Gal. 5:16)
  – *reflect*—on the mercy and love God provides (Eph. 2:4)
  – *pray*—admit to God feelings and regrets (Matt. 5:43–45)
  – *forgive*—choose to let go of resentment and bitterness (Eph. 4:31–32)
  – *avoid*—ruminating and revenge (1 Cor. 10:13; 1 Peter 1:13)
  – *give and receive*—mutual respect with those close to you (Eph. 5:22, 25)
  – *love*—even those who anger you (1 Corinthians 13)
  – *remember*—what it was like to be on the receiving end of someone else's anger (1 Sam. 19:9–10)
  – *resolve*—the anger issues (Eph. 4:26)

- Underlying issues such as deep emotional wounds that have been identified in counseling need to be considered. Make plans to work on such issues through additional counseling and support groups.
- When we learn to control our anger and forgive those who offend us, we are following the example of Jesus, who forgave each of us. Ephesians 4:31–32 says, "Let all bitterness, wrath, anger, clamor, and evil speaking be put away from you, with all malice. And be kind to one another, tenderhearted, forgiving one another, even as God in Christ forgave you."

BIBLICAL INSIGHTS 6

If you do well, will you not be accepted? And if you do not do well, sin lies at the door. And its desire is for you, but you should rule over it.

Genesis 4:7

Cain's problem with anger wasn't that he became angry. It was how he reacted in his anger.

At first, Cain's anger was a positive response, but it missed the mark. Instead of Cain becoming furious with himself, his anger turned to deadly jealousy.

Anger must be ruled or it will rule. Uncontrolled anger quickly becomes destructive. When you invite God to help you identify your anger and take positive action, anger becomes a servant rather than a master.

"Be angry, and do not sin": do not let the sun go down on your wrath, nor give place to the devil.

Ephesians 4:26–27

Note that this does not say, "Never be angry." Anger is a God-given emotion and, if handled well, will promote positive change.

Do not allow anger to cause you to act in ways that you will later regret.

Do not turn anger on yourself or pretend you are never angry.

Deal with anger as quickly (and responsibly) as possible—before the sun goes down—so that you do not "give place to the devil."

Seek to resolve differences with others respectfully. Then continue together in the Lord's work. Remember, Satan loves to use anger to divide believers.

And I became very angry when I heard their outcry and these words.

Nehemiah 5:6

Nehemiah's anger was righteous indignation because many Jews were suffering at the hands of rich countrymen who had lent them money. Expressing his anger in a healthy way, Nehemiah called a meeting of the moneylenders, who agreed to his firm requests.

When you feel anger burning beneath the surface, ask God to guide you toward a productive way of resolving the conflict.

According to the National Institute of Health, 7.3 percent (11.5–16 million Americans) experience "intermittent explosive disorder" in their lifetimes. This disorder is marked by episodes of unwarranted anger.[1]

Make no friendship with an angry man, and with a furious man do not go, lest you learn his ways and set a snare for your soul.

Proverbs 22:24–25

People may not be able to change the anger others express, but they can avoid close ties with "furious" people. Such people are ready to explode and anyone around will either catch the brunt of that fury or become similarly furious.

Choose carefully those who will be your closest friends, business partners, and spouse.

Then God said to Jonah, "Is it right for you to be angry about the plant?" And he said, "It is right for me to be angry, even to death!"

Jonah 4:9

When Jonah learned that God would spare the Ninevites, instead of rejoicing in their repentance, Jonah became angry. His anger at Nineveh's sinfulness was justified, though his selfish anger at God's mercy was not.

Perhaps, with selfish motivation, Jonah was concerned that his reputation had been ruined with the false forecast of the city's destruction. Or he may have desired a front-row seat at Nineveh's demise—after all, Assyria was Israel's enemy.

We must consider honestly the inspiration of our anger.

7 : PRAYER STARTER

Lord, we all get angry. Anger is a powerful emotion that You have given us, and Your Word teaches us clearly about the constructive and destructive force that anger is. Help us to follow Your Word, Lord, by teaching us to control our anger when we have been threatened and wronged. Bless us, God, that we might see clearly and not hurt others in our anger . . .

8 : RECOMMENDED RESOURCES

Carter, Les. *The Anger Trap: Free Yourself from the Frustrations That Sabotage Your Life.* Jossey-Bass, 2004.

Carter, Les, and Frank Minirth. *The Anger Workbook: A 13-Step Interactive Plan to Help You . . .* Thomas Nelson, 1992.

———. *The Anger Workbook for Christian Parents.* Jossey-Bass, 2004.

Oliver, Gary, and Carrie Oliver. *Mad about Us: Moving from Anger to Intimacy with Your Spouse.* Bethany House, 2007.

Websites

American Association of Christian Counselors (www.aacc.net)

Ecounseling (www.ecounseling.com)

Bitterness

PORTRAITS 1

- Becky has not been to church for over a year. The leaders in her last church sided against her when she brought them concerns over inappropriate advances by a worship leader. She has tried but cannot seem to get past the bitterness. She thought her church cared for her.
- David's father was killed by a drunk driver when David was a teenager. Life was difficult for David's family after that. The man was given only a light sentence. David is bitter at the unfairness of life.
- Adam's parents constantly belittled him as he was growing up. Now an adult, he suffers from depression and anxiety and cannot figure out why he can't get over it.
- Laura's husband does not seem interested in meeting any of her emotional needs. He is distant and cold when she tries to talk to him about it. Over time, she has given up hoping that he will ever change and sees no reason to continue in the marriage.
- Claire's boss is demanding and extremely critical. He humiliated Claire in front of her co-workers by judging her work unfairly. Claire can't seem to let it go and fantasizes about plots for revenge.

DEFINITIONS AND KEY THOUGHTS 2

- Bitterness is an attitude of *extended and intense anger and hostility*. It is often accompanied by resentment and a desire to get even. It is a result of not forgiving an offender and letting the hurt and anger grow until the pain and resentment sour the person's view of life.
- Bitterness is a sin that *destroys life*. Hebrews 12:14–15 warns that bitterness corrupts by its poison. Romans 12:17–19 commands not to seek revenge, but rather let God avenge the wrong.
- Bitterness can *be conquered only by forgiveness*. Ephesians 4:31–32 says to get rid of bitterness by replacing it with forgiveness.

Key Elements of Bitterness

- *Unresolved anger*—Ephesians 4:26 says that we can be angry without sinning. But when anger is unresolved and allowed to ruminate, it turns into bitterness.
- *Inability to grieve*—Relationships that do not live up to expectations and that fail to meet legitimate needs can result in feelings of sadness and loss. When people are unable (or unwilling) to face the reality that their needs are never going to be met by a certain relationship, the result can be bitterness. Taking time to grieve the loss is an important prerequisite to becoming free from bitterness. When people refuse to admit that the relationship will never become what they had hoped, the refusal causes bitterness. "Hope deferred makes the heart sick" (Prov. 13:12).
- *Lack of control*—When other people do not meet a person's needs, he or she can become obsessed with thoughts like, "*If they would just do this . . .*" Give it up! People may never do what someone else desires or expects, and they can't be made to. We can control only ourselves; much bitterness could be avoided if people accepted this truth.

Key Characteristics of Bitterness

resentment

obsessive thoughts of revenge

sarcasm

critical or unkind comments

self-righteousness

conflicts with others

hostility

aggressiveness in relationships

controlling behavior

3 ASSESSMENT INTERVIEW

At first, just listen to the client's story. *Show empathy by listening closely* with appropriate feedback and restating emotions to make sure you understand what the person is saying. Bitterness may not be the presenting problem a client brings to counseling, but *it is often the real problem* underneath. Gently lead the client through the following questions to help him or her come to this realization.

If any of the questions hit a nerve, bring back a memory, or upset the client, *stop the questions and deal with that issue*. Let the person talk about it further; show compassion for the pain he or she is feeling. The goal is to help, and this is the purpose of the questions. It is not necessary to have the client answer all the questions.

> Revenge has no more quenching effect on emotions than salt water has on thirst.
>
> *Walter Weckler*

Rule Outs

1. On a scale of 1 to 10 with 10 being contentment and joy and 1 being total despair, where are you today?
2. Do you use alcohol or drugs to escape your hurt and bitterness?
3. Do you feel you might hurt yourself or others? (*If you suspect that depression or substance abuse is present, you should deal with that along with the bitterness. Research shows that both issues need to be dealt with for full recovery. Refer to the sections on Addictions and Depression. If you think the person is suicidal, make out a safety contract in which he or she promises not to hurt self without first calling you. If your client calls you, take him or her to the hospital to be placed in a safe environment and get professional help. See the section on Suicide.*)

> Whatever you do, do it heartily, as to the Lord and not to men.
> *Colossians 3:23*

General Questions

1. What brought you to counseling today?
2. What things have you already tried to deal with this problem?
3. What do you hope will happen as an outcome of counseling?
4. Let's start by getting some background information that will help me get to know you better. Tell me about the family you grew up in, about your mother, father, sisters, brothers, and anyone else who lived in your home or was an important part of your life. (*Attitudes toward life are molded in the family of origin, so it's important to see who and what shaped your client into the person he or she is today. This will help you understand your client and his or her reactions, and help the client understand self.*)

    Tell me about your adult life, your job, your marriage, your children, your church. (*Ask these questions one at a time, but the general idea is to get the person talking about his or her life and how this problem has affected it.*)
5. It sounds as though you have been hurt a lot in your life. Do you feel bitter about that? (*The client may not admit to bitterness. Other feelings like anger, frustration, or disappointment may arise. You may have to help them see how these feelings can or have turned to bitterness.*)
6. When did you first notice feelings of bitterness?
7. What events led to those feelings?
8. How has this bitterness affected your quality of life?
9. Can you remember anyone else in your life being bitter?
10. How did it affect that person?
11. What effect did that person's bitterness have on you?
12. What feelings did you have when this person or event first caused offense or made you bitter?
13. Tell me why you were angry and what hurt your feelings. (*Often people feel anger when first offended because they are hurt, but underneath the hurt are expectations and underneath the expectations are needs.*)
14. What expectations did you have from the person who hurt you?

> If we could read the secret history of our enemies, we should find in each person's life sorrow and suffering enough to disarm all hostility.
> *Henry Wadsworth Longfellow*

15. What need did you have that the person failed to meet?

16. Do you think that person will ever meet your need? Why or why not?

17. Can you accept that?

18. Can you forgive the person for that? (*If forgiveness is a tough sticking point, refer to the section on Forgiveness and work through it in a separate session.*)

19. What would forgiveness look like?

20. Where else could you get your need met?

4 WISE COUNSEL

Share some information about what bitterness is. If the client does not realize that the root of his or her problem is bitterness, it will help the person see what is going on in his or her life. Share the results of bitterness and the destruction it causes.

Empathize with your client. Help him or her acknowledge legitimate needs that were not met (usually by a parent or spouse). Validate the loneliness and sadness of not having needs met. *Rephrase what your client is saying* so he or she knows you're hearing the real meaning and that you care about the pain.

Explain the importance of following the action steps to get rid of bitterness. Bitterness is a poison that will destroy the person's relationship with others and hurt his or her relationship with God. When people are bitter, they cannot experience a full and healthy relationship with God. Forgiveness is the only way to get rid of bitterness and restore relationships with God and others.

5 ACTION STEPS

1. Accept

- Make a list of the persons who have hurt you.
- Next to each name, write what you needed from that person.
- Next to that, write how it made you feel when that person did not meet your need.
- In the last column write whether you think the person will ever be able to meet your need. Be honest.
- Accept your loss and grieve it.

2. Forgive

- Ask God to help you forgive. Forgiveness is letting go of anger and your quest for revenge. Realize that you are powerless to forgive through your own strength, but God does not ask you to do something without giving you His strength and power to do it. (*Refer to the chapter on Forgiveness.*)

- Ask God to help you feel compassion for your offender. Psalm 78:38 says that God is full of compassion.

3. Break the Chain

- Bitterness often runs through families. When a parent does not meet a child's needs, that child can become bitter and is then unable to meet his or her own child's needs. The chain can continue through several generations.
- Ask God to help you break the chain with your generation. (*You may need to help your client say this prayer.*)
- (*If the client has a bitter parent, help him or her see the parent as emotionally wounded.*) Just as you would not expect a person in a wheelchair to run a marathon, don't expect someone who is emotionally troubled to meet your needs—that person cannot. Ask God to help you have empathy for him or her.

4. Look Elsewhere

- Find somewhere else to get your needs met. If you are an emotional orphan, God will provide people to meet your needs.
- Be proactive and look for those God has provided to meet your needs.
- Join a women's or men's group or look for a prayer partner.
- If your mother did not meet your need for love and acceptance, find an older woman in the church who would be willing to mentor you. She can give you the love and acceptance your mother never could. Finding a man to mentor you as a father may also meet your need.
- If your husband or wife will not meet your need for friendship and intimacy, look around and see if there is a friend (of the same sex) or family member who is willing to be your friend and kindred spirit. Give of yourself to that person and meet each other's needs.

> I imagine one of the reasons people cling to their hates so stubbornly is because they sense, once hate is gone, they will be forced to deal with the pain.
>
> *James Baldwin*

BIBLICAL INSIGHTS 6

Then Saul was very angry, and the saying displeased him; and he said, "They have ascribed to David ten thousands, and to me they have ascribed only thousands. Now what more can he have but the kingdom?" So Saul eyed David from that day forward.

1 Samuel 18:8–9

King Saul wasted his last years in hatred and anger. Fears, jealousies, murderous thoughts, and violent rage consumed him without relief. His soul was hardened and unresponsive to any message from God. He collected a legacy of evil and bitterness that finally turned into self-destruction.

People who are bitter, angry, divisive, and dark in thought and deed need to be treated with mercy and respect, but they also must be lovingly called to repentance. The church can speak truth to them while taking care not to join them on their bitter journey.

Can anyone teach God knowledge, since He judges those on high? One dies in his full strength, being wholly at ease and secure; his pails are full of milk, and the marrow of his bones is moist. Another man dies in the bitterness of his soul, never having eaten with pleasure.

Job 21:22–25

Job did not understand why he was suffering so terribly. His words here reveal the depth of his pain and the bitterness rising in his heart, but Job maintained his trust in God.

How we respond to struggles defines our attitude toward God. We can become bitter or we can press on in faith. God is faithful and will see us through any crisis.

But I say to you who hear: Love your enemies, do good to those who hate you, bless those who curse you, and pray for those who spitefully use you.

Luke 6:27–28

Loving one's enemies does not mean having affectionate feelings for them. Instead, it requires a decision to act in love toward them no matter how we feel.

We need to pray and ask Christ to take our hurt and bitterness and replace those feelings with His love.

Repent therefore of this your wickedness, and pray God if perhaps the thought of your heart may be forgiven you. For I see that you are poisoned by bitterness and bound by iniquity.

Acts 8:22–23

Bitterness is like a poison, eating away at a person's soft heart, turning it into stone—hard and unyielding.

People poisoned by bitterness, whatever the cause, can be touched by God's grace, and so we pray for them.

Pursue peace with all people, and holiness, without which no one will see the Lord: looking carefully lest anyone fall short of the grace of God; lest any root of bitterness springing up cause trouble, and by this many become defiled.

Hebrews 12:14–15

Believers need to look out for each other—helping those who are feeling weak and guiding those who are heading in the wrong direction. This will guard against "any root of bitterness" that might spring up within the fellowship.

God wants you to forgive so you can be free from the destructive power of bitterness.

When my father and my mother forsake me, then the LORD will take care of me.

Psalm 27:10

Bitterness that is allowed to take root in our lives will spring up into actions and words that cannot be taken back. Believers can avoid the root of bitterness by dealing with their feelings immediately.

When hurt or doubt is allowed to remain in one's life, it provides hospitable soil for the root of bitterness. With God's help, we can keep that root from having a place to grow, and if bitterness has already taken root, weed it out.

PRAYER STARTER : 7

Lord, I thank you that _____ has come in today to talk about this painful situation. I thank You, Lord, that while people often disappoint us, You never do. You have promised to meet all of our needs . . .

RECOMMENDED RESOURCES : 8

Clinton, Tim. *The Bible for Hope: Caring for People God's Way.* Thomas Nelson, 2007. See theme article and corresponding Scriptures on bitterness.

Cloud, Henry. *Changes That Heal: How to Understand the Past to Ensure a Healthier Future.* Zondervan, 1997.

Hybels, Bill, and Mark Mittelberg. *Becoming a Contagious Christian.* Zondervan, 1996.

Thomas, Angela. *Tender Mercy for a Mother's Soul: Inspiration to Renew Your Spirit.* Focus on the Family, 2006.

Websites

American Association of Christian Counselors (www.aacc.net)

Ecounseling (www.ecounseling.com)

Burnout

1 PORTRAITS

- Jane hung up the phone. The nursing home had called again; her mother was refusing to eat. Could Jane please come immediately? When Jane got into her car, she was surprised by the waves of anger that she felt. It seemed as though it was all up to her to take care of everything. Lately she moved in a blur from caring for her children and her husband to her students and her mother. It seemed that everyone always needed something, and lately she was beginning not to care.

- Tom was barely ever home. The new job, while lucrative, had him on the road much of the week. Travel was exhausting, so even when he was home, he barely had the energy to keep up with his two-year-old.

- Sandy is a good student—maybe too good. She's involved in a score of activities and taking advanced classes. She's starting to have difficulty sleeping, she can't relax, and at times, she can't even focus. She's starting to think that nothing she does is good enough, and so she may not even apply to college.

2 DEFINITIONS AND KEY THOUGHTS

- Western culture continues to push the limits, has become increasingly obsessed with the "pursuit of excellence," and burnout has reached *epidemic proportions*, even within the church.

- Burnout is a stressful state characterized by *physical, emotional, and mental exhaustion, chronic fatigue, and lethargy.*

- Someone experiencing burnout may

  - feel cynical toward life
  - have a strong desire to escape
  - experience a false sense of failure
  - display emotional distancing, numbing, or apathy
  - become hypercritical
  - experience negative feelings toward others
  - show inappropriate anger or sadness
  - succumb to depression

    – endure a resulting physical illness

    – abuse alcohol or drugs

- Burnout is often experienced by those in the *helping professions,* such as clergy, doctors, teachers, police officers, social workers, and others who work extensively with people. It is thought to result from the excessive demands that others place on their energy, time, and resources.

- Burnout can also be felt by *caregivers of the chronically ill* or by overburdened parents. These people often feel trapped by the demands of others, isolated, and unable to find sufficient time for rest and relief.

ASSESSMENT INTERVIEW :3

1. How are you feeling physically? (*If people are experiencing burnout, chances are they haven't been caring for themselves physically. If your client hasn't had a recent physical, recommend that he or she have one.*)
2. How are you feeling emotionally?
3. How long have you felt like this?
4. When did these feelings start?
5. What prompted you to seek help now?
6. What are the stressors in your life?
7. How large a part does each stressor play in your stress level?
8. What kind of support do you get—both with your responsibilities and for yourself personally?
9. How do you perceive yourself? (*For example, someone who feels that he or she must meet all the needs of an aging parent to be a "good" child is going to experience failure.*)
10. What do you do for fun?
11. Are you able to relax?
12. What do you do when you relax?
13. What are the activities you're currently involved in?
14. How would you prioritize these activities?
15. What can be taken out of your schedule?
16. What can be put into your schedule to help you have downtime and family time?
17. What would keep you from doing that?
18. What is the worst thing that will happen if you say no or pull out of certain responsibilities?
19. What will happen if you do nothing?

> Rest in the Lord, and wait patiently for Him. . . . Do not fret—it only causes harm.
>
> *Psalm 37:7–8*

4 WISE COUNSEL

Any *physical concerns* and issues should be addressed medically.

Try to help the counselee gain some *immediate short-term relief* from his or her responsibilities.

Try to help your counselee *mobilize family members and friends* to begin sharing more of the load. Ironically someone who is overburdened needs this help the most and is often least able to ask others to provide it.

There is both a *short-term crisis component* to helping someone who is burned out and a *longer-term component* of helping the person begin to live life in such a way that burnout doesn't recur. When someone is burned out and overstressed, immediate relief is essential—getting adequate sleep and relaxation and exercise. Then as the person begins to recover, helping him or her look at some lifestyle issues that caused burnout will be important to prevent burnout from recurring.

5 ACTION STEPS

1. Take Control

> Let the peace of God rule in your hearts, to which also you were called in one body; and be thankful.
>
> *Colossians 3:15*

- Don't relinquish control of your schedule to the whim of everyone else.
- Put a concrete plan in place to relieve yourself of some of your responsibilities. Enlist the aid of family members and friends. (*Name this as a crisis and help the counselee see his or her need for others' help and care.*)
- *For the school student*: find the balance between what is essential and what is merely "extra."
- Schedule days more sanely, humanely, and relationally.

2. Say No

- *No* is a very helpful word—and often the overworked don't know how to say it.
- While some things can't be dropped (the student has to do the homework; the businessman has to travel), there may be creative ways to schedule your time that will allow for less stress and more rest.

3. Understand God's Will

- God never guides you into an intolerable scramble of overwork—after all, Jesus didn't live that way.
- Before you say yes to any new activity, pray about it. Even if it's a good activity, now may not be the time.

4. Slow Down

- Consciously slow the pace of your life.
- Take the time you need to replenish your resources.

5. Set Priorities

- You may get less done, but you'll be doing the right things.
- When you think about what really matters, much of your frenzied activity will be seen for what it is.

BIBLICAL INSIGHTS : 6

Then God blessed the seventh day and sanctified it, because in it He rested from all His work which God had created and made.

Genesis 2:3

From the very beginning, rest has had a special significance for God. God rested, and He made the seventh day a day of rest for us as well (Exod. 20:8–11).

So the Lord said to Moses: "Gather to Me seventy men of the elders of Israel, whom you know to be the elders of the people and officers over them; bring them to the tabernacle of meeting, that they may stand there with you. Then I will come down and talk with you there. I will take of the Spirit that is upon you and will put the same upon them; and they shall bear the burden of the people with you, that you may not bear it yourself alone."

Numbers 11:16–17

Pushing hard with many hours and demands can become counterproductive. We need to set boundaries around our time and energy to protect ourselves.

God is aware of our limitations and encourages us to lighten the load by delegating responsibility to others who can help us be more productive and effective.

We should consider our responsibilities and how we can delegate to others to get the job done.

But those who wait on the Lord shall renew their strength; they shall mount up with wings like eagles, they shall run and not be weary, they shall walk and not faint.

Isaiah 40:31

In 2007, nearly half of all Americans report that stress has a negative impact on both their personal and professional lives. Stress causes more than half of Americans (54 percent) to fight with people close to them.[1]

Isaiah reminded God's people of the value of waiting on the Lord. "Waiting" does not mean inactivity; rather, it is patient service that is not overcommitted and overextended.

Many desire to "mount up with wings like eagles" but they assume that the harder they run the more likely they will fly. The harder people run the more likely they will fall. Instead, "those who wait on the LORD shall renew their strength." Such "waiting" is the antidote for spiritual burnout.

> *Come to Me, all you who labor and are heavy laden, and I will give you rest. Take My yoke upon you and learn from Me, for I am gentle and lowly in heart, and you will find rest for your souls. For My yoke is easy and My burden is light.*
>
> *Matthew 11:28–30*

Jesus says that He will take from our shoulders the heavy burdens that are burning us out and replace them with an easy yoke, a light burden.

Jesus is in touch with the burdens of life that we carry and how much they hurt and exhaust us. When we give our troubled hearts to Him, He gives us rest for our souls. That kind of rest will cure our burnout and renew our enthusiasm for Him.

> *And He said to them, "Come aside by yourselves to a deserted place and rest a while." For there were many coming and going, and they did not even have time to eat. So they departed to a deserted place in the boat by themselves.*
>
> *Mark 6:31–32*

Even our Savior, being God, was aware of His human limitations. He never seemed to be in a hurry; He didn't work twenty-four-hour days. Even as more and more people crowded to Him to hear His words and be healed, He would often withdraw into the wilderness and pray (Luke 5:15–16).

After an exhausting time of ministry, Jesus invited His disciples to take a break to refresh themselves.

A hectic schedule takes a physical, emotional, and spiritual toll on us. God knows that we need to come aside and rest a while so that we don't burn out. He will refresh us so that we can continue to serve Him. Rest and refreshment do not waste time.

7 PRAYER STARTER

Dear Lord, Your child is tired—exhausted. He [she] wants to do so much for You and feels so much responsibility, yet we know that You never call us to burn out. We pray today that You'll help _____ determine what You would have him [her] do—Your priorities, Your will. Help him [her] discern what can be let go and what should be brought in so that life is in balance . . .

One in four people report that they have been alienated from a friend or family member because of stress, with 8 percent connecting stress to divorce or separation.[2]

RECOMMENDED RESOURCES : 8

Farrar, Steve, and Mary Farrar. *Overcoming Overload*. Multnomah, 2003.

Hart, Archibald D. *Adrenaline and Stress: The Exciting New Breakthrough That Helps You Overcome Stress Damage*. Thomas Nelson, 1995.

———. *The Anxiety Cure*. Thomas Nelson, 2001.

Minirth, Frank, and Paul Meier. *Before Burnout: Balanced Living for Busy People*. Bristol Park Books, 1997.

Sala, Harold. *Making Your Emotions Work for You: Coping with Stress, Avoiding Burnout, Overcoming Fear, and More*. Harvest House Publishers, 2009.

Swenson, Richard. *A Minute of Margin: Restoring Balance to Busy Lives*. NavPress, 2003.

Websites

American Association of Christian Counselors (www.aacc.net)

Ecounseling (www.ecounseling.com)

You have created us for yourself, and our heart cannot be stilled until it finds rest in you.

Augustine of Hippo

Death

1 PORTRAITS

- Dave was forty-six and enjoying life when he was hit by a car and killed while jogging. His wife came home from work to a mysteriously empty house—and then a police car pulled into the driveway.
- Millie was recovering from a heart attack in the hospital when another massive attack occurred and her heart stopped instantly. Her son found her dead on the floor of her hospital room.
- Lilly had a terminal illness, but her death was hastened when a lengthy power outage at her parents' home stopped the respirator that kept her breathing.

2 DEFINITIONS AND KEY THOUGHTS

- *Death was not God's original desire* for humanity. God created human beings for life not death. Adam had received the breath of life (see Gen. 2:7). It was not until Adam and Eve sinned that death arrived.
- Death is difficult because it is *loss*—real and painful because a loved one is gone; symbolic because it reminds us of lost innocence, sin, and punishment.
- Death is distasteful and dreaded by humans, though God describes it as a gateway to a glorious new day. *Humans see death as an end* of a journey; God sees it as the beginning of a journey to a better life.
- Responses to death are as *different* as are individuals.
- The bereaved may *ask questions* like, "Why did God take him away?"; "Why did I get mad at her before she left the house?"; "What was I thinking when I let him go without me?"; "What if . . . ?"; "Why . . . ?"
- Sudden death can lead to a *complicated grieving process* because the suddenness often leaves feelings of anger, guilt, and abandonment.
- We now know that there are "stages" of grief as described by various theorists. On hearing of a death, two stages are particularly serious: *shock* and *denial*. *Shock* is an emotional and physical response to the news of a sudden death. The bereaved person may experience a racing heartbeat, shortness of breath, and feelings of unreality.

  Denial may follow quickly, and the bereaved person may start doing ordinary things like washing the dishes or balancing a checkbook in an attempt to

> I must not think it strange if God takes in youth those whom I would have kept on earth until they were older. God is peopling eternity, and I must not restrict him to old men and women.
>
> *Jim Elliot*

reestablish normalcy. Denial is usually broken when the person must face up to the many decisions that follow a death.

What the Grieving Person Needs

David K. Switzer has described eight needs that must be fulfilled for effective resolution of the grieving process:

1. Accept the reality and finality of the physical death.
2. Become aware of and express all the feelings about the loss or toward the deceased. Sometimes this concerns the way the person died.
3. Break the emotional ties with the deceased; that is, not act as though he or she is still physically present.
4. Break habitual patterns of speech and other behaviors that assume the deceased is physically present.
5. Affirm one's own value apart from interaction and connection with the deceased.
6. Reaffirm and therefore allow to come back to life those characteristics and behaviors that contribute to one's ongoing and growing life.
7. Cultivate both old and new relationships.
8. Rediscover meaning in life.

> For to me, to live is Christ, and to die is gain.
> *Philippians 1:21*

ASSESSMENT INTERVIEW 3

Don't be surprised by the variety of responses people have to the death of a loved one. People may do bizarre things in the moments after hearing of a death. It is common for a person to say things like, "Why not me instead?" or "I think I caused it." These are not necessarily true confessions; they are the *cries of a breaking heart.*

Don't rush the grieving process. The anguish is a necessary part of recovery.

Don't tell the person how to feel. Your presence as a loving and attentive listener is your greatest gift to the person who is overwhelmed by grief.

Rule Outs

1. Are you having any physical symptoms as a result of this death? (*Be aware of signs of physical distress; the bereaved person may need medical attention.*)
2. Are you feeling increasingly depressed and suicidal? Is the grief beginning to subside? (*After a certain amount of time, the grief should be lessening. There will always be pain, but if the person is not improving over the course of several weeks, other intervention may be needed.*)

Questions Immediately after a Death

1. Who has died and how? Were you present? (*Ask the bereaved to share with you what happened. Talking about the experience is cathartic and will help the bereaved person come to terms with the situation.*)
2. Where are other family members located? (*What kind of a support system exists for helping the person through the experience of loss?*)
3. If the deceased had children, where are they? (*Are there any other individuals who will need help dealing with the loss of the deceased?*)
4. Besides the obvious shock and pain, what else are you feeling right now? (*Probe for feelings like guilt, anger, and fear. Try to identify the source of the feelings—and then make a mental note to talk further about it at a later time.*)

Questions to Help the Grieving Person

1. What are your favorite memories about this person?
2. What did you like best about him [her]?
3. What were his [her] best qualities? What were some things that bothered or irritated you? (*This helps the person realize that the deceased person was not perfect.*)
4. When do you miss this person the most—morning or evening?
5. To whom do you talk when you think about this person?
6. What do you need from the person you're talking to that will help with your grief?
7. Do you still cry when you think of this person?
8. In what ways is your life better for having known this person?
9. In what positive ways can you keep alive the good memories and the joy of having known this person?

4 WISE COUNSEL

Some bereaved people may feel very overwhelmed by the decisions required after a death. Others will argue with family members over decisions, such as cremation versus burial or open versus closed casket. Your first job may be to *help the family and friends come to consensus.* Remind people that the wishes of the deceased, if known, are not as important after death as what will make the survivors more comfortable. If that means canceling a cremation, then encourage family members to do it.

Provide plenty of biblical images of hope, heaven, and resurrection, but *avoid being glib or superficial.* When a loved one dies, the loss is acute, and knowing that the person is in heaven is not always an immediate comfort to those who are left behind—because they *are* left behind.

When dealing with a sudden death, *identify a family friend or other volunteer who can help with some of the practical tasks* that must be done for the funeral. Help the bereaved person prioritize what needs to be done. Aid in identifying a funeral home, writing an obituary, calling other family members and friends, and other tasks. It should be noted that the process of grief and bereavement will *not be resolved by things returning to "normal,"* as the person understands it. A death always drastically changes the identity, roles, and responsibilities of the person closest to the deceased. Recovery will come as the bereaved person learns to *cope with and take on the new dynamics and tasks of daily life.*

ACTION STEPS 5

1. Focus on Basic Needs

- *Be sure to focus on basic needs—food, shelter, safety. If these needs are not met, the critical emotional issues will be even harder to handle.*
- *People who are experiencing shock may neglect hygiene, necessary medications, or meals.*

2. Discover the Best Ways of Coping

- *Assess the level of emotions present by using some of the questions suggested above.*
- *Some people process crisis emotions better by being busy while others need to be alone. Help the former to find something simple to do and help the latter find a quiet place to be alone.*

3. Seek Social Interaction

- Do not withdraw from social interactions. Find support in your friendships.
- Some friendships will be different (for example, if a spouse has died), but your friends will still want your company, even without the other person.

4. Help the Children

- *If children are involved, counsel the family on strategies for helping them.* Children often feel responsible for a sudden death, and teens can react in particularly complicated ways if a relationship with the deceased was tense.
- Children need, first of all, to feel secure. Reassure them that their family will be okay.
- *If a parent is in acute distress, try to ensure that the children are cared for by a familiar person who is calm.*
- Avoid statements that indicate to a child that God caused the death because He "wanted Mom/Dad/Grandma/Johnny in heaven with Him."

He whose head is in heaven need not fear to put his feet into the grave.
Matthew Henry

- Demystify death for children. Most funeral directors will openly answer a child's curious questions.
- Help children begin to process feelings of anger, guilt, and abandonment. They need to know that such feelings are normal.

5. Allow Time

- It will take time for the pain to subside.
- You need to truly grieve. The grieving process is healthy.
- *Remind the person, when appropriate, of the stages the grieving person goes through.*

6 BIBLICAL INSIGHTS

But now he is dead; why should I fast? Can I bring him back again? I shall go to him, but he shall not return to me.

2 Samuel 12:23

After the death of David and Bathsheba's first son, David's only consolation was that eventually he would "go to him." While the child was alive, David had begged God to spare his life. When the child died, however, David was confident that the boy was with God and he would see him again.

Christian parents who have faced the devastation of the death of a young child can take hope in David's faith that God will bring the little ones to Himself.

Precious in the sight of the LORD is the death of His saints.

Psalm 116:15

It is sad when loved ones die, and it is natural to grieve.

God says that the death of a believer is "precious in the sight of the Lord." For believers, death is merely a gateway into their home in heaven where they ultimately belong.

But now Christ is risen from the dead, and has become the firstfruits of those who have fallen asleep. For since by man came death, by Man also came the resurrection of the dead. For as in Adam all die, even so in Christ all shall be made alive.

1 Corinthians 15:20–22

Jesus brought the promise of resurrection from the dead. He accomplished this by becoming human, dying, and then rising again.

Someday in God's new creation, death itself will be destroyed: "The last enemy that will be destroyed is death" (1 Cor. 15:26).

We must always be ready to die, ready to stand before God, and ready to thank Him for all He has done in giving us salvation.

So we are always confident, knowing that while we are at home in the body we are absent from the Lord. For we walk by faith, not by sight. We are confident, yes, well pleased rather to be absent from the body and to be present with the Lord.

2 Corinthians 5:6–8

Exactly what happens after someone dies? The Bible doesn't go into much detail, but it does say that believers who die—that is, are "absent from the body"—will be "present with the Lord" (see also Phil. 1:23). They will experience a state of blessedness with God.

When Christ returns, the believers who have died will be raised and the living believers will be changed, and all will receive glorified, eternal bodies (see 1 Thess. 4:16–18).

God has promised that His people will be with Him forever. We can take hope in God's sure promise.

I have fought the good fight, I have finished the race, I have kept the faith. Finally, there is laid up for me the crown of righteousness, which the Lord, the righteous Judge, will give to me on that Day, and not to me only but also to all who have loved His appearing.

2 Timothy 4:7–8

Believers can face death with confidence, knowing that God is waiting for them.

May we all be able to say, "I have fought the good fight, I have finished the race, I have kept the faith."

Blessed are the dead who die in the Lord from now on . . . that they may rest from their labors, and their works follow them.

Revelation 14:13

This chapter of Revelation paints a picture of stark contrasts—eternal life with God or eternal life without God.

Where will you be for eternity?

PRAYER STARTER 7

Dear Lord, thank You for the life of _____. Our hearts are very heavy that he [she] is no longer here. Although this death may make no sense now, please bring sense from it, and glorify Yourself through it. Give us Your Holy Spirit as a Comforter in the minutes and hours and days to come and help us to understand each other's needs at this time . . .

8 RECOMMENDED RESOURCES

Graham, Billy. *Death and the Life After.* Thomas Nelson, 1994.

Lynch, Thomas. *The Undertaking: Life Studies from the Dismal Trade.* Penguin, 1998.

Nouwen, Henri. *Turn My Mourning into Dancing: Finding Hope in Hard Times.* Thomas Nelson, 2004.

Veerman, Dave, and Bruce Barton. *When Your Father Dies: How a Man Deals with the Loss of His Father.* Thomas Nelson, 2006.

Zimmerman, Dennis. *Healing Death: Finding Wholeness When a Cure Is No Longer Possible.* Pilgrim Press, 2007.

Websites

American Association of Christian Counselors (www.aacc.net)

Ecounseling (www.ecounseling.com)

Decision Making and the Will of God

- Gracie has always been a bright student. Now she has had a number of universities accept her application for enrollment. For the first time in her life, she feels as though she doesn't have the answer. Which school would God want her to attend?

- Casey has been dating Madison for more than two years. He is thinking of proposing to her, but with a lifelong decision such as this, he wants to make sure that this is what God would have him do.

- At forty-five Paul is not sure if he can handle another career change. A great opportunity has just surfaced, but he is wondering if his family is up for the challenge. He wishes he knew if this was God's plan.

- Mary wants to get a divorce. She's met another man and wants a counselor to tell her that it's okay for her to make that decision; she thinks the grass is much greener on the other side of the fence.

DEFINITIONS AND KEY THOUGHTS 2

- *Do not tell the person what he or she should do*, even if it seems obvious to you. The person is seeking God's will, not yours.

- Encourage the counselee to *wait on God's answer*. He will reveal His will to those who earnestly seek Him. And remember that God is much more patient than we are.

- Do not allow *superstitions* to enter into the decision-making process (such as blindly pointing to a passage in the Bible or following some dream or coincidence). God uses His Word, not luck or superstition.

- God is most interested in a *relationship* in which we lean on Him daily for our strength and guidance. He will not show a person his or her entire life's journey. He wants us to rely on Him throughout our lives.

- Decision making can be *fearful* for some people. They speak of past decisions that ended disastrously. Of course this doesn't mean that God wasn't in those earlier decisions.

- Be careful not to put too much credence in a person's feelings. *Emotions can be misleading* and may cause a person to sin. Often people will quote Psalm 37:4 and say that God wants to give them the desires of their heart. This is true only after the first half of that verse is fulfilled, which is that they should be delighting themselves in the Lord.

3 ASSESSMENT INTERVIEW

Most Christians *want to know and follow the will of God.* They just want to know without a doubt that they are doing it.

First, explain to the person you are counseling that there is a difference between God's "directive" and His "permissive" will.

Directive Will

God's directive will is His specific, absolute, unchangeable, unconditional will. Examples of God's directive will are:

Assemble with others in worship (Heb. 10:25).

Marry only another Christian (2 Cor. 6:14).

Raise children by God's standards (Eph. 6:4).

Obey and honor parents (Eph. 6:1–2).

Support one's own family (1 Tim. 5:8).

Proclaim Christ (Acts 1:8).

Meditate on the Scriptures (Ps. 1:2).

Show love to others (1 Corinthians 13).

> I will instruct you and teach you in the way you should go; I will guide you with My eye.
> *Psalm 32:8*

Permissive Will

God's permissive will is what He allows to happen. Most of what we see every day is under God's permissive will. The building of a new grocery store, falling interest rates, rising gas prices, the choices we make that glorify God, and the ones we make that do not honor God are all within God's permissive will simply because He permits them to occur.

Questions for Understanding God's Plan

Ask questions that will help the person understand that *God does have a plan and will reveal it.* It's a process that occurs slowly. Often God is fine with any number of possibilities, providing they glorify Him equally. Remember, it's much easier to see God in the rearview mirror than through the windshield. This means that as we look back on our lives, we can usually see how God was working and how He was actively involved. It's much harder to look forward and see the good that He is about to do.

1. Tell me about your relationship with the Lord.
2. Do you think that you initiated this relationship or did God reach out to you?

3. What major decisions have you made in the past?

4. How have you changed as a result of these decisions?

5. Do you believe that God was with you when you made these decisions?

6. If so, how could you tell?

7. What might happen in this current situation if you make the "wrong" decision?

8. Do you think that God will disown you if you make the wrong decision?

9. If you make the wrong decision, do you think God could change His plan to accommodate that wrong decision?

10. How might God direct you toward His will or plan in this decision?

11. How will you know if you have made the right decision?

12. Will any or all of the options you are considering bring glory to God?

13. You are searching for the unrevealed will of the Lord. Do you currently follow what you already know is the revealed will of God as described in His Word?

WISE COUNSEL : 4

Faith and action go hand in hand. It is not necessary to make a final decision hurriedly, yet we must also not become complacent and do nothing. We must engage in activities, like searching the Scriptures and prayerfully seeking counsel from mature believers.

When we have God's peace concerning a previous action, we can *receive it as God's confirmation.* This peace is a knowing, a revelation, a confirmation that God is with us and we are walking in His will. If the peace isn't present, then we had better go back to the Lord and continue to seek His will.

ACTION STEPS : 5

1. God Will Show His Will

(*Remind the person of James 1:5–6. Assure the person that God wants to reveal His will to him or her even more than the person wants to know it.*) God will speak through His Word, His people, and through prayer. Search the Scriptures, be patient, and pray through the decision at hand.

2. Be Patient

At times it may be necessary to make the decision not to make a decision. In other words allow yourself the luxury of purposely not deciding until a later time. Often God's will becomes evident after a period of time, and we have to backtrack because we rushed into a decision. During the waiting period, keep seeking God's will.

3. Be Proactive

List the major decisions that you have made in the past. List the results of those decisions. Mark the decisions that you believe God directed.

4. List Options

List as many options as you can think of regarding the current issue.

5. What's Obvious?

Are any of these options automatically outside the will of God? For example, are any illegal or immoral?

6. Keep Praying

Commit yourself to praying over your options for a specified length of time.

7. Get Wise Counsel

Ask advice from a trusted Christian friend or family member regarding this decision.

8. Make the Decision

After the specified amount of time has passed, make a decision and accept that decision as God's will.

> The Christian life is not merely a matter of getting from here to there . . . from point A to point B. Instead, God's will for us in this life is more about the journey itself.
> *Charles R. Swindoll*

6 BIBLICAL INSIGHTS

Yet there shall be a space between you and it, about two thousand cubits by measure. Do not come near it, that you may know the way by which you must go, for you have not passed this way before.

Joshua 3:4

Every day brings new experiences and new challenges that stretch our faith in God. Without God, people are left to wonder what direction to take. With God, believers can know that every new day is in His hands and He will guide according to His eternal plan.

As the Israelites followed the ark to "know the way," so we can look to God and His Word to know the way He wants us to go.

But [Rehoboam] rejected the advice which the elders had given him, and consulted the young men who had grown up with him, who stood before him.

1 Kings 12:8

Rehoboam's unwillingness to listen to the older and wiser men ultimately led to the division of his kingdom.

It is wise to seek counsel, but then we must compare that advice to God's Word. God knows the way we should go.

I beseech you therefore, brethren, by the mercies of God, that you present your bodies a living sacrifice, holy, acceptable to God, which is your reasonable service. And do not be conformed to this world, but be transformed by the renewing of your mind, that you may prove what is that good and acceptable and perfect will of God.

Romans 12:1–2

Paul used a picture to describe how believers should live, offering *themselves* to God as living sacrifices. Thus they could be transformed by the Holy Spirit and have renewed minds.

This transformation and renewal help God's people know His good, acceptable, and perfect will.

We are promised that we can know God's will for us when making tough decisions. We must humbly pray and seek His guidance, knowing that He will answer.

If any of you lacks wisdom, let him ask of God, who gives to all liberally and without reproach, and it will be given to him.

James 1:5

Sometimes we must choose between two good options. Whatever the choice, we need God's wisdom to see life from His perspective and make good decisions in difficult circumstances.

When we ask, we need to be willing to do what He says!

Now this is the confidence that we have in Him, that if we ask anything according to His will, He hears us.

1 John 5:14

How can believers know God's will as they make decisions? First, they should consider whether they truly want to know what God wants and if they truly want to follow His leadership. Then they should pray and study God's Word for guidance.

The Holy Spirit will help them interpret what God is doing in and around them in the decision-making process.

Believers learn how to seek God's will, asking not what they want, but what He wants for them. When the answer comes, believers know it and can act on it.

> In each action we must look beyond the action at our past, present and future state, and at others whom it affects, and see the relation of all those things. And then we shall be very cautious.
>
> *Blaise Pascal*

71

7 PRAYER STARTER

Thank You, Lord, that You promise to give wisdom to those who ask. _____ needs wisdom today to make the right decision. He [she] wants to know Your will and wants to do what You would have him [her] do, but it's just not clear right now . . .

8 RECOMMENDED RESOURCES

Eldredge, John. *The Journey of Desire.* Thomas Nelson, 2001.

Friesen, Garry, and J. Robin Maxson. *Decision-Making and the Will of God: A Biblical Alternative to the Traditional View.* Multnomah Books, 2004.

Gire, Ken. *Weathering the Grace of God: The Beauty God Brings from Life's Upheavals.* Vine Books, 2001.

Hinson, Ed. *Using Your Spiritual Gifts.* American Association of Christian Counselors Life Enrich Video Series. See www.aacc.net for more information.

Websites

American Association of Christian Counselors (www.aacc.net)

Ecounseling.com (www.ecounseling.com)

Depression

PORTRAITS 1

- Each morning Angela struggles to find the energy to get out of bed. She feels listless and down. Her kids need her, but she can't summon the energy to even interact with them—much less prepare meals or clean the house.
- George is having a hard time thinking clearly. He lost his job and just can't seem to crawl out of the hole he feels that he's fallen into. He doesn't interview because he's so down, so he sits around at home and plays on the computer. And he just keeps spiraling downward.

DEFINITIONS AND KEY THOUGHTS 2

- Depression can have a variety of meanings because there are different types of depression. Clinical depression as a disorder is not the same as brief mood fluctuations or the feelings of sadness, disappointment, and frustration that everyone experiences from time to time and that last from minutes to a few days at most. Clinical depression is a more serious condition that lasts weeks to months, and sometimes even years.

  Misdiagnosis of depression is common. It can often be misdiagnosed as anxiety, which is a common affect in many types of depression or other mood disorders. Accurate assessment is the first step to proper treatment.

- Depression is *on the rise*. People born after 1950 are ten times more likely to experience depression than their predecessors. Those between ages twenty-five and forty-five have the greatest percentage of depression, though adolescent groups have the fastest rate of depression growth (*source*: *A Woman's Guide to Overcoming Depression*; see Recommended Resources).

- *Women are twice as likely* to experience depression as men.

- According to the National Institutes of Health, depression causes inestimable pain for both those enduring the disorder and persons closest to them. It is said that depression destroys the lives of the victims and of their family members unnecessarily. Most sufferers *do not seek treatment* or believe their depression to be a treatable illness (*source*: National Institutes of Mental Health, http://www.nimh.nih.gov/publicat/depression).

> Thirty-five million Americans (more than 16 percent of the population) suffer from depression severe enough to warrant treatment at some time in their lives. In one given period, thirteen to fourteen million people experience the disorder.[1]

73

- Depression differs from sadness, which is a God-given reaction to loss that serves to slow people down so they can process grief. When one is sad, self-respect remains intact, intrinsic hope is maintained, and relief comes after crying and receiving support.

Types of Depression

- *Clinical/major depression* is distinct in that symptoms are so severe that they disrupt one's daily routine.
- *Dysthymic disorder* is a chronic, low-grade depression.
- *Bipolar disorder*, previously known as manic depression, is a type of mood disorder with severe changes in affect. A person may have periods of euphoric elatedness contrasted with periods of severe major depression.
- *Seasonal affective disorder (SAD)* is a severe onset of "winter blues" when one experiences depression, most often believed to be due to lack of sunlight (or vitamin D).

Causes of Depression

- Depression can be caused by *many life issues,* including anger; failure or rejection; family issues, such as divorce or abuse; fear; feelings of futility, lacking control over one's life; grief and loss; guilt or shame; loneliness or isolation; negative thinking; destructive misbeliefs; and stress. This is sometimes referred to as "*reactive depression.*" With this, the depression symptoms may be lowest in the morning and increase throughout the day. *Note*: Persistent reactive depression will change one's chemical balances and may compound depression.
- *Medical and biological factors* can also facilitate depression: inherited predisposition to depression, thyroid abnormalities, female hormone fluctuations, serotonin or norepinephrine irregularities, diabetes, B-12 or iron deficiencies, lack of sunlight or vitamin D, a recent stroke or heart attack, mitral valve prolapse, exposure to black mold, prescription drugs (antihypertensives, oral contraceptives), and recreational drugs (such as alcohol, marijuana, cocaine). When rooted in the biological, it is sometimes referred to as "*endogenous depression.*" With this, sufferers often feel worse in the morning.

Anxiety in
the heart of
man causes
depression, but
a good word
makes it glad.

Proverbs 12:25

Symptoms of Depression

- Symptoms are many, including decreased energy, fluctuating body weight, depleted concentration, irritability, bouts of crying, hopelessness/despair, a disinterest in pleasurable activities, social withdrawal, and thoughts of suicide.
- The Bible is replete with examples of depression with a variety of reasons and results: David wrote of his depression caused by unconfessed sin (Psalms 38; 51). God used depression to get Nehemiah's attention (Nehemiah 1–2). Job's devastat-

ing losses led him to curse the day he was born (Job 1–3). Elijah was so depressed over the situation with Israel's leaders that he wished to die (1 Kings 19).

ASSESSMENT INTERVIEW 3

Rule Outs

1. If 10 is extreme sadness, and 1 is feeling well, where are you today on a scale of 1 to 10? (*If the client is on the low side, find out what is causing the sadness. The issue to address may not be depression but other concerns.*)
2. Are you using drugs or alcohol?
3. Are you currently taking any medications?
4. When is the last time you had a thorough physical examination? (*If the counselee hasn't seen his or her doctor recently, give a medical referral.*)
5. Do you have significant mood swings? (*Ask about the existence of mania or hypomania and, if they exist, give a psychiatric referral.*)

General Questions

1. How long have you felt depressed?
2. What was happening in your life when you first became depressed? (*Someone who is depressed needs acceptance and gentleness. The counselee may already be feeling as if he or she has failed in some way. Begin by listening to your counselee's story without judgment.*)
3. Have you been depressed before?
4. Do you have a family history of depression?
5. Do you have difficulty concentrating?
6. Have you lost interest in pleasurable activities?
7. Have you noticed changes in your eating or sleeping patterns?
8. Are you dealing with guilt or fear about anything? (*Fear is prevalent in many kinds of depression—anxiety and depression coexist in 70 percent of those diagnosed with depression.*)
9. What do you see in your future?
10. Have you had any thoughts about injuring yourself or suicide? (*Sometimes the thoughts are vague, such as "It would be better if I were not here." Pay particular attention to anything indicating a means for carrying out these thoughts. Someone who is suicidal and imagines having an automobile accident has both a plan and a means to carry it out.*)

> Depressed Christians certainly should continue praying, reading the Bible, confessing sin and pursuing holiness, but unless God or a professional Christian counselor says otherwise, don't assume the depression is caused by a spiritual problem. That type of thinking can keep a depressed Christian from seeking professional help.[2]

4 WISE COUNSEL

The most dangerous symptom of depression is *suicidal ideation*. If, as a result of your questions, you discover that the counselee desires to hurt him- or herself, do not hesitate to involve other family members or a mental health professional if necessary. See also the section on Suicide.

If you recommend that your client see a physician, *make sure he or she understands that it is okay to take medications* if needed to get depression under control. Communicate that using medication doesn't mean that the counselee is weak or lacks faith.

5 ACTION STEPS

1. Watch Physical Health

- *(If there would be no health risks, assign your counselee to moderate exercise such as a brisk walk.)* Research shows that thirty minutes of moderate daily exercise is very helpful in elevating mood; therefore I am assigning a daily brisk walk and I'll be checking up. Find a partner to walk with—it makes it harder to avoid the activity if someone is waiting for you.
- Have a medical checkup and work with a doctor on a diet program. Better eating habits (for example, less sugar and more vitamins) can be a big help.

2. Get Behind the Scenes

- *Assure the client that you will help them deal with whatever situation might be behind the depression.*
- *(If the counselee has recently suffered a significant loss, acknowledge that loss and begin to help him or her grieve.)* It's okay to feel upset, but you must also look to the light. Your loss is painful but future happiness in Christ is yours.
- Think honestly about what might be other deep sources of the depression.
- Keep a journal in which you write down thoughts that occur over the next couple of weeks regarding what is behind the depression.
- Carry a "daily mood log" and record the times when you feel most depressed. Write down what is happening and what you are thinking at those times.

3. Begin Clear Thinking

- *Challenge the counselee's statements and beliefs. For example, your counselee may say, "I'm totally worthless. I have nothing to give to anyone." Ask pointed questions to draw out the fact that this person does indeed have value.*
- Over the next week prepare a list of ten things you like about yourself—and three of them have to be physical characteristics. I will ask you to tell me those ten things.
- Very few things are really hopeless, and very few situations are "all bad."

> Out of the depths I have cried to You, O Lord; Lord, hear my voice! Let Your ears be attentive to the voice of my supplications. . . . I wait for the Lord, my soul waits, And in His word I do hope.
>
> *Psalm 130:1–2, 5*

4. Get Social Support

- Who are your friends? Are they people who help you counter the depression?
- What social groups are you currently involved in? (*Social isolation will only further his or her depression.*)
- What is your level of church involvement? Who at church could be of help and support?

5. Pay Attention to Spiritual Issues

- Do you have any unconfessed sin that is promoting the depression?
- Do you need to forgive someone as a means of moving toward personal health?
- Are you motivated to connect with Christ? (*When one is motivated by something other than God, frustration and depression can ensue.*)
- Do you believe that God can both remove your depression and provide complete happiness (or joy)?

> Depression is not something you can just "snap out of." It's caused by an imbalance of brain chemicals, along with other factors. Like any serious medical condition, depression needs to be treated.[3]

BIBLICAL INSIGHTS 6

But [Elijah] went a day's journey into the wilderness, and came and sat down under a broom tree. And he prayed that he might die, and said, "It is enough! Now, LORD, take my life, for I am no better than my fathers!"

1 Kings 19:4

Life has highs and lows, and as in a mountain range, the lows often come right after the highs. Like Elijah, we may scale the heights of spiritual victory only to soon find ourselves in the dark valley of depression.

While certain forms of clinical depression should be professionally treated, many depressed feelings are part of life's ups and downs.

Like Elijah, we should listen for God's "still small voice" (1 Kings 19:12) to comfort us.

Then as [Elijah] lay and slept under a broom tree, suddenly an angel touched him, and said to him, "Arise and eat." Then he looked, and there by his head was a cake baked on coals, and a jar of water. So he ate and drank, and lay down again.

1 Kings 19:5–6

Depression can drain energy, twist values, and assault one's faith.

Depression can affect anyone.

God provided care to Elijah on many levels. He provided food so that Elijah regained his physical and emotional strength. An angel touched Elijah, confirming to Elijah that he was not alone. Also, twice, God encouraged Elijah to rest.

> *Why are you cast down, O my soul? And why are you disquieted within me? Hope in God, for I shall yet praise Him for the help of His countenance.*
>
> *Psalm 42:5*

Depressed feelings may cause some people to turn away from God. Others, like David, allow those disquieted, depressed feelings to make them "hope in God," remembering His goodness.

During such times, living by faith takes on new meaning.

Depressed people must learn to trust what they cannot feel or see. They must understand that happiness comes from communion with God, not anything on the earth.

> *To console those who mourn in Zion, to give them beauty for ashes, the oil of joy for mourning, the garment of praise for the spirit of heaviness; that they may be called trees of righteousness, the planting of the LORD, that He may be glorified.*
>
> *Isaiah 61:3*

The Bible recognizes the heaviness of depression. God's love and understanding reach out to those who are depressed and discouraged.

God promises to give consolation, beauty in place of ashes, oil of joy in place of mourning, and a garment of praise instead of a spirit of heaviness.

> Besides the obvious impairments in mood and relationships, untreated depression affects multiple areas of a person's life. It is one of the top three causes of disability and diminished work productivity.[4]

7 PRAYER STARTER

Lord, at times we all feel downhearted. Today _____ feels like he [she] is walking in darkness with no way out. I pray, Lord, that You will provide healing and help us discern what is going on deep in his [her] heart. If there is deep pain or loss, guilt or shame, help us to have the discernment to bring it into the light and confess it by Your grace . . .

8 RECOMMENDED RESOURCES

Anderson, Neil, and Joanne Anderson. *Overcoming Depression.* Regal Books, 2004.

Burns, David. *The Feeling Good Handbook.* Plume Books, 1999.*

Hart, Archibald D., and Catherine Hart Weber. *A Woman's Guide to Overcoming Depression.* Revell, 2007.

Minirth, Frank, and Paul Meier. *Happiness Is a Choice: The Symptoms, Causes, and Cures of Depression.* Baker Books, 2007.

Tan, Siang-Yang, and John Ortberg. *Coping with Depression.* Baker Books, 2004.

Websites

American Association of Christian Counselors (www.aacc.net)

Ecounseling (www.ecounseling.com)

*Note: This is not written from a Christian perspective but offers relevant and insightful material.

Discouragement

1 PORTRAITS

- Mark has worked two jobs most of his adult life just to make ends meet. He has three children and a wife who works in the home and has a part-time job outside the home. Recently Mark lost the higher paying of his two jobs. If that weren't enough, their older son was suspended from school the same week, having drugs in his possession. Mark blames himself for not being at home enough.

- Lila is a young woman who has been out of college and in the workforce for almost five years. All her college friends are married, and she longs for a husband and family. This is all she has ever dreamed of. She had a relationship for almost seven years with a Christian high school sweetheart. She blames herself for the breakup, and wonders, *What if*? She sits at home most nights alone in her tiny apartment. A married friend is worried sick about her and doesn't know how to help her.

2 DEFINITIONS AND KEY THOUGHTS

- Discouragement is a *feeling* of despair, sadness, or lack of confidence. A discouraged person is disheartened. Three underlying causes contribute to discouragement:

  - lack of confidence in ourselves
  - lack of confidence in God
  - lack of hope for the future

- Because discouragement is a feeling or emotion, it can *play games* with our minds. We must learn how to control our minds, and thus our discouragement, and lean on God for strength.

- Joshua was challenged with discouragement as he led the people of Israel into the Promised Land. God told Joshua, "Be strong and of good courage" (Josh. 1:6).

- God also reminded Joshua that *the key to overcoming discouragement was a personal relationship with Him.* The Lord told Joshua: "This Book of the Law shall not depart from your mouth, but you shall meditate in it day and night, that you may observe to do according to all that is written in it. For then you will make your way prosperous, and then you will have good success" (Josh.1:8).

- Discouraged people often blame themselves or God and ask, *What if . . . ?* This is Satan's trap, his way of trying to have us think, *I blew it* or *God isn't capable.*

- God has a much bigger picture for our lives than we could ever imagine. *Challenges along the way are God's way of refining us*, preparing us for the bigger and better picture—the first prize.

- If not dealt with, discouragement *can lead to depression*, which can stop people in their tracks. People must be taught how to deal with discouragement before it becomes depression.

- Discouragement reveals an *unwillingness to trust God*. It can be dealt a deathblow when people consistently cast all their cares on God.

- Discouragement can be *caused by many different circumstances and feelings*:

  - shouldering one's own worries, cares, and fears; then collapsing under the weight
  - out of control events
  - circumstances that were within one's control but were handled poorly
  - failure—either occurring in the present, in the past, or a perceived potential for failure in the future

> There are three stages in the work of God: Impossible; Difficult; Done.
>
> *Hudson Taylor*

ASSESSMENT INTERVIEW : 3

1. What are some things or events that make you discouraged?
2. Do you have control over these things or are they out of your control?
3. Describe yourself using three adjectives.
4. Describe what you think someone else would say about you (a friend, a parent, a coach). (*Note to questions 3 and 4: Sometimes there is an underlying problem of lack of self-confidence that leads to discouragement. If you suspect such a problem, it needs to be addressed.*)
5. When you feel discouraged, what do you do?
6. Do you have a direction or plan for your life?
7. What do you see yourself doing three years from now, five years from now?
8. Is failure an option for you? What does God think about failure?
9. Envision yourself failing at something. How does that make you feel?
10. Envision yourself succeeding at something. How does that make you feel?

WISE COUNSEL : 4

Discouragement ought to be the first indication that *it is time to pray*. People may become discouraged as they become overwhelmed and begin to neglect prayer (ironically this is when they need to be relying on God more).

Help the person understand that God uses our trials to shape our personal and spiritual lives for the better, and for His glory. Paul tells us, "We know that all things work together for good to those who love God, to those who are the called according to His purpose" (Rom. 8:28).

Many times what leads to discouragement are *events that are out of control*. This is where faith in God comes in. Realizing that God sees the events in our lives before we do should help us not feel so overwhelmed.

There are times when discouragement is a result of *something the client could have controlled* (such as flunking college or being late to work). These events should be seen as wake-up calls and opportunities to improve, not hopeless or disastrous events.

Often the discouraged will need someone to be *accountable* to if this has been a lifelong struggle.

The person needs to be helped to see discouragement as an *opportunity to grow in Christ* and rediscover the person God designed in His image. Help the client to see discouragement as a time to *step back and look at life* and perhaps change some goals or behaviors (consider whether the unachieved goals are in keeping with God's plan for the person's life).

Help the person understand that feelings of discouragement will likely *creep into his or her life from time to time*; this is normal because of our human nature. Share with the person that even when one has confidence in the abilities and greatness of God and has a better grip on handling challenges, it doesn't mean discouragement will never come again.

> Look, the LORD your God has set the land before you; go up and possess it, as the LORD God of your fathers has spoken to you; do not fear or be discouraged.
>
> *Deuteronomy 1:21*

5 ACTION STEPS

1. Be Realistic

Understand that discouragement is a part of life and often is a result of things or events that are out of our control. This does not mean that we are failures.

2. Give Discouragement to God

When we have confidence in Him, we gain confidence in ourselves. God sees events before we do.

3. Rethink Goals

Pray and ask God for a fresh direction. After prayer and consideration of God's will, make plans for an optimistic future.

4. No "What Ifs"

Stop considering what might have been. This type of thinking will only bring defeat.

5. Don't Focus on Feelings

Stop using feelings to determine how to handle discouragement. Feelings can change drastically with our mood. We must focus on change and doing it with God's help.

6. Keep a Journal

Call your journal "Discouragements That Become Encouragements." Document each discouragement and what was done with God's help to turn it around.

7. Be Ready

Be ready for what God may have in mind for you. When you have confidence in God, you will gain confidence in yourself. This will be a huge step toward overcoming discouragement.

BIBLICAL INSIGHTS : 6

The steps of a good man are ordered by the LORD, and He delights in his way. Though he fall, he shall not be utterly cast down; for the LORD upholds him with His hand.

Psalm 37:23–24

Following God, having our steps "ordered by the LORD," does not guarantee success in every endeavor. In fact, some lessons that God wants to teach can come only through failure.

When God's people fall, however, He does not allow them to be "utterly cast down." Instead, He helps them back up so they can learn what He wants to teach them and move on toward success.

The only real failures are those who give up on God and refuse to get up and go on.

For a righteous man may fall seven times and rise again, but the wicked shall fall by calamity.

Proverbs 24:16

Failure is never final until a person quits trying. As the person continues to try, failure is really no more than a setback, a possibility to learn from mistakes and try again.

Failure is a part of the human experience. It can be painful and embarrassing but it can also be a great teacher. God's definition of success does not preclude failure but it includes a willingness to refuse to quit, to learn from one's mistakes, and to try again. Failure can be our greatest teacher.

And let us not grow weary while doing good, for in due season we shall reap if we do not lose heart.

Galatians 6:9

Paul encourages believers to "not grow weary while doing good."

Why are you cast down, O my soul? And why are you disquieted within me? Hope in God, for I shall yet praise Him for the help of His countenance.

Psalm 42:5

We must never allow discouragement to make us grow idle. Our good works are valuable to God.

Being confident of this very thing, that He who has begun a good work in you will complete it until the day of Jesus Christ.

Philippians 1:6

We won't be perfect until we are with Christ.

In the meantime, when we feel discouraged or distressed by our failures, we just need to remember that God won't give up on us. He began His good work in us and will complete it when we meet Him face-to-face.

Casting all your care upon Him, for He cares for you.

1 Peter 5:7

Casting our cares on God takes a great amount of trust and humility. We need to give Him all of our cares—not just the ones we think are big enough or important enough. God will even shoulder the cares that we have brought on ourselves—we can give them *all* to Him.

His shoulders are big enough to carry all of our fears, worries, and troubles. When we give our cares to God, we can brush off our discouragement and get back to work. We have much to do for God!

7 PRAYER STARTER

Dear Lord, Your child is discouraged today. He [she] feels unable to get past this, unable to do better. He [she] feels that he [she] has disappointed You and doesn't know where to turn. Help _____ see that You are the God of second chances. Show _____ the path You want him [her] to go, the changes You want him [her] to make as a result of this discouraging time . . .

8 RECOMMENDED RESOURCES

Clinton, Tim. *Moving On: Disappointment with God and Life and the Recovery of the Heart.* American Association of Christian Counselors Life Enrich Video Series. See www.aacc.net for more information.

Solomon, Lon. *Brokenness: How God Redeems Pain and Suffering.* Red Door Press, 2005.

Wilkinson, Bruce. *The Dream Giver.* Multnomah Books, 2003.

Websites

American Association of Christian Counselors (www.aacc.net)

Ecounseling (www.ecounseling.com)

Divorce

- Jennifer was served with divorce papers after her husband had an affair with a co-worker. She was devastated and begged him to attend counseling, but he has no interest in saving the marriage.
- Doug's wife walked out two years ago, leaving him alone to care for their three-year-old son. "She didn't want to be a mother anymore," he says. He wonders if he should file for divorce and move on with his life.
- Emily's husband has beaten her since they were married five years ago. He always apologizes, and she always takes him back, but then it happens again and the cycle is repeated. "As a Christian, I feel I have to stay with him," she explains, "but I'm tired of being a punching bag."
- Luke and Cathryn fight constantly over everything. "I'm worried our fighting is hurting the children," Cathryn sighs. "I think they'd be better off if we'd divorce. At least they would have a peaceful home."

DEFINITIONS AND KEY THOUGHTS 2

- Divorce and recovery will be something *today's pastors will deal with much more* than their predecessors.
- According to the 2000 census, for some U.S. ethnic populations, single-parent households outnumber homes with a married-couple family.
- Research by The Barna Group shows that 35 percent of married people endure a divorce, and 18 percent of divorced people are divorced multiple times. Multiple divorces are extraordinarily common among born-again Christians—23 percent are divorced two or more times.
- Almost half (46 percent) from the Baby Boomer generation have undergone a marital split, and millions more are expected to divorce in the next ten years. As for younger generations, they are likely to reach similar numbers. It is estimated that somewhere between 40 and 50 percent of marriages that begin this year will end in divorce.

Age at Marriage for Those Who Divorce in America

Age	Women	Men
Under 20 years old	27.6%	11.7%
20 to 24 years old	36.6%	38.8%
25 to 29 years old	16.4%	22.3%
30 to 34 years old	8.5%	11.6%
35 to 39 years old	5.1%	6.5%

From http://www.divorcerate.org/

> Children feel that their childhood has been lost forever. Divorce is a price they pay as forfeiture to their parents' failures, jeopardizing their future lives.
>
> *Dr. Judith Wallerstein*

- For marriages with children, Wallerstein and Blakeslee (in their book *The Good Marriage*) state from clinical experience that many children continue to battle with consequential unhappiness even ten to fifteen years after the divorce of their parents.

- Although Christian churches try to dissuade congregants from divorce, the rate of divorce among Christians is identical to the non-Christian population (35 percent). This data is not from those recently converted to faith, for data shows such divorces rarely occur before the married persons have accepted Christ as their Savior.

- *Divorce is a death* in every sense of the word—the death of a marriage, a family, and a dream. No one, especially a Christian, enters marriage expecting the marriage to end in divorce.

Scriptural View of Divorce

- Malachi 2:16 says that the *Lord hates divorce.* The rest of the verse reveals that Malachi was speaking to men who were disloyal to their wives. God's compassion toward the injured party is clear.

- Romans 12:15 says that we should "weep with those who weep." People recovering from the trauma of a broken marriage *need the church* to:

  - share in their sorrow
  - offer compassion
  - give reassurance that their church family will not reject them
  - impart hope that God will somehow bring good out of this
  - offer opportunities to serve in the church

Biblical Reasons for Divorce

- *Sexual activity outside the marital covenant* breaks the marriage vow. In Matthew 19:9 Jesus said that if a spouse has committed this type of sin, the other spouse is free to divorce and remarry. This does not mean divorce is required in instances where sexual sin has been committed, but it is permitted.

- Some maintain that *the abandonment* of a believer by a nonbelieving spouse leaves the believing spouse free to divorce the deserter (see 1 Cor. 7:15).

Reasons for Separation

- *Physical abuse* is not addressed in the Bible as a reason for divorce, but nowhere does Scripture specifically command a woman to stay in a home where she or her children are being physically abused. Separation (not divorce) is necessary for physical safety. Restoration should be predicated on *true repentance and by a significant change* in the abuser's behavior that lasts for an extended period of time. The church can serve as a protector of the abused by helping them find a safe place to stay, counseling, providing economic assistance, and using church discipline to hold the abusive spouse accountable.
- *Mental or verbal abuse* is not a biblical reason for divorce, although in some cases, such as severe belittling and demeaning behavior, it can be a cause for separation. Restoration should follow the pattern established for physical abuse (above).
- *Chemical addictions* to drugs or alcohol that result in harmful behavior to the spouse or children can be a reason for separation. Restoration should follow the pattern established for physical abuse (above).
- *Physical neglect*, such as not providing appropriate food, clothing, shelter, or supervision for the children, or physical abuse can result in life-threatening situations. The spouse should remove the children or the addict from the home to provide a safe environment for the children. Restoration should again follow the pattern outlined above with the church functioning in the role of a safe haven.

Consequences of Divorce

- Divorce creates *new problems* in exchange for the old ones (see under Wise Counsel below).
- Divorce *devastates children*. Research shows that, for most children, the pain they feel from the breakup of their home is just as painful ten years after the divorce as it was at the time of the divorce. The pain follows them into adulthood and affects their personalities and life choices.

ASSESSMENT INTERVIEW 3

For Couples Contemplating Divorce

When a couple comes to counseling with divorce as an option, *you are usually the last stop before a lawyer.*

Rule Outs

1. Do either of you have reason to believe that you are in physical danger from the other?
2. Has there been any type of abuse (physical, verbal, or sexual) to either of you or your children? (*If there has been physical or sexual abuse, the first step is to get the abused spouse and children away from the abuser and to a safe place.*

Counseling cannot begin until this takes place. After the abused person is safe, the couple can meet for counseling with the counselor and a representative of the church, such as an elder or pastor, present. It is a good idea if both genders are represented in the core counseling times.)

General Questions

1. What has prompted you to come to counseling at this time?
2. What do you hope the outcome of counseling will be?
3. Tell me about your marriage. How long have you been married?
4. Do you have any children?
5. How did you meet?
6. What first attracted you to each other?
7. How did you know this was the person you wanted to marry?
8. What was your first fight about?
9. When did the problems that bring you here today first arise?
10. What have you tried already to solve these problems?
11. Do you feel there is any hope for reconciliation?
12. Do you both want a divorce? Why or why not?
13. What would it take for you to want to reconcile?
14. Do either of you think you have biblical grounds for divorce?
15. What are they?
16. Are you both believers?
17. How is your walk with the Lord?
18. Tell me about your background, your parents, and your siblings. What was growing up like for you?
19. Are there any divorces in your family or among your friends?
20. What do you think divorce will accomplish for you?
21. How do think the divorce will affect your children?
22. Would you like to see what the Bible says about divorce?

For a Victim of Divorce—A Person Divorced against His or Her Will

When a victim of divorce comes for counseling, it is a positive sign that he or she feels worthy of help, even though the person's *self-worth may have been demolished* by the divorce.

Reinforce his or her decision by reminding the person that the Bible says only *the wise seek counsel* (Prov. 12:15).

> God does not hate divorced people—He hates the cruelty of divorce. Divorce does not eliminate problems; it just substitutes a new set of problems.
>
> *Author unknown*

Rule Outs

1. On a scale of 1 to 10, with 10 being joy and 1 being hopelessness, where would you put yourself? (*You will want to rule out the presence of clinical depression.*)

2. Do you feel down much of the day on most days?

3. Have you had any thoughts of hurting yourself or others? (*If you feel the client is a danger to self or others, refer him or her to a professional counselor immediately.*)

General Questions

1. What brought you here today?
2. What do you hope the outcome of counseling will be?
3. Tell me about your marriage. How did you meet your spouse?
4. What attracted you to him or her?
5. Did you notice any character qualities that gave you concern?
6. Did your feelings change during the marriage? How?
7. How did your parents feel about your spouse?
8. When did you first realize there were problems?
9. How did your spouse tell you he or she wanted to end the marriage?
10. What were your feelings?
11. What did you say and do?
12. Who did you go to for help?
13. Were they helpful?
14. What was the reaction of your family? Your spouse's family?
15. Do you have any children? How old are they?
16. How did they react when they heard?
17. How are they doing now?
18. What feelings have you gone through? Be honest.
19. Have you been able to talk about your feelings to anyone?
20. How do you express your anger?
21. Do you go to a support group?
22. What support do you have around you?
23. How are you and your children doing financially?
24. How does that make you feel?
25. What is your relationship with the Lord like?
26. Do you feel the Lord has rejected you or forgotten about you?
27. Let's see what the Bible says about that.

A girl had watched her mother verbally abuse her father for years. When she became an adult, she asked her dad, "Why do you put up with this? Why don't you leave her?" Her father gently replied, "The Bible says that men should love their wives as Christ loved the church. I don't think I've loved your mother that much yet. Do you?"

4 WISE COUNSEL

For Couples Contemplating Divorce

Share what God says about divorce. Explain that *God hates divorce* because of the hurt and devastation it brings to people. He still loves the people involved.

Make clear that the only biblical reasons for divorce are constant sexual sin (by one or both of the partners in violation of the marital covenant) and abandonment.

Make it clear that people are not commanded to divorce in these situations but are allowed to. *Forgiveness and restoration* are also an option when true repentance is embraced by the partner who has violated the marital covenant.

Empathize with the pain and hurt both spouses are going through, but share with them the new problems divorce will bring:

- financial difficulty of providing for two households
- probability of custody battles
- stress of single parenthood, with no one to help
- guilt from seeing the children's world torn apart
- dealing with sending children back and forth between the parents
- anger
- grief
- depression
- hopelessness

> When couples who are contemplating divorce because they cannot get along ask if they should stay together for the sake of the children, the typical answer is, "Absolutely."

For Victims of Divorce

Assure the counselee that *God sees his or her troubles. It grieves Him* to see the person hurt like this (Isa. 40:27–28).

Using the Scripture under Biblical Insights, let victims of divorce know that God loves them and totally accepts them. He *understands their feelings of betrayal and rejection* because He was also betrayed and rejected.

Explain *the importance of grieving* and the time it takes.

Grieving usually takes *two to five years and consists of five stages*: denial, anger, bargaining, depression, and acceptance. A person usually goes through these stages many times in different order until healing occurs.

Validate the evil done against the victim. Emphasize that, though the person is a victim, he or she can *become a survivor*.

Give hope that *God can bring good* out of this (Rom. 8:28).

Share with the person that other people may judge him or her unjustly; the victim will be tempted to feel shame because of the divorce. It is important that he or she *not accept that shame*. The person must put it back on the spouse who wronged him or her. Express that the person will never be truly healed and released until he or she *forgives self and the spouse*. As long as he or she lives with anger and resentment, the victim is not free from these feelings. (For more, see the section on Forgiveness.)

ACTION STEPS : 5

For Couples Contemplating Divorce

1. Put the Divorce on Hold

- Wait for a time and attend marriage counseling if you have not yet done so.
- Begin to meet with a trained marriage mentoring couple who can encourage and instruct you.
- Considering the devastation a divorce causes for all involved, isn't it worth your best efforts to save this marriage if you can? At the end of the marriage mentoring and counseling, you can revisit your decision and see if there is any reason to be hopeful.

2. Go to Marriage Mentoring and Counseling

- (*Have on file the names of several good Christian marriage counselors who have a record of success in helping couples restore their marriages.*) Call one of these recommended counselors.
- Work with pastoral staff to determine how and when to utilize marriage mentoring and professional counseling.

3. Read Books

- *Suggest to the couple the list of books at the end of this article.*
- Many people were once where you are today and they now have healthy and fulfilling marriages. It is helpful to read what has helped others.

> There were approximately 2,230,000 marriages in 2005—down from 2,279,000 the previous year, despite a total population increase of 2.9 million over the same period.[1]

For Victims of Divorce

1. Go to a Recovery Group

- Start attending a divorce recovery group. Many larger churches have these groups. (*Research and recommend.*)
- Some groups last a specific number of weeks and some are 12-step programs that meet every week indefinitely.

2. Go to Counseling

- Start individual counseling on a weekly basis. You need someone to whom you can be accountable.
- Make a commitment to meet with a counselor once a week.

3. Make No Major Decisions

- Do not make any major life decisions for at least a year without running it by your counselor or pastor.
- This helps guard against making poor decisions while you are still emotionally vulnerable.

4. Develop No New Relationships

- Do not rush into any new dating relationships.
- Focus on letting God fill the emptiness inside you. You need to heal before entering another relationship.

5. Pursue Church Involvement

- Get involved in church and join a Sunday school class.
- Seek out friends of the same sex to whom you can talk and with whom you can do activities.
- When you feel up to it, serve and help others.

6 : BIBLICAL INSIGHTS

They said to Him, "Why then did Moses command to give a certificate of divorce, and to put her away?" He said to them, "Moses, because of the hardness of your hearts, permitted you to divorce your wives, but from the beginning it was not so."

Matthew 19:7–8

8.1% of coupled households consist of unmarried heterosexual partners, according to *The State of Our Unions 2005*, a report issued by the National Marriage Project at Rutgers University. The same study said that only 63% of American children grow up with both biological parents—the lowest figure in the Western world.[2]

God has always intended each married couple, one man and one woman, to remain married for life (Gen. 2:24). Moses had indeed permitted divorce (Deut. 24:1) but only because of the "hardness" of human hearts.

Divorce is permissible, but marriage vows should not be taken lightly.

God would have couples do their best—with His help—to keep their marriage intact. If a divorce occurs, God's compassionate love can heal even the deepest wounds.

When a man takes a wife and marries her, and it happens that she finds no favor in his eyes because he has found some uncleanness in her, and he writes her a certificate of divorce, puts it in her hand, and sends her out of his house.

Deuteronomy 24:1

God desires marriages to stay together. Because sin has infected all relationships, however, some marriages do not survive.

Moses's commands regarding divorce were given in a culture where a man could divorce his wife verbally and leave her with no property or rights. These commandments regulating divorce in Israel protected those left most helpless—the woman and her children.

The Bible does not give people an easy way out of their commitments. People are expected to honor their commitments.

The woman answered and said, "I have no husband." Jesus said to her, "You have well said, 'I have no husband,' for you have had five husbands, and the one whom you now have is not your husband; in that you spoke truly."

John 4:17–18

As of 2003, 43.7% of custodial mothers and 56.2% of custodial fathers were either separated or divorced. And in 2002, 7.8 million Americans paid about $40 billion in child and/or spousal support (84% of the payers were male).[3]

Divorce is not an unforgivable sin. As painful as divorce is for all involved and as heartbreaking as divorce is for those who face it without wanting it, God can touch broken hearts and lives and make them whole again.

When possible, couples should seek every option they can to avoid divorce.

At times, however, the unthinkable occurs. God is there to help us pick up the pieces.

If any brother has a wife who does not believe, and she is willing to live with him, let him not divorce her. And a woman who has a husband who does not believe, if he is willing to live with her, let her not divorce him. For the unbelieving husband is sanctified by the wife, and the unbelieving wife is sanctified by the husband; otherwise your children would be unclean, but now they are holy. But if the unbeliever departs, let him depart; a brother or a sister is not under bondage in such cases. But God has called us to peace. For how do you know, O wife, whether you will save your husband? Or how do you know, O husband, whether you will save your wife?

1 Corinthians 7:12–16

When one spouse becomes a Christian and the other doesn't, the believing spouse should stay in the marriage.

Paul explained that the marriage bond is so strong that a believer should not willingly break it. Through that union, the unbeliever may become a Christian. In any event, the believer can have a positive influence on the spouse and children.

PRAYER STARTER 7

Lord, we know that You hate divorce. You hate what it does to people. You hate the death it causes of a marriage, a family, a dream. And yet, it is a sad reality. We want Your will, Lord. We want what is best for all concerned. I pray today for . . .

RECOMMENDED RESOURCES 8

Carter, Les. *Grace and Divorce: God's Healing Gift to Those Whose Marriages Fall Short.* Jossey-Bass, 2004.

Clinton, Tim. *Before a Bad Goodbye.* Thomas Nelson, 1999.

Hart, Archibald D. *Helping Children Survive Divorce.* Thomas Nelson, 1997.

Wallerstein, Judith S., and Sandra Blakeslee. *The Good Marriage: How and Why Love Lasts.* Grand Central Publishing, 1996.*

Whiteman, Tom. *Divorce Recovery: For Those Starting Over Again.* American Association of Christian Counselors Life Enrich Video Series. See www.aacc.net for more information.

Websites

American Association of Christian Counselors (www.aacc.net)

Ecounseling (www.ecounseling.com)

Note: This is not written from a Christian perspective but offers relevant and insightful material.

> The divorce rate in 2005 (per 1,000 people) was 3.6—the lowest rate since 1970, and down from 4.2 in 2000 and from 4.7 in 1990.[4]

Domestic Violence

PORTRAITS 1

- Marge stared in the mirror at the new bruise on her face. She had never imagined that this would be happening to her. She knew her husband, Paul, was sorry; he had told her so again and again last night after he had seen the marks on her face where he had hit her. This morning before he left for work, he had promised that it wouldn't happen again if she would just give him another chance.

- Janet didn't know what to do. The wedding was only weeks away and she had always thought that she and Randy had made such a good couple. But lately he was becoming more controlling of her time and demanded to know where she was going when he wasn't with her. He was also getting jealous when some of her other friends spent time with her. But last night had been the worst. When she had disagreed with him, he had actually grabbed her arms and shaken her. She had been afraid. But surely he would calm down once they were married, wouldn't he?

- Tom was afraid. Marsha had always had a temper and would occasionally slap him when she got angry. But last night she had been drinking and when she attacked him, she really tried to hurt him. Tom knew he couldn't fight back but he didn't know how much more of it he could take.

> In homes where partner abuse occurs, children are 1,500 times more likely to be abused.[1]

DEFINITIONS AND KEY THOUGHTS 2

The U.S. Office on Violence Against Women (OVW) defines domestic violence as a "pattern of abusive behavior in any relationship that is used by one partner to gain or maintain power and control over another intimate partner." Domestic violence can happen to anyone regardless of race, age, sexual orientation, religion, or gender. It can take many forms such as physical abuse, sexual abuse, emotional abuse, economic abuse, and psychological abuse (www.ovw.usdoj.gov/domviolence.htm).

Domestic violence or intimate partner violence (IPV) may follow a three-step circular pattern.

1. *Tension builds* until the abuser loses control.
2. *Battering occurs.* The batterer sometimes feels that the victim deserves it or

that he or she needs to teach the victim a lesson. Rationalization about the battering and minimization of the consequences of the abuse are common.

3. *Remorse.* The batterer is sorry and asks for forgiveness. The tension is gone and he or she asks for reconciliation. The batterer may make promises that "it will never happen again" and behave in very loving and contrite ways.

- The third stage of the cycle looks a great deal like true repentance. However it is due only to an absence of tension and the feeling on the part of the abuser that the victim has "learned her [or his] lesson." When this situation changes and the tension again increases, the battering can recur.
- Domestic violence is fueled by the *batterer's need to control*. When the victim tries to break the cycle, she or he can be in danger of more battering.
- *Biblical headship* in a marriage is based on love and servant leadership, not on the man's control over his wife and certainly not on physical coercion.
- Abusers and victims of domestic abuse often *grew up in abusive homes*.
- Many of the predictors of domestic violence are *present in the dating relationship*. Some of these predictors are:

    – use of force or violence to solve problems
    – a male abuser's need to prove himself by acting tough
    – rigid ideas of what men and women should be like
    – the victim's fears of the abuser's anger

- In public, abusers can often be charming and personable but *behave entirely different in private*. In counseling sessions, abusers can seem quite reasonable and can try to influence you, portraying their wives as irrational or rebellious and wanting you to see their side.

Consequences

Physical

Women with a history of IPV report 60 percent higher rates of all health problems than do women with no history of abuse. IPV victims report lasting negative health problems, such as chronic pain, gastrointestinal disorders, and irritable bowel syndrome, which can interfere with or limit daily functioning. The more severe the abuse, the greater its impact on a woman's physical and mental health, resulting in a cumulative effect over time. IPV also affects reproductive health and can lead to gynecological disorders, unwanted pregnancy, premature labor and birth, and sexually transmitted diseases including HIV/AIDS. IPV victims have a higher prevalence of sexually transmitted diseases, hysterectomy, and heart or circulatory conditions.

Psychological

Abused girls and women often experience adverse mental health conditions, such as depression, anxiety, and low self-esteem. Women with a history of IPV experience increased levels of substance use, and antisocial and suicidal behavior.

Social

Children who witness IPV are at greater risk of developing psychiatric disorders, developmental problems, school failure, violence against others, and low self-esteem. Women in violent relationships have been found to be restricted in the way they gain access to services, take part in public life, and receive emotional support from friends and relatives.

Vulnerability of Victimization

Several factors are related to IPV: history of physical abuse, prior injury from the same partner, having a verbally abusive partner, economic stress, partner history of alcohol or drug abuse, childhood abuse, being under the age of twenty-four, marital conflict, male dominance in the family, poor family functioning.

ASSESSMENT INTERVIEW 3

If a couple comes into counseling together and you *suspect abuse, speak to each separately* to get an accurate understanding of the situation. To avoid putting the victim in danger, simply say that it is *your practice* to speak to each member of the couple individually.

Rule Outs

1. Do your fights ever get physical? (*This is an easier question to answer than one about violence or abuse.*)
2. Do either of you use alcohol or drugs?
3. Do you feel safe with your spouse? (*If you have any questions about the presence of abuse, do not try to address marital issues with the couple together until the issue of safety is thoroughly addressed.*)

General Questions

1. Has your spouse ever hurt you physically or tried to physically intimidate you?
2. If yes, when was the last time it happened?
3. How often does the abuse happen?
4. Have you ever tried to get help?
5. What have you done to get help?
6. Has it worked?
7. Does your spouse go through the cycle of tension, battering, and then remorse? (*See Definitions and Key Thoughts above.*)
8. Describe what usually happens.
9. Are you afraid for your children's safety?
10. Do you have a plan for safety if the abuse happens again?

> Estimates indicate more than 1 million women and 371,000 men are stalked by intimate partners each year. Intimate partner violence occurs across all populations, irrespective of social, economic, religious, or cultural groups. However, young women and those below the poverty line are disproportionately affected.[3]

4 WISE COUNSEL

The first issue is safety. Working out a plan of safety with the victim is essential. Sometimes what keeps a victim in the abusive situation is the lack of *resources to escape*. Be sure you investigate this need.

5 ACTION STEPS

The following steps are specific actions for the counselor to take.

1. Provide for Safety

- Reassurance of the person's safety (and that of any children involved) is the first priority.
- Empower the victim to separate from their abuser if necessary.

2. Have a Plan

- Help the person develop a plan for the next time abuse occurs.
- Be sure the victim has numbers to call—police, a family shelter or hotline, and a trusted friend or counselor. These numbers should be in an easily accessible place.
- If the victim decides to leave, where will they go? Who will they call?
- Advise the victim to have bags with essentials packed and in an easily accessible location so he or she and the children can leave quickly if needed.
- The victim should photocopy important documents and have them packed as well.
- Think through how the victim can access money, car keys, and important documents if she does need to leave suddenly.
- If he or she needs to leave at some point after an abusive incident, tell them that no argument or discussion should happen at this point, but she should calmly exit and go to a location they have predetermined with the people at that location (if the place is with a friend or family member).

> 85–90% of domestic violence victims are women.[4]

3. Follow Up

- After the first session, put a follow-up plan in place for the victim to get continued help.

4. Provide Reassurance

- Reassure the person that abuse is never "deserved" and is always wrong.

- A husband's role of headship in a marriage never includes the right to control or abuse. A wife's role never includes the right to control or abuse, nor does it include submitting to abuse.

5. Assess Relationships

- Assess how much support the person has and encourage him or her to reach out to others for help.
- A victim of abuse is often isolated, both out of shame over the situation and the abuser's need to control.

BIBLICAL INSIGHTS 6

And Moses and Aaron gathered the assembly together before the rock; and he said to them, "Hear now, you rebels! Must we bring water for you out of this rock?" Then Moses lifted his hand and struck the rock twice with his rod; and water came out abundantly, and the congregation and their animals drank.

Numbers 20:10–11

Moses acted in anger. He did not obey God and was punished by not being allowed to lead his people into the Promised Land (Num. 20:7–12).

Anger can be the most damaging of all emotions, causing people to say or do things they regret. Out-of-control anger can ruin friendships and marriages and even cause nations to go to war.

Some people end up living forever with the consequences of choices made in a moment of heated anger. People who struggle with destructive anger must find help to discover alternative ways to manage it. This begins by turning it over to God.

> During the six months following an episode of domestic violence, 32 percent of battered women are victimized again.[5]

Then [Abimelech] went to his father's house at Ophrah and killed his brothers, the seventy sons of Jerubbaal, on one stone. But Jotham the youngest son of Jerubbaal was left, because he hid himself.

Judges 9:5

The tragic story of Abimelech pictures extreme violence used for selfish reasons. This illegitimate son of Gideon and a concubine (Judg. 8:29–31) brought disaster on the rest of Gideon's family.

Violence and murder became his way of dealing with all threats to his power (Judg. 9:22–49). In the end, however, his violent ways resulted in his own destruction (vv. 50–56).

Violence doesn't really resolve anything and ultimately leads to more violence.

And you, fathers, do not provoke your children to wrath, but bring them up in the training and admonition of the Lord.

Ephesians 6:4

> As many as 324,000 women each year experience intimate partner violence during their pregnancy.[6]

Parents ought to be careful in their training and discipline not to provoke their children "to wrath." In other words, sometimes a parent's discipline can be overly harsh, unfair, unloving, or irresponsible, causing children to become angered, discouraged, and resentful.

Parents who discipline fairly, consistently, and lovingly are raising their children well.

Fathers, do not provoke your children, lest they become discouraged.

Colossians 3:21

Although children are commanded to obey their parents, this does not give parents permission to be cruel or unreasonable in their treatment of their children.

Parents who nag, belittle, or deride their children destroy their self-esteem and discourage them.

The purpose of parental discipline is to train children. Consistent discipline, administered with love, will help children grow into responsible adults.

7 PRAYER STARTER

Today we're worried and frightened, Lord. Your children are in need of great help. One needs help handling anger so that he no longer is abusive; the other needs help to know how best to deal with this situation and get her husband the help he needs . . .

8 RECOMMENDED RESOURCES

Kroeger, Catherine Clark, and Nancy Nason-Clark. *No Place for Abuse: Biblical and Practical Resources to Counteract Domestic Violence.* InterVarsity Press, 2001.

Nason-Clark, Nancy, and Catherine Clark Kroeger. *Refuge from Abuse: Healing and Hope for Abused Christian Women.* InterVarsity Press, 2004.

Stewart, Donald. *Refuge: A Pathway Out of Domestic Violence and Abuse.* New Hope Publishers, 2004.

Vernick, Leslie. *The Emotionally Destructive Relationship: Seeing It, Stopping It, Surviving It.* Harvest House, 2007.

Websites

American Association of Christian Counselors (www.aacc.net)

Ecounseling (www.ecounseling.com)

Eating Disorders

PORTRAITS 1

- Lindsay had binged a few times during middle school and early high school. She didn't like vomiting, so she used laxatives afterward and exercised a lot.
- Madeline and Maggie were twelve-year-old twins whose anorexia got started in part because of their intense competition with each other. They obsessed over who ate the least and exercised the most.
- Don was a seminary student who found that he was very good at keeping track of food intake. After he graduated, his food obsession went with him to his job as a youth pastor.
- Jennifer would binge and purge for weeks every time she started dating someone new or broke up with a boyfriend. After getting married in her early twenties, her binging stopped for a while. When it returned, she started getting cavities from the vomiting and she finally decided she had to tell her husband.

DEFINITIONS AND KEY THOUGHTS 2

- Persons with eating disorders are characterized by a primary *obsession with food* (either eating a lot or not eating enough) and compulsive behaviors related to eating. Often these behaviors are illegitimate attempts to gain control and deal with *anxiety and stress.*
- Compulsive overeating and milder forms of obsession with food or weight can also be considered eating disorders if the practices produce *unhealthy and obsessive behaviors* and/or altered thought processes or body image.

> Estimates indicate that one-third of American women and 15 percent of men will have an eating disorder or related problem at some time in their lives.[1]

Anorexia Nervosa

- Anorexics (those with *anorexia nervosa*) *starve themselves* to feel thin.
- Even when weighing twenty to thirty pounds below the lowest recommended weight for their age and height, anorexics *still believe they are fat.* Body image is extremely distorted.

The treatment needed is a transformation from a worldview in which self-worth comes from appearance or achievement to one that values people as unique individuals. A person's faith often helps in this spiritual transformation.[2]

- Anorexics consider hunger pangs to be good—evidence of their success at weight loss. They *obsess over what they eat* and how much they exercise.
- Approximately 30–35 percent of college-age women have a diagnosable eating disorder.
- Some estimates indicate that as many as 20 percent of anorexics may *die of starvation*.
- Most anorexics are *girls between the ages of fourteen and eighteen*. A symptom of the disorder is that they stop menstruating or never start.
- Many anorexics come from homes where parents held them to *high or perfectionistic standards*, which they were successful in meeting early in life. They may resort to anorexia when standards become unclear, for example when rigid parental standards are challenged by permissive societal expectations.
- The attempt at perfection is fueled by several fears:

  - fear of fat
  - fear of failure
  - fear of being less than perfect
  - fear of rejection
  - fear of losing control

Bulimia Nervosa

- Bulimics (those with *bulimia nervosa*) *binge on high-calorie, fatty, and/or sweet foods,* secretively eating hundreds or thousands of calories at a sitting. Afterward, to counteract the effect of this eating, they *self-induce vomiting*, overdose on laxatives, or exercise excessively.
- Bulimia tends to occur in girls in *late adolescence*, such as the last years of high school and early college.
- Bulimia can lead to complications related to *electrolyte imbalances and destruction of tooth enamel*.
- Bulimics are often of *normal weight*. While they are worried about fat, they do not suffer from the severe distortion of body image that plagues anorexics.
- Unlike anorexics, bulimics are often not particularly thin, yet they are similarly *obsessed with food and fat*.
- While anorexics feel they are right in their extreme diets, bulimics know that their bingeing and purging is *not normal*.

Common Barriers to Treatment

There are often multiple barriers that keep a person from receiving proper treatment for an eating disorder.

Access: Sometimes finding treatment from someone who specializes in eating disorders is difficult.

Considering It an Act of Will: There are emotional, spiritual, and interpersonal complexities involved in the healing of eating disorders. Persons with an eating disorder cannot simply "will themselves" out of it.

Denial: Persons with eating disorders can have distorted body images and may deny the level of harm they inflict on themselves.

Fear of Treatment: Treatment involves discomfort, and facing pain and hurt, and it can be a difficult and frightening process. This prevents some persons with eating disorders from seeking treatment.

Financial Barriers: Unfortunately, many treatments for eating disorders are expensive.

Idols: With eating disorders, food is not about sustenance; it is a preoccupation and obsession similar to idolization. Their world and priorities revolve around food.

Lack of Faith: Persons with eating disorders may not believe any person or treatment can help with their affliction.

Minimizing the Problem: Many delay treatment because they minimize the grasp the problem has on their lives, and they believe it might go away on its own.

Pride: It's not easy to admit to self, others, and God that something is out of control.

Shame and Guilt: Secrecy and shame may shroud eating disorders for long periods of time. It is very hard for persons to admit there is a problem. It is embarrassing to admit to not eating or to binging and vomiting.

> Outcome studies suggest that treatment promotes adequate recovery in 75 percent of patients with eating disorders.[3]

Warning Signs

Secretive behavior coupled with trips to the bathroom after eating

Laxative or diuretic abuse

Heart palpitations

Depression

Social withdrawal

Restrictive dieting

Frequent and obvious weight fluctuations

Preoccupation with body weight and appearance

ASSESSMENT INTERVIEW 3

You will probably be *approached by a family member* who is concerned about a girl's eating. Your questions need to be probing but nonjudgmental. The family members might be inclined to *blame themselves* for the eating problem or to deny the problem.

First, *rule out immediate medical problems*. Then ask the remaining questions. Some are directed at family members, while others are for the person who is having eating problems. We have used female pronouns because some 90 percent of people with eating disorders are girls or women.

Rule Outs

1. If you [your loved one] have been starving yourself [herself], how long have you [has she] been doing it?
2. What do you [does she] weigh? (*If her weight is 10 percent or more below the lowest recommended weight for her age and height, she should be taken to a doctor for a thorough medical exam. Medical conditions are always a significant concern for those with eating disorders.*)
3. If you [your loved one] purge by vomiting, how long has this been going on? (*If she has done this frequently, she should have medical and dental exams to rule out medical conditions caused by vomiting.*)

Questions for the Caring Adult

1. What statements does this person make related to body image and fat?
2. Does this person view herself as fat, even if she is very thin?
3. Has this girl been asked to gain weight? If so, how did she respond?
4. How long has she been starving herself/bingeing and purging/overeating?
5. What was childhood like for her? Are there issues of control or perfectionism in the home?
6. Is this girl facing a transition (*such as from middle school to high school, from high school to college, from a familiar neighborhood and school to a new one*)?
7. How has this girl been influenced by social norms related to beauty?
8. Have you noticed her being particularly sensitive to such expectations?

Questions for the Counselee

1. Do you ever feel helpless? If so when?
2. How do you handle such feelings?
3. Describe a time when you felt angry, frustrated, or afraid. How did you express those feelings?
4. What were meals like in your family of origin?
5. In your home, was there much focus on food while you were growing up?
6. Has anyone ever told you that you're beautiful? Who and when?
7. How did that make you feel?
8. Why do you think the person said that?

Between 40 and 60 percent of high school girls diet.[4]

Between 30 and 40 percent of junior high girls are concerned about their weight.[5]

9. Describe your relationship with your parents and siblings. What kind of a child were you?

10. Do you sometimes feel as though you aren't good enough?

11. What advantage does weight loss (purging) afford you? How does it make you feel about yourself?

12. What disadvantages have you seen from those actions?

WISE COUNSEL 4

Do not attempt to treat an individual whose symptoms are affecting her health. A girl whose eating disorder is endangering her life or well-being should be in the hospital or an inpatient treatment program.

Even if the person with the eating disorder must be hospitalized, there is also a *family that is hurting*. Focus on them and their needs. Help them avoid blaming themselves or their child. Instead, help them have hope for recovery.

Keep reminding everyone involved that *God is always working* and there is always hope for recovery. Eating disorders are very difficult but not impossible to overcome.

Watch for *evidence of suicidal feelings* (see section on Suicide) and get help immediately if you see signs.

If the behavior has gone on for some time, you will do best to *seek the assistance of a professional* who is a specialist in eating disorders. The young woman's *health will continue to be compromised* until she gets help.

ACTION STEPS 5

1. Identify a Target Weight

- It is important to identify an ideal weight and target weight. Ideal weight refers to the best weight for a person when the person's height and body type are taken into account. The body mass index (often abbreviated as BMI) is the most accurate measure of ideal weight, but few persons can easily work with this index.

- A target weight is the lowest safe weight; it is the bare minimum you want someone with an eating disorder to be at. Target weight is calculated as 90 percent of midpoint of the ideal weight. It is best to have agreement on a target weight with a doctor or dietician because persons with eating disorders often try to negotiate this number.

> Forty percent of nine-year-old girls have dieted.[6]

2. Focus on Relationships

- You will want to build a positive relationship with the person with the eating disorder. These individuals tend to have a very hard time being open and accepting help. You will need much patience and you will need to be willing to speak the truth. Let the young woman know that she must be willing to hear the truth.

- Encourage family members to show unconditional love to the person with the eating disorder. Do not criticize or compare or ask questions in a manner that causes the person to feel condemned.
- Healing relationships with people and with God are essential to the recovery process.

3. Take the Focus off Food

- Unless the girl is in immediate danger from starvation or electrolyte problems, examine what weight loss means to this person, what eating stands for, and what she most fears about eating.
- Help the family to take the focus off food at home. They need to see that focusing on food is part of the disease, not the solution.

4. Watch for Triggers

- Help the young woman to see what triggers her bingeing behaviors and try to identify situations that aggravate it.
- Help her see what is behind her actions. Chances are, some kind of anxiety and stress are driving these actions.

5. Change Thinking Patterns

- Gently question the girl's thinking. Help her begin to see the lies behind the behaviors that are trapping her.

6. Examine Perfectionism

- Examine her perfectionism. Chances are she holds herself to standards to which she does not hold her loved ones.
- Help her examine these standards and how they square with God's truth revealed in Scripture.

7. Keep a Journal

- Encourage the person to write in a journal about her feelings and the events of each day. She may have difficulty identifying feelings. Help her view her feelings as normal and acceptable.

BIBLICAL INSIGHTS 6

Now the mixed multitude who were among them yielded to intense craving; so the children of Israel also wept again and said: "Who will give us meat to eat? We remember the fish which we ate freely in Egypt, the cucumbers, the melons, the leeks, the onions, and the garlic; but now our whole being is dried up; there is nothing at all except this manna before our eyes!"

Numbers 11:4–6

Preoccupation with food can indicate an eating disorder. When people become overly focused on food, their dependence on God suffers.

The Israelites, while not having an eating disorder, did experience a "perspective disorder" because of their focus on food. Their preoccupation with foods they did not have caused them to lose sight of God's miraculous and loving provision of manna.

When people become preoccupied with anything other than God, they can lose their perspective of God's care for them. People with eating disorders need to refocus on their worth in God's eyes and be thankful for God's provision.

Only one in ten people receives treatment for their eating disorder. The majority of people who do, don't receive the adequate care they need.[7]

Put a knife to your throat if you are a man given to appetite.

Proverbs 23:2

Some people attempt to fill the emptiness in their lives with drugs, alcohol, sex, money, or even hard work. Others use food, and such people find themselves trapped in emotional eating—leading to such problems as obesity and bulimia.

There is nothing wrong with food. There must be a balance, however, between enjoying what God has provided and using food to meet emotional needs and thus allowing it to control one's life.

Self-control, a fruit of the Spirit, applies to many areas of life, including eating. God desires to fill any emptiness, helping us to lead balanced, healthy lives.

All things are lawful for me, but all things are not helpful. All things are lawful for me, but I will not be brought under the power of any. Foods for the stomach and the stomach for foods, but God will destroy both it and them. Now the body is not for sexual immorality but for the Lord, and the Lord for the body.

1 Corinthians 6:12–13

Some who face a difficult eating disorder—whether it is an addiction to food or an addiction to going without food—understand the power of that addiction. God provided food for the animals and people He created to sustain them. Food is meant for sustenance—"foods for the stomach and the stomach for foods."

A food obsession takes the focus off God and puts it on one's food or stomach—both of which will eventually no longer be needed.

People who struggle with eating disorders should seek Christian professional guidance to gain a proper perspective and pattern for eating.

7 PRAYER STARTER

Dear Lord, thank You that _____ is seeking help. Please help her to accept herself and to know that she is loved. Help her family to get beyond their concern or guilt so they can work on showing love to their child. Please comfort this family, Lord, and be very close to them. Heal their hearts and minds, and protect _____ from medical problems. Please be with them every step of the way to healing . . .

8 RECOMMENDED RESOURCES

Organizations

Gurze Books specializes in eating disorder publications (1-800-756-7533 or www.gurze.com).

Remuda Ranch provides inpatient and residential programs for women, girls, and boys suffering from anorexia, bulimia, other eating disorders, and related issues. Their Christian programs offer hope and healing to patients of all beliefs (800-445-1900 or www.remudaranch.com).

Books

Alcorn, Nancy. *Starved: Mercy for Eating Disorders.* WinePress, 2007.

Costin, Carolyn. *The Eating Disorder Sourcebook.* 3rd ed. McGraw-Hill, 2006.

Davidson, Kimberly. *I'm Beautiful? Why Can't I See It?: Daily Encouragement to Promote Healthy Eating and Positive Self-Esteem.* Tate Publishing, 2006.

Dillinger, Jesse. *Reasonably Thin.* Thomas Nelson, 1998.

Jantz, Gregory L. *Hope, Help, and Healing for Eating Disorders: A New Approach to Treating Anorexia, Bulimia, and Overeating.* Shaw Books, 2002.

Websites

American Association of Christian Counselors (www.aacc.net)

Ecounseling (www.ecounseling.com)

National Eating Disorders Association (www.nationaleatingdisorders.org)

Envy and Jealousy

PORTRAITS 1

- Carolyn spends most of her days looking for new ways to decorate her home. Her husband, Tom, complains that they are never able to get ahead because of Carolyn's constant spending.
- Although Jill has advanced education and a successful career, she finds herself resenting Lindsey's ability to entertain with such elegance and style. She thinks, *If I had that much time on my hands, I would be able to entertain like Martha Stewart also!*
- Maria can't seem to control her tongue. She feels it is almost impossible to resist the temptation to pass along to her friends the latest "scoop" on someone in the church.
- Sue was thankful that the friendship with Dana was one in which they could commiserate over the hardships and trials they were both experiencing. Now that Dana seems to be receiving one blessing after another, Sue finds that she is resentful that Dana's life has taken a turn for the good.
- Jealous of her sister, her friends, and her neighbors, the young wife was now jealous of her husband's new co-worker. Wallowing in anger and self-pity, she was allowing her jealousy to consume her emotions and taint her marriage. Feeling smothered and wrongly accused, her husband was pulling away in frustration. She was becoming panicky, predicting that her husband would leave her or have an affair, but she was behaving in a way that increased the odds of her dark predictions coming true.

> The envious man thinks that, if his neighbor breaks a leg, he will be able to walk better himself.
>
> *Helmut Schoeck*

DEFINITIONS AND KEY THOUGHTS 2

- Jealousy and envy are siblings, the perverse children of a *toxic mix* of anger, anxiety-based insecurity, and an obsessive habit of comparing oneself (usually poorly) with others.
- There is also a *root of fear* in most jealousy—the fear of losing the love or praise of one's object of love or affection.
- *Envy* wants what someone else has.
- *Jealousy* is being fearful that something one has attained will be taken. Jealousy also involves a triangle—three people, one of which is the jealous person becoming fixated on a (usually misperceived) rival, who is viewed as competing for the attention of the third person.

- Scripture says that love as "strong as death" will produce powerful jealousy that is "as cruel as the grave" (Song of Sol. 8:6).
- Envy may be defined as *wanting what someone else has*, whether it is status, possessions, lifestyle, relationships, or characteristics.
- Left unchecked, envy can develop into *malice, contempt, and destruction* of others (see 1 Sam. 18:9 to see envy in the life of Saul).
- Envy manifests itself in the *resentment* of others' prosperity.
- Envy will be *evident in one's dislike of another*. The envious person will not necessarily be aware that the dislike is prompted by envy.
- Envy is fueled by the *expectation of deserving* more success and recognition than another person. Envy, therefore, is *closely linked to pride and greed*.
- *Envy is the opposite of love*. Love rejoices over the good of another. Envy seeks the destruction of another for the benefit of oneself.
- Envy is ultimately a *rebellion* against one's own finiteness and God's provision. When people struggle with envy, they reject God's provision as well as how God uniquely created them to be.
- Scripture tells us that the Lord is "a jealous God" (Exod. 34:14), but the Lord's jealousy is righteous. God is jealous for the church (2 Cor. 11:2). Paul warns us, however, not to provoke the Lord to jealousy (1 Cor. 10:20–22).

> Envy is a symptom of lack of appreciation of our own uniqueness and self-worth. Each of us has something to give that no one else has.
>
> *Anonymous*

Causes of Envy and Jealousy

Dissatisfaction with God's Provision: The person may see only what God *hasn't* provided rather than what God has provided.

Comparison with Others: From early on, many have been conditioned to see themselves only in comparison to others—being smarter than, not as attractive as, more popular than, and so on.

Pride: Envy is driven by the false notion that a person "deserves" to have a life focused on his or her own personal gain and satisfaction.

Low Self-Esteem or Seeking Significance: When people don't feel good about themselves, they will constantly seek to soothe their pain by seeking significance in their circumstances rather than finding their deepest needs met by Jesus Christ.

Value of Worldly Gain: People may seek money, status, appearance, talents, or achievements as evidence of their value and "place" in the world.

Expressions of Envy and Jealousy

Envy can be disguised in a multitude of ways. Here are the most common manifestations:

Resentment toward Others: The person may be highly critical and judgmental of another person or persons.

Competition in Relationships: The desire to be the "top dog" in relationships may be indicative of a struggle with envy. The person may exhibit a drive toward overachievement and exhibit a superior attitude toward others.

Depression: The person may become highly self-critical because he or she has not achieved what is desired and what the other person has.

Lack of Contentment: We live in a culture in which the media bombards us with the false notion that achieving more material gain will lead to greater happiness. A person struggling with envy is rarely content with what God has provided.

Gossip about Others: Envious people constantly criticize the object of their envy.

Idolizing or Putting Others on a Pedestal.

Dissatisfaction with Life: People who are jealous often have thoughts of *If only . . .*

Stages of Envy and Jealousy

Initial Stage: The first stage of envy is desiring what someone else is or has.

Scorn or Disdain: When a person does not face his or her own envy, it can *lead to scorn or disdain* for another person, simply because this person is a reminder of what is lacking. This is expressed in contempt.

Malice: Envy can also *develop into malice.* People desire to destroy the good they see in another's life, believing that if they cannot have what another person has, they will destroy any pleasure the other person has from it.

Domination of Relationships: Jealousy, when carried to extremes, can dominate a relationship. Some spouses, having faced abuse or abandonment in their childhood, bring this pathology into a marriage. *Unresolved issues* from one's past can be the impetus for developing a vicious cycle of dysfunctional jealousy.

A Consuming Cycle: A chronically jealous partner will use self-pity, lies, threats, and other manipulations to control a relationship. When the other resists, the jealous person reacts by becoming more controlling. As time goes by, this cycle gains speed and heads toward disaster.

> Charity rejoices in our neighbor's good, while envy grieves over it.
>
> *Thomas Aquinas*

ASSESSMENT INTERVIEW 3

Often other issues mask envy. A person may speak of *the unfairness of life* or *express resentment* toward someone else. The person may have a *need to always be the best* at every task undertaken.

Be aware that the issue of resentment may also be a *lack of forgiveness* in which the person experienced hurt from someone else and desires revenge.

Listen to the core issue. Is it that the person is resentful toward what someone has done to him or her? Is it because someone else has achieved something that he or she has not?

Do not label the person as being "envious" or "jealous." Listen and acknowledge the person's struggle and experience.

1. What is the situation that has prompted such difficult feelings for you?

2. Do you get upset when others advance in their career or social standing?

3. Do you find that it is difficult for you to celebrate the blessings of some of those around you?

4. Do you sometimes feel that God has disappointed you in His provision?

5. Do you find yourself often thinking, *If only I* _____ (fill in the blank with what you wish were different in your life)?

6. Where do you find that most of your money goes?

7. Do you feel secretly pleased when someone you admire experiences a setback?

8. Do you sometimes want to sabotage another's blessings?

9. Do you struggle with feeling critical and/or judgmental of others?

10. Do you find that you are not content unless you are the "best" at something?

11. Do you struggle with depression?

12. Would you identify more with the best and brightest rather than with those on the fringe of a group?

13. Do you find that you tend to put others on a pedestal?

14. Tell me about your marriage.

15. How do you feel about your spouse's friendships or activities?

16. Has your spouse ever given you reason to doubt his [her] faithfulness or love for you?

O, beware, my lord, of jealousy; it is the green-eyed monster which doth mock the meat it feeds on.

Shakespeare, Othello, Act III, Scene 3

4 : WISE COUNSEL

The core to overcoming envy or jealousy is *threefold*:

> understanding God's love
>
> being content with His provision
>
> loving others as God loves you

Envy and jealousy are *futile attempts* to fill one's deepest longings for significance and security by seeking what someone else has or by controlling what someone else does.

The person who is struggling should be gently and consistently pointed to the *love and sufficiency of Jesus Christ*.

In addition, *offer encouragement* until the person is willing to address this issue and look honestly at his or her own sin.

ACTION STEPS : 5

1. Be Honest

- We all deceive ourselves in a multitude of ways. While we may not feel we are experiencing envy or jealousy, these feelings may be disguised in many different forms, such as criticism, contempt, gossip, self-pity, and manipulation.
- Ask God to reveal your motivations and feelings. Write down in a journal or private notebook what God has shown you in your heart.
- Confess your heart attitudes to Christ.

2. Focus on Jesus Christ

- God sees you as His own beloved child.
- Commit yourself and the day to God, asking for His guidance and presence throughout the day.

> Envy is counting the other fellow's blessings instead of your own.
>
> *Harold Coffin*

3. Develop a Lifestyle of Gratitude and Worship

- Count your blessings.
- Read the Psalms as personal prayers, praising God for all He is and what He has done.
- At the end of each day, reflect on the unexpected blessings you received throughout the day. Thank God for His constant love and care.

4. Avoid Activities That Encourage Comparison

- Spend time in malls only when there is a specific item you need to purchase.
- Read books that encourage reflection on the beauty of life and external blessings we have as believers (for example, *The Best Is Yet to Come* by Greg Laurie, *Future Grace* by John Piper, and *Envy* by Bob Sorge).
- Minimize exposure to magazines, TV, and other media that focus on material gain.

5. Interrupt Feelings of Envy

- Pray for God's blessing to be poured out on the person whom you envy and give thanks for God's provision for that person.
- Remind yourself of Jesus's counsel that "one's life does not consist in the abundance of the things he possesses" (Luke 12:15). Ultimately, "things" are shallow substitutes for the presence of God in your life.
- Remind yourself of who you are as one of God's chosen children. "From the beginning [God] chose you for salvation through sanctification by the Spirit and belief in the truth" (2 Thess. 2:13).

113

- Ask yourself what it is about the person that causes you to envy him or her. Does this person have strong social skills? Is he or she deeply compassionate? Thank God for the redeeming qualities you see in this person and ask God to form those qualities in your own heart. Then you will move from envy to admiration. Affirm and give thanks for the qualities that God has established in your own heart.

6. Interrupt Feelings of Jealousy

> A sound heart is life to the body, but envy is rottenness to the bones.
>
> *Proverbs 14:30*

- Be honest with yourself—back off from controlling or manipulative statements.
- Spend time with God. Immerse yourself in prayer and God's Word. Ask Him to transform your need for security into dependence on and confidence in Him.
- Transform your mind. Instead of allowing your anxious thoughts to lead to dark suspicions, ask God to cleanse your heart and mind. Ask Him to help you truly love—"love does not envy . . . thinks no evil" (1 Cor. 13:4–5). Remember all the positives in your relationship with the person of whom you are jealous. Do something—right then—to show your love. Make a call; send an email.

7. Grow

- Create a plan to develop the gifts and abilities God has uniquely given you.
- Evaluate your spiritual gifts and talents.
- Practice spiritual disciplines. Examples are: prayer, fasting, solitude, study, sacrifices, worship, fellowship, meditations, and memorization.
- Spend time memorizing Scripture; make a commitment to fast and pray for a particular situation in your life.
- Ask God to bring believers into your life who can encourage you in your relationship with Christ.

8. Consider Follow-Up

- *For some people, a chronic struggle with envy may be indicative of deeper unresolved pain from their past in which working with a professional therapist might be the best course of action.*

6 BIBLICAL INSIGHTS

This is the law of jealousy . . .
> *Numbers 5:29*

The ancient Israelites had a complex ritual for dealing with jealousy. Their detailed process (Num. 5:11–31) recognized the destructive potential of a jealous husband or wife. The most important part was that they dealt with this issue before the Lord (v. 30).

Jealousy can destroy any relationship, and in a marriage, it can drive in a wedge of mistrust.

Protection from the wedge of jealousy begins with honesty. Each spouse should honestly consider his or her own tendency toward jealousy, answering the question, "What makes me jealous?"

Each spouse should honestly tell his or her feelings. Then they can discuss what they could do for each other to alleviate those feelings. Complete honesty and trust will help to obliterate jealousy.

Then Saul was very angry, and the saying displeased him; and he said, "They have ascribed to David ten thousands, and to me they have ascribed only thousands. Now what more can he have but the kingdom?"

1 Samuel 18:8

Saul became jealous of David's victory over Goliath and the national attention that it received. The young warrior had upstaged the king. Saul's jealousy led to anger, resentment, fear, and attempted murder.

Like a seething cauldron ready to tip at any moment, uncontrolled jealousy can lead to destruction. We must take our jealousy to God, asking Him to help us appreciate others' talents while showing us how best to use our own.

For I am jealous for you with godly jealousy. For I have betrothed you to one husband, that I may present you as a chaste virgin to Christ.

2 Corinthians 11:2

The word *jealous* can be used positively or negatively. Paul said that he was "jealous for" the Corinthian believers "with godly jealousy." Paul's jealousy was not for his own reputation but for the Corinthians' eternal safety.

Human jealousy, however, often has a less than noble focus—such as another's looks, wealth, popularity, or power—and it is harmful to all involved.

Believers must be careful not to allow ungodly jealousy to harm themselves or others.

Therefore, laying aside all malice, all deceit, hypocrisy, envy, and all evil speaking . . .

1 Peter 2:1

Believers should be so grateful to the One who called them to be holy that they desire to be holy in every aspect of their conduct (1 Peter 1:15).

This means "laying aside all . . . envy" because envy has no usefulness in God's kingdom. Envy causes hurt, dissension, and division.

People who compare themselves to others will feel either superior or inferior. God wants us to stop comparing our looks, possessions, jobs, or abilities with those of others and to focus on being His child and serving Him.

> For where envy and self-seeking exist, confusion and every evil thing are there.
>
> *James 3:16*

115

7 PRAYER STARTER

We want to thank You, first of all, for Your great blessings in Your child's life. He [she] knows that You have done great things, but today he [she] struggles with the pain of desiring more. Help him [her] today, Lord, to understand the great gifts he [she] has from Your hand and the great contributions he [she] can make to Your kingdom. Help him [her] learn contentment . . .

8 RECOMMENDED RESOURCES

Clinton, Tim. *The Bible for Hope: Caring for People God's Way*. Thomas Nelson, 2007.

Clinton, Tim, Archibald D. Hart, and George Ohlschlager. *Caring for People God's Way: Personal and Emotional Issues, Addictions, Grief, and Trauma*. Thomas Nelson, 2006.

Laurie, Greg. *The Best Is Yet To Come: Faith for Today, Hope for the Future*. Multnomah, 2005.

Piper, John. *Future Grace*. Multnomah, 2005.

Sorge, Bob. *Envy: The Enemy Within*. Regal Books, 2003.

Websites

American Association of Christian Counselors (www.aacc.net)

Ecounseling (www.ecounseling.com)

Fear and Anxiety

PORTRAITS : 1

- Janice was always on the alert. Her timid voice and shy manner indicated she was on constant watch for potential hazards. As an only child born to a single mother, Janice felt she was born to be her mother's scapegoat. When she was young, Janice can remember waiting for her mother to come home and feeling her whole body become tense. She never knew what would happen when her mother returned. As an adult, Janice was always wary of potential harm. She even found that she became tense when there was nothing to be anxious about.

- Nadine was considered a loner. Little did anyone know that this facade was a mask for a deep fear of being in groups. Nadine found that she would become overwhelmed with panic when she was in a restaurant eating with her co-workers. Even though it seemed irrational, she would fear saying something foolish, spilling food on her shirt, or beginning to stutter. When she was alone with one person, she was fine, but in a group, even making eye contact with someone seemed painful.

> For God has not given us a spirit of fear, but of power and of love and of a sound mind.
>
> *2 Timothy 1:7*

DEFINITIONS AND KEY THOUGHTS : 2

Fear

- While most people experience fear as a negative emotion, *fear also has a positive component.* If you find that you have turned down a one-way street and see a car heading directly at you, fear triggers an autonomic response that sends a signal to your brain to "flee" the potentially dangerous situation.

- Fear becomes a problem when a person is *afraid of things that are not real* or when the feeling of fear is *out of proportion* to the real danger present.

- Fear is an emotion that draws a person into a *self-protective mode.*

- More often than not, fears are related to *what a person perceives* as a threat to his or her safety and security. The person may fear losing his or her job, having his or her home burglarized, or having conflict in a relationship.

Anxiety

- *Anxiety is a constant fearful state,* accompanied by a feeling of unrest, dread, or worry. The person may not be aware of what is creating the fear.

- Anxiety is aroused by *a number of factors*:

  – external situations (viewing the nightly news, a fast-paced lifestyle)

  – physical well-being (lack of sleep, blood sugar imbalance)

  – modeling (parents who were highly anxious)

  – trauma (in situations that may be similar to experiences of the past that caused great pain)

- Anxiety's *symptoms* can include inability to relax, tense feelings, rapid heartbeat, dry mouth, increased blood pressure, jumpiness or feeling faint, excessive perspiring, feeling clammy, constant anticipation of trouble, and constant feeling of uneasiness.

Both faith and fear sail into the harbor of your mind, but only faith should be allowed to anchor.

Anonymous

Phobias

- Phobias are *fears of specific things*.
- Phobias are fears that are *out of proportion* to the object, situation, or activity feared. For example, one may have a fear of spiders. A person exhibits a phobia when he or she sees a small spider on the ceiling of a room and refuses to enter the room ever again.

Panic Attacks

- Panic attacks are *sudden, overwhelming, fearful reactions,* with feelings of impending doom.
- In a panic attack, the person feels *out of control*. Symptoms include being paralyzed by the flight-or-fight response, shortness of breath, racing heartbeat, sweating, dizziness, nausea, diarrhea, ringing ears, choking, vertigo, and becoming homebound in fear of another attack.
- The person generally has *no clear idea* of what prompted the reaction and then becomes afraid of another episode occurring.
- The sufferer may feel as if he or she is *going crazy* or is having a heart attack.

Note: More than three attacks in a month or the onset of a person refusing to go out of the house may indicate the need for some professional assistance.

Relational Fears

- There are four major relational fears that people experience that can significantly alter their quality of life: fear of failure, fear of rejection, fear of abandonment, and fear of death or dying.

ASSESSMENT INTERVIEW : 3

1. When do you find yourself feeling afraid or anxious?
2. How long and to what extent has this fear or anxiety been occurring for you?
3. What situation/object/person causes you the most distress?
4. Do you find there are times when you are more anxious than others? If so, when?
5. Of the things that cause you fear, which seem reasonable and which seem more unreasonable?
6. When do the feelings of anxiety go away?
7. How have you tried to cope with the anxiety?
8. Do you have any health problems and/or medications that may contribute to the anxiety?
9. What would your life be like if you were free of this anxiety?

WISE COUNSEL : 4

Fear and anxiety are *defused by knowledge.* The more a person can defuse the perceived threat, the less anxiety he or she will experience.

Generally, the fearful person has established an *irrational belief system* that is creating anxiety for him or her. *Try to gain an understanding* of what lies or deceptions are contributing to the anxiety.

Most anxiety reactions are *learned behavior.* Be intentional in your efforts to encourage the person to develop hope that he or she will be able to overcome the anxiety or fears by learning new behaviors rooted in truth.

Anxiety can be *contagious.* Those who experience strong anxiety tend to elicit anxiety reactions in those who are around them. You need to be aware of your own anxiety level and how you cope personally with anxiety when it occurs.

Be patient with the person as he or she sorts through the feelings of fear. Changing patterns takes time.

ACTION STEPS : 5

1. Change Thought Patterns

- It is important to dispute negative thoughts and lies with the truth of Scripture (Phil. 4:8).

2. Focus on God

- *Help the person move his or her focus from fear to the character of God (1 Peter 5:7).*
- God wants you to trust and relinquish all fears to Him, especially through prayer (Phil. 4:4–6).
- To have peace, keep your thoughts on God (Isa. 26:3).

3. Watch for Triggers

- *Assist the person in trying to minimize activities and input that induce anxiety.*

4. Move Forward

- *Help the person learn from setbacks and resolve to continue to face down the fears.*
- *Gently encourage the person to take careful steps to face their fears.*
- When you are becoming afraid, move your focus to the external world and others rather than the internal feelings of anxiety.

5. Develop Relationships

- *Assist the person in finding supportive, positive relationships.*

6. Be Patient

- Growth takes time.
- God will work in your life to overcome the anxiety that is keeping you from living life to the fullest.
- Try to keep an eternal perspective.

> Do the thing you fear to do and keep on doing it . . . that is the quickest and surest way ever yet discovered to conquer fear.
>
> *Dale Carnegie*

6 BIBLICAL INSIGHTS

If you should say in your heart, "These nations are greater than I; how can I dispossess them?"—you shall not be afraid of them, but you shall remember well what the LORD your God did to Pharaoh and to all Egypt: the great trials which your eyes saw, the signs and the wonders, the mighty hand and the outstretched arm, by which the LORD your God brought you out. . . . You shall not be terrified of them; for the LORD your God, the great and awesome God, is among you.

Deuteronomy 7:17–19, 21

The Christian life is not easy. Believers face difficulties, pain, suffering, and sorrow. In situations that seem impossible, they sometimes become afraid.

God told Israel not to be afraid when the battle seemed too great. Instead, they should remember what He had done for them in the past and take heart.

We must look at our fearful situations in the light of what God has already done for us, remembering that "the great and awesome God" will be going into battle with us.

Trust in the LORD. . . . Delight yourself also in the LORD. . . . Commit your way to the LORD. . . . Rest in the LORD, and wait patiently for Him; do not fret because of him who prospers in his way, because of the man who brings wicked schemes to pass.

Psalm 37:3–5, 7

David encouraged God's people to trust in the Lord, delight themselves in Him, commit their way to Him, and wait patiently for Him to act.

Trusting focuses our faith and deepens our commitment.

Delighting in God means that we experience pleasure in His presence.

Committing our way to God means entrusting everything in our lives to His guidance and control.

Waiting patiently is sometimes difficult but it often is the ultimate test of our trust in God.

Surely He shall deliver you from the snare of the fowler and from the perilous pestilence. He shall cover you with His feathers, and under His wings you shall take refuge; His truth shall be your shield and buckler. You shall not be afraid of the terror by night, nor of the arrow that flies by day, nor of the pestilence that walks in darkness, nor of the destruction that lays waste at noonday.

Psalm 91:3–6

When believers are afraid, they can run to a "refuge"—God Himself.

No place could be more safe than with God! Believers can trust that God will protect them in their times of fear.

This does not imply that God's people will never suffer or face difficulty, but it does promise that they need not be afraid for they are in God's hands.

Trust in the LORD with all your heart, and lean not on your own understanding; in all your ways acknowledge Him, and He shall direct your paths.

Proverbs 3:5–6

It's one thing for people to trust God with their eternal destiny; it is quite another for them to trust God to handle the challenges and difficulties of daily life.

God promises to direct, or straighten, our paths. We need to trust God to help us handle the difficult situations we face, even in cases where we can't begin to see how He could do it.

If we really want to know God's will for our lives, or even for our actions in a particular situation, we must begin by trusting that God cares about every aspect of living and that He will provide what we need.

A 2008 study suggests that intellectually demanding challenges like crossword puzzles or chess may be more successful at keeping worry-prone people from worrying than supposedly relaxing pastimes like watching TV or shopping.[1]

7 : PRAYER STARTER

Today a precious child of Yours is frightened, Lord, frightened about the fear that has taken hold of his [her] life and left him [her] feeling helpless and hopeless. He [she] wants to serve You, Lord, but this anxiety is debilitating him [her] to the point that he [she] can barely function. We need the healing touch of Your hand, Lord, and wisdom to handle this anxiety . . .

8 : RECOMMENDED RESOURCES

Clinton, Tim. *The Bible for Hope: Caring for People God's Way.* Thomas Nelson, 2007.

Clinton, Tim, Archibald D. Hart, and George Ohlschlager. *Caring for People God's Way: Personal and Emotional Issues, Addictions, Grief, and Trauma.* Thomas Nelson, 2006.

Hart, Archibald D. *The Anxiety Cure.* Thomas Nelson, 2001.

Young, Ed. *Know Fear: Facing Life's Six Most Common Phobias.* Lifeway Christian Resources, 2003.

Websites

American Association of Christian Counselors (www.aacc.net)

Ecounseling (www.ecounseling.com)

Forgiveness

- Zach cannot bring himself to attend his parents' fiftieth wedding anniversary. Their lack of interest in his life and his family has hurt him so much that he wants nothing to do with them—let alone to honor them for fifty years of marriage.
- Becky cannot sleep at night. She keeps having nightmares about her mother, who abused her as a child. Even though her mother has been dead for ten years, Becky still cannot forgive her for the pain.
- Joanne's "best friend" lied about her to her boyfriend, causing him to break up with her. Now Joanne's friend and her former boyfriend are dating. Every time Joanne sees them at school, she feels betrayed all over again and can't stop thinking about it.
- Tom finds out his co-worker has been criticizing him to the boss and making negative comments about his work. The boss has elevated his co-worker and demoted Tom. Tom can't stop thinking of ways to get even with his co-worker.

> It takes two to reconcile but only one to forgive.

DEFINITIONS AND KEY THOUGHTS 2

What Forgiveness Is and Is Not

Unforgiveness is a state of resentment, bitterness, hatred, hostility, anger, fear, and stress toward an individual who has transgressed against another in some way. *Unforgiveness is a cancer that eats away at the very soul of a person.*

Forgiveness occurs when the cold feelings of unforgiveness are changed to warm, loving, compassionate, caring, and altruistic emotions because of a heartfelt transformation.

In Luke 7:40–47 Jesus tells us the truth that those who have been forgiven much love much.

Explain to the person you're counseling the following definitions and parameters of forgiveness. Forgiveness

- does not mean that any wrongs done to you were acceptable.
- does not diminish the evil done against you, nor is it a denial of what happened.
- is a key part of not letting those wrongs hurt you any longer.

123

- does not take away the consequences the other person will face because of his or her sin.
- is letting go of your desire to hurt the other person. Simply put, forgiveness means you "cancel a debt."
- is a difficult and uncomfortable process. When you make a decision to forgive, God provides the grace and strength to forgive and to maintain a heart of forgiveness.
- is not weakness. It is the most powerful thing you can do. Refusing to forgive allows Satan to continue to hurt you; forgiveness stops the destructive power of Satan in one's life.
- is not reconciliation. It takes two to reconcile but only one to forgive.
- does not depend on the other person's actions, and it is not probationary (for example, saying, "I will forgive you as long as you aren't drinking").
- does not require you to become a "doormat" nor does it require you to allow the offender to hurt you again.
- is a gift you *give* to the offender. Trust, on the other hand, *must be earned*. You must set boundaries.
- does not wait for the offender to repent. Unlike God, who provides forgiveness when we repent, humans cannot demand repentance before granting forgiveness.
- is about how much you trust God to take care of you.
- is experiencing empathy for the offender, humility about your own sinfulness, and gratitude for being forgiven by God and others.

> Human power alone is not sufficient to reach full forgiveness. There is an element of forgiveness that is divine. It cannot be reached without God.
>
> *Frank Minirth*

Reasons to Forgive

- Forgiveness sets you free to move on with your life.
- It refuses to let the person who hurt you have any power over your life.
- It opens up your relationship with God (see Matt. 5:43–48).
- It keeps you from becoming bitter and thus protects those around you.
- It keeps you from becoming like the person who hurt you.
- Unforgiveness doesn't hurt the perpetrator at all; it hurts only *you*.
- Scripture commands us to be forgiving (Matt. 18:21–35).

3 ASSESSMENT INTERVIEW

When a person seeks help to forgive, it is because the inability to forgive has started to *disrupt his or her personal, emotional, or spiritual life.*

The inability to forgive (due to the stress it creates) may be the source of physical problems, such as lack of energy, sleeplessness, headaches, joint pain, or back pain. It also may be the root cause of *depression or anxiety.*

Sometimes the person *does not realize* that the origin of his or her problem is a lack of forgiveness. Therefore, a counselor may need to gently lead him or her to this knowledge.

Consider the following assessment questions:

1. Can you tell me about your background?
2. What do you think is the source of your concern?
3. What led you to come to counseling?
4. What do you hope to accomplish?
5. What incident or incidents are you having trouble forgiving?
6. How did the incident(s) make you feel?
7. What can you tell me about the person who hurt you?
8. What have you already tried to do to help you forgive?
9. How have you protected yourself from being hurt again by this person?
10. How can you tell that you haven't forgiven this person?
11. Did you ever see any examples of forgiveness in your home while you were growing up?
12. When is the first time you can remember someone offending you? How did you handle it?
13. Can you see a pattern in how you respond when people offend you?
14. Do those responses help or hurt you?
15. What does God say about forgiveness?
16. What do you think forgiveness is?

> When you don't forgive someone, in some way that person is in jail, and you are the warden. You're incarcerated, too, because you have to make sure the prisoner stays there.
>
> *Kerney Franston*

WISE COUNSEL 4

Share with the person some *information about real forgiveness* as described above. Often a person has not forgiven because he or she doesn't understand what forgiveness is.

Forgiveness is best understood as an act and a process. When a person forgives, his or her heart will begin to heal. We can forgive when we realize that we have been forgiven by God (Eph. 4:31–32).

If the person doesn't want to let the offender "off the hook," explain that forgiveness *lets* the counselee *off the hook* and protects him or her from the destructive power of unforgiveness, setting the person free to move on with life.

Identify Emotions

Empathize with the person and acknowledge the evil that has occurred. Encourage the person to grieve the offense and the losses that have resulted from any wrong committed against him or her. Explain that hurt and anger are not sinful; they are normal responses to an offense.

It is important to identify and express one's feelings toward the offense committed; how the person felt during the offense and how he or she feels now.

Set Boundaries

Work with the person to decipher what must be done to keep the offender from hurting the counselee again. This involves the way in which the person maintains an ongoing relationship with the offender. For instance, he or she can be polite (safe boundaries) without being a best friend (unsafe boundaries). Likewise, he or she can listen without taking advice.

Minimize time with unsafe people. Unsafe people are those who hurt without regard for the damage it creates in another's life.

Do not look for approval from a person who will likely cause pain.

Help the person recognize that he or she does not need another's approval to live a free and fulfilling life. The only approval he or she needs is God's.

Recognize God's Hand

Know that God can use the offense to promote personal and spiritual growth and dependence on Him for His plan and glory.

Ask for the intervention of the Holy Spirit to heal the emotional wounds of the client.

Ask God to help the client love the offender. It is said that any action that is not motivated by compassion is sinful. Since those who transgress are often lost, broken, or hurting, even the one who was wronged can feel pity and compassion for the offender.

Praying for the offender will help the client's feelings move from wanting revenge to not wanting harm and finally to wanting the best for the transgressor. When the client reaches the latter stage, he or she will know real freedom.

5 ACTION STEPS

Everett Worthington Jr., author of *The Handbook of Forgiveness*, has developed a useful acrostic for navigating the process of forgiveness. It is known as R-E-A-C-H:

Recall the Hurt

- It is difficult but necessary to recall the hurt.
- *Don't minimize or deny the person's pain.*
- *Don't make excuses for the offender.*
- Recalling your hurt is not for the purpose of finger-pointing but a means to objectively review what has occurred.
- Journaling is a great way to work through anger and hurt. It organizes your thoughts and helps you acknowledge the truth in clear black and white.
- Sometimes writing a letter to the offender is helpful, but *don't mail the letter.*

Empathize with the Person

- Write a letter as if you were the offender. You should write about thoughts, feelings, insights, and pressures. Make this a letter of apology. How difficult is it to do this?
- By placing yourself in the shoes of the person who transgressed, you can begin to understand why the person did what he or she did.
- This does not remove blame from the individual but does serve to show that people who hurt are often hurting deeply themselves.

Altruistic Gift of Forgiveness

- Think about the "giving" of forgiveness. Think of a time when you did something wrong and were forgiven. Reflect on the wrongdoing and guilt you felt. How did it feel to be forgiven? Would you like to give that gift of forgiveness to the person who hurt you?
- Write a blank check of forgiveness. Write in your journal that this day you have released the offender from the debt he or she owes you.
- You may want to write down the offenses the person has done and then write "Canceled" or "Paid in Full" over them.
- Through this step, also recall the great mercy and grace of God toward you.

Commit Publicly to Forgive

- Write a certificate or letter of forgiveness stating that you will not ruminate on the wrongs done to you anymore, but don't send it.
- By participating in some outward expression of forgiveness, such as writing a letter, you will be more prone to remember that you have forgiven and are thus freed from the plague of "unforgiveness."
- Tell your family and/or friends about your decision to forgive. By disclosing your forgiveness to others, you will be held accountable to your decision to forgive the transgressor.

Hold on to Forgiveness

- Hold on to forgiveness when doubts arise.
- There is a difference between remembering a transgression and lacking forgiveness.
- Make "Stones of Remembrance." After God parted the Jordan River so the Israelites could go through on dry land, God told Joshua to have each tribe choose a stone to be piled up as a memorial to what great things God had done that day. Those stones served as a remembrance for the people and their children in times to come (Joshua 4). It is good to have something "concrete" to help you remember the day you set your offender free.

> There is a difference between mental forgiveness and gut forgiveness. For example, when a person has had an affair, frequently the wronged spouse will choose to forgive with the head right away, but it will take the gut months to catch up.
>
> *Charles Stanley*

127

- Remember to forget! When Corrie ten Boom was reminded of an offense some-one had done to her, she responded, "I distinctly remember forgetting that." Though you may never really forget, you can remember that you forgave.

6 BIBLICAL INSIGHTS

He shall restore its full value, add one-fifth more to it, and give it to whomever it belongs, on the day of his trespass offering. And he shall bring his trespass offering to the LORD, a ram without blemish from the flock, with your valuation, as a trespass offering, to the priest.

Leviticus 6:5–6

The Old Testament offerings were designed so that the offender could receive God's forgiveness. But the wrongdoer also had to take responsibility for his or her behavior by making restitution to the person who had been wronged.

We too must take responsibility for the effects of our sins on others. We need to be reconciled not only to God, but also to those whom we have wronged. Biblical law holds us responsible for our own behavior.

And when [David] had called for Absalom, he came to the king and bowed himself on his face to the ground before the king. Then the king kissed Absalom.

2 Samuel 14:33

Despite all that Absalom had done, David allowed for the possibility of recon-ciliation by forgiving his son. Absalom, however, had no tears, no repentance, no change of heart. Indeed, Absalom would eventually try to take his father's throne (2 Sam. 15:10).

One person can forgive, but it takes two to reconcile. Forgiveness does not guarantee reconciliation. Forgiveness, however, does put salve on those who are willing to let go of the hurt and wrongs done by others.

I, even I, am He who blots out your transgressions for My own sake; and I will not remember your sins.

Isaiah 43:25

When the guilt of past sins weighs us down, we must remember that when we seek forgiveness, God "blots out" our transgressions and forgets our sins.

Blotting out sins is wiping the slate clean. Whatever sins we have committed, God promises to erase them. He knows what we have done but He treats us as though we have never sinned.

Because God has forgiven us, we must forgive ourselves.

Then Peter came to Him and said, "Lord, how often shall my brother sin against me, and I forgive him? Up to seven times?" Jesus said to him, "I do not say to you, up to seven times, but up to seventy times seven."

Matthew 18:21–22

> When did Jesus forgive you for your sin? Two thousand years ago on the cross. Two thousand years before you came and begged his forgiveness, forgiveness was there—ready, rich, full and free.
>
> *Joseph M. Stowell*

Don't even keep count; just keep on forgiving.

Jesus then told a parable about a man who, after receiving great forgiveness for a large debt he owed to someone, refused to forgive a person who owed him a small debt. Jesus was illustrating that we sinners have been graciously forgiven by God—and are being forgiven daily, over and over again.

We should be just as gracious in forgiving others. To refuse to forgive shows that we have not understood how much God has forgiven us.

But if you do not forgive, neither will your Father in heaven forgive your trespasses.

Mark 11:26

Jesus stated that God's forgiveness of us is somehow related to how we forgive others. When we accept God's forgiveness of all the wrongs we have done Him, we should be so grateful that we willingly offer that same kind of forgiveness to those who have wronged us.

To refuse to forgive others shows that we do not appreciate the forgiveness God offers us.

PRAYER STARTER 7

Lord, Your servant has been deeply hurt. He [she] wants to let go, to be free of the pain, but he [she] is finding it very difficult. The emotions go all over the place and he [she] doesn't want this pain affecting one more waking moment. Please help him [her] let this go. Please help him [her] forgive the offender as he [she] has been forgiven by You. Please give him [her] life once again . . .

RECOMMENDED RESOURCES 8

Clinton, Tim. *The Bible for Hope: Caring for People God's Way*. Thomas Nelson, 2007.

Clinton, Tim, Archibald D. Hart, and George Ohlschlager. *Caring for People God's Way: Personal and Emotional Issues, Addictions, Grief, and Trauma*. Thomas Nelson, 2006.

Kendal, R. T. *Total Forgiveness*. Charisma House, 2007.

Stoop, David. *Forgiveness: Getting beyond Your Past and Pain*. American Association of Christian Counselors Courageous Living Video Series. See www.aacc.net for more information.

———. *Forgiving the Unforgivable*. Regal Books, 2005.

Worthington Jr., Everett L. *Handbook of Forgiveness*. Brunner-Routledge, 2005.

Websites

American Association of Christian Counselors (www.aacc.net)

Ecounseling (www.ecounseling.com)

Grief and Loss

1 PORTRAITS

- Mark didn't know what was the matter—it had been almost two years since his wife, Sue, had died and he felt as if nothing had changed. He still couldn't believe that she was really gone. After Sue's accident, Mark's friends were supportive and his church had brought meals and had prayed for him, but nothing had seemed to help. There were days, more of them than he cared to admit, when he thought it would have been better if he had been in the car with Sue and had died too.
- Tina couldn't seem to stop crying. She was angry with herself for agreeing to move and her husband, Bill, for forcing them to move a thousand miles from family and friends. She missed everyone, her church, the friends she had grown up with, and most of all her family. She didn't want to be here and certainly didn't want to make friends. The phone bill was huge but she didn't care. She just wanted to go back home.
- Rob couldn't drive past the hospital without feeling that sick clenching feeling in his gut. He had spent hours watching his dad struggle with cancer. Rob just couldn't seem to care about anything else—his days, and sometimes nights for that matter, had revolved around doing whatever he could to make sure his dad made it, and now his dad was gone.

2 DEFINITIONS AND KEY THOUGHTS

- Grief is *intense emotional suffering* caused by a loss.
- Grieving is like entering the valley of shadows. Grief is not fun. It is *painful*. It is *work*. It is *a lingering process*. It is a healing journey that can last anywhere from one to three years, and for some a lifetime. Some people never get through the process of grieving.
- A *sudden death* can be more difficult to grieve because there is no warning and no chance to say good-bye and begin to prepare for the loss.
- Grief is not always just about death. It can also be faced in a *divorce, life transition, disaster, or misfortune*.
- Grief is actually a *complex set of emotions*, all of which are "normal." People who are grieving may experience their loss psychologically through feelings, thoughts, and attitudes; socially as they interact with others; and physically as it affects their health.

- Often friends don't know how to help someone who is grieving and may try to "*cheer him up*" or "*get her mind off her loss.*" This can actually add to the burden as the person who is grieving has to either avoid friends or "fake it" rather than have the chance to share his or her true feelings.

- Sometimes loss is cumulative and *awakens memories of early losses* that were never fully grieved.

- Someone who is grieving may experience *intense feelings of guilt* for aspects of the relationship with the person who has died or the grieving person may feel as if he or she is being punished.

- Sometimes the feelings of anger and sadness are *projected onto God* and the grieving person experiences God as distant and uncaring.

- Often sadness and loss can *intensify during certain times of the year*, such as the month that the person died, family holidays, and the person's birthday or anniversary.

> When you feel that all is lost, sometimes the greatest gain is ready to be yours.
>
> *Thomas à Kempis*

Stages of Grief

Grief can be felt in many different ways. Grief has several stages that were originally identified by Elisabeth Kübler-Ross (*On Death and Dying*):

1. *Denial or shock:* Intellectually, bereaved people may comprehend what has happened, but their emotions may not experience the pain yet; they may feel numb.
2. *Anger:* Often this anger is released toward others. The bereaved may even get angry with God. Grieving people become preoccupied with memories of what has been lost and may withdraw for a time.
3. *Bargaining:* In the case of impending death, the grieving individual may bargain with God for more time—a time of negotiations.
4. *Depression:* A time of sadness, disconnection. Bereaved people beat themselves up emotionally as they blame themselves for not somehow preventing the loss. They feel disorganized and don't know how to move on with life. Depression may set in.
5. *Acceptance:* Reorganizing their life, filling new roles, and reconnecting with those around them are all healthy and important facets of the healing process. A key part of this process is the ability to learn how to feel and express the pain more truly without denial and avoidance.

As helpful as it may be to learn about these stages, they are not neatly packaged states that a person experiences sequentially; rather, they are a cycle, and the bereaved may experience more than one at a time.

The goal of grieving is *not to get things back to normal.* After a loss, one's entire life may change. The goal is to find and accept a new "normal."

3 ASSESSMENT INTERVIEW

Rule Outs

1. To determine if the grieving process has cycled downward into a debilitating depression ask: "On a scale of 1 to 10, with 1 being great and 10 being extremely depressed, where would you put yourself today?" (*If depression is evident, see also the section on Depression.*)
2. Do you have any thoughts of hurting yourself? (*If suicidal tendencies are evident, see the section on Suicide and get other help immediately.*)

General Questions

Note: These are directed toward someone who is grieving over a death, but could be recast for the person who is grieving loss for other reasons.

1. Who has died?
2. What are your favorite memories of this person?
3. Was the death especially traumatic? (*For example, was it a sudden accident or death at home?*)
4. Where were you when the death occurred? (*Listen for ways that the person may be blaming him- or herself or feeling guilty for what has happened. For example, was he or she driving the car that had the accident? Was he or she the passenger who survived a car accident while the other person did not? Process those feelings with the grieving person.*)
5. How did you feel after the death?
6. What emotions have you had since the death?
7. What emotions do you currently feel most often?
8. Does this loss remind you of any other loss that you have experienced?
9. Who else knows what you have been going through? Who is supporting you emotionally and spiritually?
10. What does the loss mean for you personally?
11. At what level are you functioning right now? Tell me about a typical day.
12. When are your best times?
13. When are your worst times?

> Yea, though I walk through the valley of the shadow of death, I will fear no evil; for You are with me; Your rod and Your staff, they comfort me.
>
> *Psalm 23:4*

4 WISE COUNSEL

Address any issues the person may have of *wanting to die* or not having a reason to live and give a referral for immediate professional care and/or medication, if necessary.

Assess how the person is *functioning in daily life* and what help he or she might need. Reassure the person that the process will *take time* and that the range and intensity of emotions he or she is experiencing are normal.

Remind the grieving person that everyone's grieving experience is unique, while at the same time *normalizing the process* by identifying it as one you have seen with all persons suffering some important loss.

ACTION STEPS 5

1. Be Patient

- Give yourself the time it takes to heal emotionally.
- Keep a routine, get lots of rest, and try not to attempt too much but direct your energies toward healing.

2. Maintain Friendships

- Let others comfort you and share in your journey toward healing.
- Do not become isolated from people but rather seek meaningful connection with others.
- Make a list of friends to call.
- Locate a grief support group.

3. Feel the Pain

- The intensity of your pain is normal and eventually it will begin to subside. The pain will probably never disappear completely, but it will become bearable.
- Trying to avoid the "terrible pain" only prolongs the grief.
- Trying to avoid a loss by hiding the feelings will only cause problems in other areas—emotionally, spiritually, or physically.
- Dealing with loss in a healthy manner can be a major avenue to growth and life-transforming change.
- You must move forward by experiencing the grief, while at the same time rejoining the living through acts of giving and receiving.

> We are healed of grief only when we express it to the full.
> *Charles R. Swindoll*

4. Realize Grief Is Normal

- Grief encompasses a number of changes. It appears differently at various times, and it comes and goes in people's lives.
- It is a normal, predictable, expected, and healthy reaction to a loss.
- *Grief is each individual's personal journey, and his or her manner of dealing with any kind of loss—no matter how minor or severe it may appear to others—must be respected. It should be gently challenged only when prolonged in a manner that is detrimental to the person and his or her relationships.*

5. Heal

- *Help the grieving person process any guilt and anger he or she is feeling.*
- *Help him or her redirect energy from excessive "if onlys" and wishing that things could be different to a focus on healing.*

6 BIBLICAL INSIGHTS

Then David lamented with this lamentation over Saul and over Jonathan his son.

2 Samuel 1:17

Expressing sorrow is a healthy response to grief. David poured out his sorrow in words that honored the anointed king and his son.

Putting grief into words is a healthy way to handle the pain and to honor those who have died.

He is despised and rejected by men, a Man of sorrows and acquainted with grief. And we hid, as it were, our faces from Him; He was despised, and we did not esteem Him. Surely He has borne our griefs and carried our sorrows; yet we esteemed Him stricken, smitten by God, and afflicted.

Isaiah 53:3–4

In every pang that rends the heart, the Man of Sorrows has a part.

Michael Bruce

Isaiah's words communicate the suffering of the One who loved us and died for us.

In our deepest moments of grief and loss, we need only look to Him on the cross and realize that He understands. He alone can heal the wounded heart.

Jesus said to her, "I am the resurrection and the life. He who believes in Me, though he may die, he shall live. And whoever lives and believes in Me shall never die. Do you believe this?"

John 11:25–26

Because of sin, death comes to all (Rom. 5:12–14). Many try to ignore death, not wanting to think or talk about it. But feared or embraced, expected or not, death still occurs.

Jesus experienced those emotions at the death of His good friend Lazarus. Jesus knows the pain of loss and deep sorrow. He knows the incredible power of death.

It is natural to feel sad and mourn the death of a loved one. But in our times of sorrow, we can let Jesus hold us in His compassionate arms, knowing that He understands.

But I do not want you to be ignorant, brethren, concerning those who have fallen asleep, lest you sorrow as others who have no hope. For if we believe that

Jesus died and rose again, even so God will bring with Him those who sleep in Jesus.

1 Thessalonians 4:13–14

The Thessalonian believers wondered what was happening to their fellow believers who had died.

Believers have the ultimate assurance. We believe that Jesus died, rose again, ascended, and is coming back; and we also believe that He will bring with Him those who have died.

One day, all believers will be reunited in the grandest reunion ever seen!

And God will wipe away every tear from their eyes; there shall be no more death, nor sorrow, nor crying. There shall be no more pain, for the former things have passed away.

Revelation 21:4

Revelation describes a better time and a better place where grief and loss will not exist: heaven.

No matter what we experience here, God promises a perfect future with Him. Through the hard times of today, we can trust this hope for the future.

PRAYER STARTER 7

Lord, we wish we understood Your thoughts, Your plans, but sometimes we admit that we just don't get it. We don't understand why You would take a loved one from us. We don't understand why You would allow this to happen when You knew what it would do. Yet, Lord, we want to trust You . . .

RECOMMENDED RESOURCES 8

Clinton, Tim. *The Bible for Hope: Caring for People God's Way.* Thomas Nelson, 2007.

———. "An Invitation to Comfort" CD. Maranatha Music, 2008.

Clinton, Tim, Archibald D. Hart, and George Ohlschlager. *Caring for People God's Way: Personal and Emotional Issues, Addictions, Grief, and Trauma.* Thomas Nelson, 2006.

Dunn, Bill, and Kathy Leonard. *Through a Season of Grief: Devotions for Your Journey from Mourning to Joy.* Thomas Nelson, 2004.

Kübler-Ross, Elisabeth. *On Death and Dying.* Macmillan, 1969.

Lewis, C. S. *A Grief Observed.* HarperOne, 2001.

Wright, H. Norman. *Recovering from Losses in Life.* Revell, 2006.

Websites

American Association of Christian Counselors (www.aacc.net)

Ecounseling (www.ecounseling.com)

Guilt

1 PORTRAITS

- For the first ten years of her marriage, Lydia lived in a house on the street behind her parents. She visited them every day, and her mother helped babysit her children. She was always very close to her parents. Then her husband got a job in a new location. Lydia feels tremendous guilt over moving away from her parents, who had become quite dependent on her.

- When Glen was nine years old, he was told to go home right after school to check on his great aunt, who lived with them. He got asked by a friend to go play football in the park and decided his great aunt would be fine for a bit longer. When he arrived home an hour late, there was an ambulance at the front door. Aunt Muriel had suffered a heart attack. She passed away that day, and Glen carried the guilt with him into his adult life.

- Marjorie stole some money years ago from a previous employer. It wasn't a lot of money, and she had gotten away with it undetected. However, recently she became a Christian and feels a lot of guilt over what she did.

As far as the east is from the west, so far has He removed our transgressions from us.

Psalm 103:12

2 DEFINITIONS AND KEY THOUGHTS

- Guilt is a *feeling of deep regret or remorse* caused by feeling responsible for something.

- Guilt can *lead to shame* if the feelings of guilt are based on an act or acts that were thought to be wrong.

- There is a difference between *feeling guilty* and *actually being guilty.* If a moral law has been violated, a person is guilty, regardless of whether or not he or she feels guilty. On the other hand, just feeling guilty doesn't mean that a moral law has been violated.

- It is important to clarify whether the guilt is caused by a *sinful act* or *from regret.*

- *True guilt* is caused by sin and is God's way of calling us to repentance and restitution.

- *False guilt* is guilt we place on ourselves because of regret for past acts, failure to live up to our own or someone else's expectations, or even causes that are unknown to us.

- Just to add a twist of complexity, sometimes the guilt can *appear to be false or invalidated* but underneath there is some sin that has been committed.

Dealing with False Guilt

- Often obsessive feelings of guilt over a situation in which the person committed no identifiable sin come from a sense of unworthiness rooted in *the person's childhood*. He or she may have been blamed or punished for things that he or she didn't do, or may have been called worthless.
- It helps for the individual to *tell his or her story*, not to ask forgiveness but to verbalize his or her feelings and get them out in the open.
- It may help for the person to *verbalize those feelings to the one* who makes him or her feel guilty. Often the person on the receiving end will affirm that he or she had no reason to feel guilty and this can provide some relief. This *can backfire*, so prepare the person for that possibility.
- If not comfortable sharing with the other person, the client needs to deal with the guilt by *giving it to God* (this is necessary anyway). This is the first step to healing.
- A person with extreme guilt over something that was not a sinful act needs to work on squaring his or her views of self and behavior with the truth as revealed in Scripture so that he or she can be *released to a life of peace and freedom in Christ*. This process will help the person experience a closeness to God that will enable him or her to realize the depths of God's love and mercy.

> If we confess our sins, He is faithful and just to forgive us our sins and to cleanse us from all unrighteousness.
> *1 John 1:9*

Dealing with True Guilt

- Guilt caused by sin requires an understanding of *confession and forgiveness*.
- This kind of guilt is healthy when *triggered by the Holy Spirit working in the conscience*. The individual should desire to do something about the sinful behavior.
- Confession, request for forgiveness, and/or restitution must happen if possible (that is, if the person hurt is still alive, or if restitution is able to be made in any form).

ASSESSMENT INTERVIEW 3

Rule Outs

1. What brought you to counseling today?
2. Are your feelings of guilt causing physical or emotional problems?

General Questions

First, seek to identify if the guilt is true or false, then proceed with the correct set of questions below.

1. What do you feel guilty about?
2. When did this event occur?
3. What have you done about the feelings of guilt related to this event?
4. Did you commit a sin in this act?

Questions if It Is True Guilt

1. Is this guilt affecting your life today? If so, how?
2. What have you done to deal with your sin?
3. What can you do to rectify the situation—confess, apologize, make restitution?
4. Have you shared this guilt with anyone?
5. If you have confessed your sin, do you feel forgiven by God?
6. Do you think that you understand God's grace?

Questions if It Is False Guilt

1. Since no sin was committed, why do you think that you still carry feelings of guilt?
2. Have you shared this guilt with anyone?
3. Tell me about your childhood. How were you disciplined as a child?
4. How was/is your self-image? How might it affect the way you experience guilt?
5. How might the way you were raised affect the way you feel guilt?
6. Have others made you feel guilty? If so, how?
7. Do you think it would help to talk to these people? Why or why not?

4 WISE COUNSEL

A person who seeks help for false guilt probably has *issues of unworthiness and self-worth*. These often are rooted in childhood. If people were always made to feel that they could not do anything right or were always being blamed for things that were out of their control, then they have more than likely carried these feelings into adult life. They need to be reminded of *God's unconditional love*. Letting people talk about their past provides an opportunity to begin the healing process.

The person dealing with true guilt needs to be given action steps that will pave the way for *confession, forgiveness, and restitution*.

Guilt can trap a person into a life of *unfulfillment and heartache*. The person will never be free to experience God's best until the guilt is released.

5 ACTION STEPS

1. Pay Attention to the Feelings

- Guilt, like physical pain, is a signal that something is wrong.
- Go to God in prayer and ask for insight and wisdom.

2. Determine the Source

- Are the guilt feelings because of sin or because of some issues that were out of your control?
- Seek God patiently. Just because you feel guilty doesn't mean you have sinned; yet, you may need to let God peel back some layers to reveal a sin long forgotten that needs to be resolved.
- If the guilt feelings are out of your control, you still need to find a way to resolve them.

3. Identify True Guilt

- If you are feeling guilty because you have committed a sin, what steps will you take to receive forgiveness from God?
- What steps will you take to receive forgiveness from and/or make restitution to the person?
- If an apology or restitution cannot happen (for example, the person has passed away), then plan a way to deal with the guilt. Write a letter to the person and do a "ceremony" of sorts when your guilt can be given to God.
- Realize that "telling all" can be a way of inflicting more pain on others. Permanent relief from moral guilt comes from God's forgiveness, not necessarily public confession. The scope of the confession should not exceed the scope of the sin.

> The most marvelous ingredient in the forgiveness of God is that he also forgets, the one thing a human being can never do. Forgetting with God is a divine attribute; God's forgiveness forgets.
> *Oswald Chambers*

4. Identify False Guilt

- If the guilt is self-worth related, make a list of all the things God has done for you, including paying the price to save you. (*Note: provide suggestions and Scripture to back it up.*)
- Continuing to punish yourself for being human is useless. Do what you can and move on.

5. Move On

- Once you've confessed, apologized, and/or made restitution, don't beat yourself up anymore. Leave it with God.
- Turn off the mental tape player. Satan, not the Holy Spirit, is the accuser (Rev. 12:10). Satan wants to create feelings of condemnation resulting in unnecessary guilt. Turn him off!
- Keep a "guilt pot." Anytime you feel guilt creeping in, write that guilt feeling on a piece of paper and throw it in the pot. (The pot will remind you that God is the Potter, always at work on you, and you are merely the clay—Isa. 64:8.)

> Good works never erase guilt.
> *Erwin W. Lutzer*

6. Keep Active

- Do things for other people.
- Practice being forgiving in your relationships.
- By providing encouragement to someone else, you will receive encouragement back and this will increase your feelings of self-worth.

6 BIBLICAL INSIGHTS

So he said, "I heard Your voice in the garden, and I was afraid because I was naked; and I hid myself."

Genesis 3:10

Adam already knew he had sinned. He felt that inner awareness of wrongdoing called *guilt*, given by God as an internal corrective.

It could have brought Adam to repentance and confession. Instead, Adam tried to cope with guilt and shame by avoidance and denial.

As long as we blame others and refuse to take responsibility for our wrong actions, we remain mired in sin. Guilt cuts us off from God's redemptive healing.

God invites us to own our sin and confess it to Him. When we do so, God is "faithful and just to forgive us our sins and to cleanse us from all unrighteousness" (1 John 1:9).

At the evening sacrifice I arose from my fasting; and having torn my garment and my robe, I fell on my knees and spread out my hands to the LORD my God. And I said: "O my God, I am too ashamed and humiliated to lift up my face to You, my God; for our iniquities have risen higher than our heads, and our guilt has grown up to the heavens."

Ezra 9:5–6

Despite our mistakes and failures, God is willing to meet us at our point of need.

Sometimes we can make amends by specific actions; at other times we must suffer the consequences of our sin. But through repentance, we can experience God's grace and love.

Then Jesus said to those Jews who believed Him, "If you abide in My word, you are My disciples indeed. And you shall know the truth, and the truth shall make you free. . . . Most assuredly, I say to you, whoever commits sin is a slave of sin. And a slave does not abide in the house forever, but a son abides forever. Therefore if the Son makes you free, you shall be free indeed."

John 8:31–36

> The purpose of being guilty is to bring us to Jesus. Once we are there, then its purpose is finished. If we continue to make ourselves guilty—to blame ourselves—then that is sin in itself.
>
> *Corrie Ten Boom*

No truth is more glorious to imprisoned people than to be told that they are no longer condemned but are set free! Christ brings that good news.

Often, however, believers who have been set free still keep themselves behind bars. They feel guilty about their past or guilty that they cannot be perfect in this life.

Guilt can be good when it helps us know when we have done something wrong. But guilt can also keep people from being able to rejoice in their new life or to bring others to Christ. That kind of guilt is a prison. We needn't stay locked up if Christ has set us free.

There is therefore now no condemnation to those who are in Christ Jesus, who do not walk according to the flesh, but according to the Spirit.

Romans 8:1

Not keeping the law perfectly leads to condemnation. Since no one can keep God's law perfectly, all people are condemned. The law brings guilt because people realize they are powerless to keep it.

Christ's death on the sinner's behalf, however, sets us free.

If Christ no longer condemns us, then neither should we condemn ourselves.

PRAYER STARTER : 7

Guilt can be so powerful. On the one hand, we know You use it, Lord, to show us where we have gone wrong, where we need to confess, ask for forgiveness, or make restitution. On the other hand, it can also become like a prison that keeps us from living for You . . .

RECOMMENDED RESOURCES : 8

Beam, Joe. *Getting Past Guilt: Embracing God's Forgiveness.* Howard Books, 2003.

Clinton, Tim. *The Bible for Hope: Caring for People God's Way.* Thomas Nelson, 2007.

Clinton, Tim, Archibald D. Hart, and George Ohlschlager. *Caring for People God's Way: Personal and Emotional Issues, Addictions, Grief, and Trauma.* Thomas Nelson, 2006.

Humbert, Cynthia Spell. *Deceived by Shame, Desired by God.* NavPress, 2001.

Wilson, Sandra. *Released from Shame: Moving Beyond the Pain of the Past.* InterVaristy Press, 2002.

Websites

American Association of Christian Counselors (www.aacc.net)

Ecounseling (www.ecounseling.com)

Homosexuality

1 PORTRAITS

- Tim painfully recalls feeling different from his brothers. "I remember feeling so alone," he recalls. "While my brothers were out competing in sports, I was quite content in my room drawing." He continues, "My dad and I never got along. He was a high pressure 'corporate type' and was always putting me down for my 'sissy' interests. As I got older, I became increasingly aware of a longing for other men. I fought fantasies of being hugged and touched by another man. Finally, in college, I decided that I couldn't battle these feelings anymore and gave in to having sex with men. Yet even then, I realized it wasn't the sex I was wanting, but love."

- Leah was the youngest daughter with five older brothers. She recalls seeing pictures of herself in preschool dressed by her mom in overalls and T-shirts. With the exception of her ponytail, it was difficult to determine if she was a boy or girl. In grade school Leah often received the brunt of her brothers wrestling competitions. She despised being born a girl. In high school Leah developed a close friendship with a girl named Emily, who was two years older and took a special interest in Leah. Leah experienced tenderness from Emily that she had never experienced from her mom or anyone growing up. Emily's care for her awakened within Leah a deep need to be loved. With time, they developed a sexual relationship. As the relationship progressed, Leah started to see not only how controlling Emily was but how dependent on her Leah had become. Somehow Emily's love was not enough to take Leah's deep soul pain away.

- Henry spoke in a quiet and controlled manner as he shared the recent news of his son "coming out." "Sure, Jay and I have had a difficult relationship, but I just saw it as his own willfulness. He always seemed to want to push me away. I see this as just another attempt to rebel against everything my wife and I believe in."

2 DEFINITIONS AND KEY THOUGHTS

- Homosexuality refers to an orientation and a behavior. The homosexual orientation is a condition in which a person is *sexually attracted* to members of the same sex. Homosexual behavior refers to any sexual activity between members of the same gender. Female homosexuality is generally called lesbianism.

- Homosexuality and lesbianism are rooted in *a variety of psychological, biological, social, and spiritual factors.*

- Research indicates that homosexuality may have its roots in a *breakdown of relationship with a same-sex parent*, creating a deficit in the child's sense of identity and feelings of being loved.

  – *Male homosexuality* has some correlation to an *absent or detached father and an overinvolved, controlling mother.* As a result, the child overidentifies with his mother while at the same time craving the attention and affection of his absent father.

  – *Lesbianism* may be related to an *emotionally or physically absent mother,* resulting in an overidentification by the daughter with her father and a craving for affection from women. Lesbianism can have roots in verbal, physical, or sexual abuse from the opposite sex (possibly a father), creating distrust of men and a feeling of safety and nurture in relationships with women.

- *Other factors* that may play a part in the development of same sex preferences are:
  – sexual abuse

  – fear of the opposite sex

  – exposure to pornography

  – seduction by peers

  – willfulness or rebellion

  – moral relativism

  – molestation pedophilia

- *Experimentation in the adolescent years* can cause confusion for teenagers as to their sexual identity as they seek to meet legitimate needs for love through sexual involvement with same-sex partners.

- Currently research does not support the existence of a "gay" gene, and *no conclusive evidence for the biological basis* of homosexuality has been found. Even in the case of such evidence being discovered, such would only prove what is already known—that people are fallen beings, physically, emotionally, and spiritually imperfect. An inborn tendency toward a particular sin does not justify that sin; it reinforces the need for a Savior.

- Homosexual behavior, like all human behaviors, is *a matter of choice.* People choose what to do with their desires.

- Homosexuality and lesbianism, from a medical and spiritual perspective, can be redeemed. *These persons can find healing from past wounds and experience redemption from sinful behavior* patterns as they seek to live in obedience to God.

- God's intent for sexual expression is within a covenant marriage between a man and a woman (see Gen. 2:24; Heb. 13:4). Hence, adultery and fornication are denounced in Scripture, along with homosexual behavior.

- In the Old Testament, homosexual behavior is condemned as an "abomination" (Lev. 18:22; 20:13).

> There is a huge difference between *loving a homosexual* and *supporting homosexuality.*

143

- In Romans 1:24–27 the practice of homosexuality is referred to as an unnatural state rooted in fallen human nature. Homosexual behavior is condemned as "vile" and "shameful." In 1 Corinthians 6:9–10 and 1 Timothy 1:9–11, Paul lists homosexual practices alongside drunkenness, fornication, murder, and other vices.

- In 1 Corinthians 6:11 Paul preaches to former homosexuals and celebrates their deliverance with the words: "Such were some of you. But you were washed, but you were sanctified, but you were justified in the name of the Lord Jesus and by the Spirit of our God."

3 ASSESSMENT INTERVIEW

If the Person Is Struggling with Homosexuality

1. Are you a follower of Jesus Christ? (*This question may be addressed later in the interview. It's important to discover if the client is having a crisis between sexual temptation and their faith.*)

2. Since you are a believer, do you want to change your homosexual behavior? (*For many, what has kept them in the homosexual lifestyle is ambivalence and fear—ambivalence because the homosexual lifestyle has temporarily numbed deeper emotional pain. They are afraid of becoming vulnerable to further hurt by dealing with their deep pain and whatever caused it.*)

3. Are you experiencing distress over your homosexual behavior?

4. Are these just homosexual "feelings" or have you participated in homosexual behavior? (*If the person has had homosexual sex, it is important that he or she begin the process of seeking forgiveness and repentance by confessing past behavior and restoring moral fences.*)

5. If you have been acting out your sexual desires, how long has this pattern been occurring? (*Evaluate the extent of the involvement in the homosexual arena—has it been in only one relationship, many relationships, an allegiance to the homosexual lifestyle?*)

6. Tell me about your family life. What was your relationship with your mom like?

7. Tell me about your relationship with your dad.

8. Have you ever experienced any of the following:

   – fear of the opposite sex

   – exposure to pornography

   – seduction by peers

   – willful rebellion

9. Are you part of a local church or Christian fellowship? (*If so, does the church provide support for those who are seeking healing from the homosexual condition?*)

If the Person Is the Parent of a Homosexual

1. What has been your reaction to finding out about your son's [daughter's] sexual orientation? (*The person may have a variety of reactions, such as feeling shock, betrayal, sadness, and/or fear.*)
2. Describe what your relationship has been with your son [daughter] in the past.
3. Describe your relationship at the current time.
4. What has your son [daughter] communicated to you are his [her] expectations of you now that he [she] has shared this information?
5. How do you feel about your own role in this situation? (*It is important to evaluate how the person is seeing his or her own effectiveness as a parent. There may be guilt or regret as to how he or she parented this child.*)
6. How do you feel your son [daughter] is handling this?
7. Does your son [daughter] feel free to express his [her] feelings to you?

WISE COUNSEL 4

It is important to evaluate *your own perceptions and feelings* regarding homosexuality. If you have fear, anxiety, or anger toward homosexuals, then you should not counsel a person with this condition. Unconditional love of the homosexual and a genuine regard for the client's personhood are critical.

Homosexuals seeking counseling may have *repressed many fears, anxieties, hostilities, and painful memories.* They may have believed it was unsafe to share with anyone their true feelings but found it too unbearable to face them alone. Therefore, it is crucial that you *communicate a deep respect for the person.*

The pathway to healing from homosexuality is long and not easy but is extremely rewarding. Ultimately the course of healing and redemption for the homosexual is found in a *deep and radical obedience to Jesus Christ,* while at the same time facing honestly the wounds and sins of the past.

The outcome of the healing journey is to be a person who walks with integrity, *willing to sacrifice all fleshly desires* to be identified deeply with Christ.

ACTION STEPS 5

If the Client Is Homosexual

1. Seek Help from a Professional Counselor or Pastor

- *Ultimately the person will need to work with a counselor or pastor who has training in this arena.*

2. Address the Issues

Explain that in counseling with the professional, the client will need to address particular issues in the process of healing:

- Submit your sexuality to God, seeking forgiveness for behavior and choices.
- Choose to change behavior—terminate homosexual relationships and choose not to frequent places where homosexual relationships or activity are encouraged.
- Find healing of your full identity in Christ and accept yourself as a child of God.
- Deal with the guilt of your past.
- Face the pain of the deficit in relationship with the same-sex parent or of opposite-sex abuse.
- Establish healthy same-sex friendships.
- Embrace your identity as a heterosexual.

If the Person Is the Parent of a Homosexual

1. Examine Your Heart

- God does not view one sin as more heinous than others. We have all sinned and fall short of God's glory.
- Examine your own heart before God and be aware of your own personal struggles and temptations so that you are prepared to show your child the same love and forgiveness God has shown you.

2. Avoid Condemnation

- The core of the homosexual struggle is deep feelings of rejection.
- "Coming out" is not an intentional act to hurt the parent. More often than not, the child has kept secret the feelings he or she has struggled with so as not to hurt the parent.

3. Avoid Lecturing

- Avoid lecturing on all the risks and problems with homosexuality.
- Rarely does someone respond positively when being told what he or she shouldn't do.

4. Maintain the Relationship

- Let your child know that you want to maintain a relationship.
- Acceptance of your son or daughter does not mean agreement with his or her choices.

To address the issue of homosexuality is to enter deeply into God's experience: loving the person, hating the sin, and remaining steadfast to God's standards. We know that even when our best efforts to persuade the people we love have failed, God's power is still more than able to accomplish His purposes.

Joe Dallas

- Withdrawing your love and affection will only make the relationship more difficult.

5. Pursue Dialog

- Talk with your child and listen. It may be tough but try to get your child to share the reasons behind his or her choices.
- As you dialog, you will become more comfortable sharing your concerns about the gay lifestyle. And your child may be more open to listening once you have listened.

6. Pray Constantly

- Pray diligently for God's truth and compassion to speak into your son or daughter's heart.

7. Find a Support Group

- You may want to join an organization that seeks to minister to homosexuals and where parents can learn more about God's redemptive plan for healing.

8. Maintain Boundaries

- You can still have boundaries in your home. Just as you would not allow your child's opposite-sex boyfriend [girlfriend] to sleep with your child on visits, this must not happen with a homosexual partner either.
- Even if they consider themselves "married," you must stand by your values, especially if younger siblings are still in the home.

BIBLICAL INSIGHTS 6

Now before they lay down, the men of the city, the men of Sodom, both old and young, all the people from every quarter, surrounded the house. And they called to Lot and said to him, "Where are the men who came to you tonight? Bring them out to us that we may know them carnally."

Genesis 19:4–5

In spite of efforts by some of today's gay theologians to revise and reinterpret Sodom's story, the clear message of Genesis 19 has always referred to homosexual violence. It is generally thought that the Sodomites also practiced bestiality, sex with children and adolescents, heterosexual rape, and adultery, along with other unspeakable forms of sexual perversity and violence. The severity of their punishment shows us God's perspective about the horrors of their behavior.

Though both homosexuality and rape are consistently condemned in the Scriptures, they are not isolated from other sexual sins or sin in general. Whether heterosexual sin or homosexual sin, God calls us to forsake all sexual sin and to know the transforming power of His redeeming and healing grace. To choose otherwise puts us in the company of the citizens of Sodom.

You shall not lie with a male as with a woman. It is an abomination.

Leviticus 18:22

This charge against homosexual relations appears in a section of Scripture that includes rules against marital infidelity and bestiality.

This is one of a number of passages in both Testaments that, taken together and interpreted plainly, reveal that homosexual conduct is a great offense to God. It is called "an abomination" and was punishable by death. Clearly, homosexual practices violate God's law.

For this reason God gave them up to vile passions. For even their women exchanged the natural use for what is against nature. Likewise also the men, leaving the natural use of the woman, burned in their lust for one another, men with men committing what is shameful, and receiving in themselves the penalty of their error which was due.

Romans 1:26–27

Paul says homosexuality is "against nature," against what God planned for sexual relations. God created marriage and sexual relations to be between a man and a woman (Gen. 2:24).

Homosexual acts are called shameful, and those who live that lifestyle will receive "the penalty of their error."

God will forgive and strengthen those who turn away from homosexuality and seek to honor Him with their lives.

And even as they did not like to retain God in their knowledge, God gave them over to a debased mind, to do those things which are not fitting; being filled with all unrighteousness, sexual immorality . . . who, knowing the righteous judgment of God, that those who practice such things are deserving of death, not only do the same but also approve of those who practice them.

Romans 1:28–29, 32

Some say that homosexuality is a lifestyle choice or a genetic predisposition—and when confronted with this passage in Romans, some say that these words were meant only for the culture of that day. When dealing with the Old Testament passages condemning homosexual activity (Lev. 18:22; 20:13), the same argument is often made.

What is clearly a moral issue in both the Old and New Testaments cannot be relegated to the past as just a cultural law. The Bible condemns homosexual conduct because it goes against God's plan for a natural sexual relationship between a man and a woman in marriage.

As with any sin, the actions of homosexuality can be forgiven, and its powerful temptations can be overcome. God will forgive and accept anyone who desires to be set free from homosexuality.

PRAYER STARTER : 7

Lord, You love Your precious child. You created him [her] and You have a plan for his [her] life. He [She] is struggling today with the sin nature and feels helpless to overcome its desires . . .

RECOMMENDED RESOURCES : 8

Clinton, Tim. *The Bible for Hope: Caring for People God's Way.* Thomas Nelson, 2007.

Clinton, Tim, Archibald D. Hart, and George Ohlschlager. *Caring for People God's Way: Personal and Emotional Issues, Addictions, Grief, and Trauma.* Thomas Nelson, 2006.

Dallas, Joe. *Desires in Conflict: Hope for Men Who Struggle with Sexual Identity.* Harvest House, 2003.

———. *When Homosexuality Hits Home: What to Do When a Loved One Says They're Gay.* Harvest House, 2004.

Haley, Mike. *101 Frequently Asked Questions about Homosexuality.* Harvest House, 2004.

Jones, Stanton L., and Mark Yarhouse. *Ex-Gays?: A Longitudinal Study of Religiously Mediated Change in Sexual Orientation.* IVP Academic, 2007.

Websites

American Association of Christian Counselors (www.aacc.net)

Ecounseling (www.ecounseling.com)

Loneliness

1 PORTRAITS

- John is a man of fifty who has just lost his wife of twenty years. They never had any children and did most everything together. John feels alienated from the friends he and his wife, Jenny, had together. Loneliness has overcome him.
- Mary can't stand going to all her friends' weddings. These are not happy occasions for her. It has been five years since she graduated from college and she longs to be married. She spends most evenings alone in her tiny apartment.

2 DEFINITIONS AND KEY THOUGHTS

- Loneliness is a human response to being alone because God created humans with *a need for relationships*.
- Loneliness:
  - is an uncomfortable feeling of *isolation*
  - is a negative feeling of being *disconnected* from others
  - causes a person to feel *alienated*
  - happens when a person feels there is *no one* with whom to share joys and disappointments
  - can result in an overwhelming feeling *of sadness*
  - can cause a person to become *despondent* if nothing is done about it
- From the moment of birth, *humans seek attachment and connection*.
- Since humans were made in the image of a triune God (who exists in relationship), humans too were *made for relationship*. This is evidenced in Genesis 2:18, where God sees Adam alone in the Garden of Eden and says it is "not good."
- Humans need both *intimacy with God* (vertical relationship) and *intimacy with other people* (horizontal relationship).
- When humans inherited a sin nature, *intimacy was tainted*. Adam and Eve clothed themselves, blamed each other, blamed God, and refused to accept responsibility for their disobedience. Through Christ, people can discover the path to genuine intimacy again.
- Due to our sin nature, *intimacy is difficult to achieve* and people often experience loneliness.

> The man who lives by himself and for himself is apt to be corrupted by the company he keeps.
>
> *Charles Henry Parkhurst*

Types of Loneliness

Situational Loneliness

- A response to physical or emotional separation.
- Death, divorce, life transitions, and personal mobility are the *most common causes* of situational loneliness.
- In situational loneliness, *intimate relationships are severed, changed, or forever disrupted* in some way.
- The loneliness may be *brief and contained or deep and overwhelming.*
- The person knows there are those who care, whose support is, perhaps, only a phone call away, but the *situation (a job or school) demands separation.*
- The *intense longing* that accompanies the separation is compelling and sometimes overwhelming.
- When the separation is *extensive* (such as through death), the loneliness is *more difficult to handle.*

Emotional Loneliness

- *Emotional separation* can also lead to loneliness.
- People can feel lonely when they are surrounded by those with whom they perceive *little or no intimate connection.* The loneliest people are often *in crowds.*
- This sense of *disconnectedness* accentuates the loneliness and often leads to greater despair.
- This kind of loneliness is often felt as a *form of anxiety*, driving some to frantic efforts at *superficial connection.*
- When physical separation is coupled with emotional separation, the loneliness can seem unbearable.

Chronic Loneliness

- *Chronic loneliness* can result from persistent feelings of not belonging or being understood.
- Chronic loneliness is often rooted in deeply held personal beliefs of social deficits.
- The person feeling chronically *alone and isolated* has *no hope of "connecting"* again in the future.
- Chronic feelings of loneliness can lead to *deep personal isolation and despair, often* ending in suicide or angry, violent alienation.

> Americans are far more socially isolated today than they were two decades ago, and a sharply growing number of people say they have no one in whom they can confide, according to a comprehensive new evaluation of the decline of social ties in the United States.[1]

> The world's greatest tragedy is unwantedness; the world's greatest disease is loneliness.
>
> *Mother Teresa*

ASSESSMENT INTERVIEW 3

1. Do you feel alone even when you are in a room full of people?
2. Does the loneliness ever go away?
3. When it does, what are you doing?

4. What would a typical day be like for you?

5. Have you prayed about and confessed your loneliness to God?

6. Do you feel that God understands your loneliness?

7. Do you blame yourself for your loneliness?

8. Do you have a friend you can share these feelings with?

9. Talk about another period in your life when you were lonely.

10. Do you remember what you did or what got you out of the loneliness the previous time?

11. Do you think you could change your loneliness in a similar way now?

12. Tell me about any of your outside involvements.

13. Tell me about your interests and hobbies.

4 : WISE COUNSEL

The client needs to understand the source of loneliness. Perhaps his or her loneliness is based on a perception, not an unchangeable circumstance. Perceptions can be changed once the person sees the cause of the loneliness. Is the person feeling lonely because of a mistaken perception of the situation? Can the situation be changed?

A person's loneliness may be a healthy part of the grief process as he or she deals with a loss. This is natural and can pass if the person does not let the loneliness cause complete isolation from others.

It sounds like a paradox, but there may be times God requires a person to be alone to move away from loneliness.

The experience of loneliness can cause people to draw closer to God and to others. If we are dealing with loneliness, we need to reach out to God and to others.

God will bring people into our lives at various times. A person might not always have the same trusted friend to confide in. People will come and go.

5 : ACTION STEPS

1. Recognize the Feeling

- *Have the person experiencing loneliness express the feeling during counseling.*
- Put your thoughts and feelings in writing—possibly in a journal—as a way to determine the source of your loneliness.
- Make some social and spiritual changes to move out of loneliness (for example, become more involved in the community; devote time to communion with God every day).

2. Seek God

- Lonely times can draw one closer to God. God wants His children to be dependent on Him for everything.
- While social relationships are still lacking, for the time being, enjoy your relationship with God. He is the closest friend you will ever have. He will never leave and never disappoint you (see Heb. 13:5).
- Focus on the positive and cherish the fact that God has a will for each day and each stage of life.

3. Get Involved

- Join a church committee, Bible study, community organization, support group, sports team, or hobby club.
- Volunteer. Volunteering for some community agency is a great way to help others and at the same time engage in meaningful relationships.
- Do more than just attend church. Try hosting a meeting, prayer group, or Bible study in your home.
- Search (with your counselor) to find others who are seeking healthy, close, active, and meaningful friendships.
- When at a social event, identify the person who looks loneliest and start there.

4. Be Confident

- Loneliness will be overcome in time.
- Remember that no one is truly alone if he or she has God.

Human beings need both vertical intimacy (with God) and horizontal intimacy (with people) in order to be fulfilled. Without those relationships, they are vulnerable to the complex set of emotions described as "loneliness."

Miriam Stark
Parent

BIBLICAL INSIGHTS 6

I have become a stranger to my brothers, and an alien to my mother's children.

Psalm 69:8

Loneliness is a heavy burden; people can feel alone even when surrounded by others.

Even in his loneliness, reflected in the verse above, David found that God was near; therefore, he was not alone at all.

When our courage and strength fail, when people seem to have abandoned us, we can take comfort in knowing that God is always with us. When we know Him, we are never alone.

Fear not, for I am with you; be not dismayed, for I am your God. I will strengthen you, yes, I will help you, I will uphold you with My righteous right hand.

Isaiah 41:10

God reminds His people that in their loneliness and inadequacy they need not fear or be dismayed. Why? Because He is their God and because He is with them, holding them in His "righteous right hand."

Everyone feels lonely at times. Sometimes, however, loneliness can become so desperate that it causes fearfulness. Then fear can draw the lonely person's attention away from God.

Feelings of loneliness can be helped. Lonely people can attend church (Heb. 10:25), be a friend to someone else (Prov. 18:24), listen to Christian music, and pray for God to work in and through them to take away the lonely feelings.

Now Pashhur the son of Immer, the priest who was also chief governor in the house of the LORD, heard that Jeremiah prophesied these things. Then Pashhur struck Jeremiah the prophet, and put him in the stocks that were in the high gate of Benjamin, which was by the house of the LORD.

Jeremiah 20:1–2

As we read Jeremiah's prayer journal, we see into the life of an intensely lonely man. On the pages, anger, resentment, and self-loathing jostle with praise and confidence. But the fact that he continued to communicate with God meant that he knew he wasn't completely alone.

The intensity of his feelings did not obliterate the deeper reality of God's presence. As overwhelming as his gripes and challenges were, he still found comfort in having Someone to whom he could gripe.

When we think that we are alone facing the greatest challenges of our lives, the Spirit of God within us will continue to shape us and draw us out to live for God.

Let your conduct be without covetousness; be content with such things as you have. For He Himself has said, "I will never leave you nor forsake you."

Hebrews 13:5

When people feel lonely, they feel as though they don't belong, that no one cares, and that they are unloved and unwanted. When believers feel lonely, they need to remember God's great promise, "I will never leave you nor forsake you."

No matter how painful or difficult our situation, no matter how alone we feel, God is there. We can look to Him for deliverance, commit the situation to His care, and take comfort in His presence. God is always with us.

The soul hardly ever realizes it, but whether he is a believer or not, his loneliness is really a homesickness for God.

Hubert Van Zeller

We are born helpless. As soon as we are fully conscious we discover loneliness. We need others physically, emotionally, intellectually; we need them if we are to know anything, even ourselves.

C. S. Lewis

PRAYER STARTER :7

Your child has come today with a burden, Lord. He [She] is facing what You called "not good" from the very moment of creation—people should not be alone. He [She] knows he [she] has You, dear Lord, and I pray that during this lonely time, Your presence and friendship will be all the more real to him [her]. Then I pray that You will show him [her] places he [she] can serve, people he [she] can help, things he [she] can do to break out of this pattern . . .

RECOMMENDED RESOURCES :8

Clinton, Tim. *The Bible for Hope: Caring for People God's Way*. Thomas Nelson, 2007.

Clinton, Tim, Archibald D. Hart, and George Ohlschlager. *Caring for People God's Way: Personal and Emotional Issues, Addictions, Grief, and Trauma*. Thomas Nelson, 2006.

Clinton, Tim, and Gary Sibcy. *Why You Do the Things You Do: The Secret to Healthy Relationships*. Thomas Nelson, 2006.

Zavada, Jack. "Lying on God's Couch: Loneliness Therapy for Christian Singles," About.com: Christianity, 2009. http://christianity.about.com/od/singlesresources/a/lonelytherapy.htm.

Websites

American Association of Christian Counselors (www.aacc.net)

Ecounseling (www.ecounseling.com)

Love and Belonging

1 PORTRAITS

- Kathy has jumped from church to church. No matter where she goes, she just doesn't seem to fit in.
- Ben grew up without a dad, a fact that plagues him daily. Often he wonders what it would have been like to have grown up with both parents.
- Sue would like to meet new people but she doesn't seem to have the necessary skills to do so. She ends up staying at home to avoid being embarrassed.

2 DEFINITIONS AND KEY THOUGHTS

Love is being so completely oriented to another—in thought, feeling, and behavior—that their best interests and desires become as important, if not more so, than your own.

- 1 Corinthians 13:4–8 describes several characteristics of love:

  - Love suffers long and is kind.
  - Love does not envy.
  - Love does not parade itself.
  - Love is not puffed up.
  - Love does not behave rudely.
  - Love does not seek its own.
  - Love is not provoked.
  - Love thinks no evil.
  - Love does not rejoice in iniquity.
  - Love does rejoice in the truth.
  - Love bears all things.
  - Love believes all things.
  - Love hopes all things.
  - Love endures all things.
  - Love never fails.

> Above all things have fervent love for one another, for "love will cover a multitude of sins."
>
> *1 Peter 4:8*

- In Romans 12:9–10, Paul writes "Let love be without hypocrisy. . . . Be kindly affectionate to one another with brotherly love." Paul continues on, speaking about love's other remarkable qualities (vv. 11–21):

  – Love is fervent in spirit and service, strong and intense.

  – Love is joyful, patient, prayerful, generous, and hospitable.

  – Love blesses persecutors, refusing revenge.

  – Love is compassionate and humble.

  – Love is peaceable.

  – Love overcomes and destroys evil.

  – Love hates or abhors what is evil.

- All people need to feel like they *belong*. Ephesians 1:4–6 states explicitly that we are chosen for belonging with God, "just as He chose us in Him before the foundation of the world, that we should be holy and without blame before Him in love, having predestined us to adoption as sons by Jesus Christ to Himself, according to the good pleasure of His will, to the praise of the glory of His grace, by which He made us accepted in the Beloved."

- Truly happy and contented people will attribute their well-being first to God, and then to their *friends and family*. What they're saying is, "I have been blessed by the love I have been able to receive from others."

- While everyone has an emotional need for love and belonging, the *level of that need may vary* from person to person. Some are perfectly content with feeling loved by and belonging to a few close people, while others thrive on being loved and accepted by a wide variety of people.

- We all need to be loved and accepted, but *no one will be loved by everyone*. A person may receive love from a number of individuals yet *be focused on the one person* who will not accept him or her.

- When we love others, regardless of whether it's warranted or not, we are *freeing ourselves to be loved* as well.

Love Languages

- In his book *The Five Love Languages*, Gary Chapman describes five different "love languages" or ways that people say, "I love you" (see Recommended Resources at end of chapter). Based on these adapted questions from that book, we need to help the client determine his or her love language:

  – *Words of Affirmation*. Do you need verbal praise and encouragement? Do you thrive on verbal praise, tone of voice, kindness, and thank yous? Do you love it when people compliment you to your face and to others (directly and indirectly)? Do you love getting notes and emails? Do you need verbal affirmation? Do you do this for others you care about?

  – *Quality Time*. Do you love having people's undivided attention? Do you like it when people come over and just hang out? Do you like to plan activities to do with others? Do you like quality conversations? Do you enjoy the

> If you judge people, you have no time to love them.
> *Mother Teresa*

> To love is to be vulnerable.
> *C. S. Lewis*

give-and-take of asking questions and listening? Do you really like to get inside people's heads and find out what they're thinking?

– *Gifts.* Do you like visual symbols of love? Gifts can come in any shape or size—maybe someone just brings you a cup of coffee at work or tosses a candy bar your way. The cost doesn't matter; it's truly the thought that counts. Do you find yourself doing this for others?

– *Acts of Service.* Do you like to *do* things for others, and have them help you out as well? Someone steps in to help on a project; someone washes your car; someone makes you dinner—and you eagerly do the same types of things for your friends.

– *Physical Touch.* Are you a "toucher"? Do you give pats on the back and hugs—all of which mean nothing but friendship? Do you appreciate that kind of physical touch from others?

> The greatest happiness of life is the conviction that we are loved—loved for ourselves, or rather, loved in spite of ourselves.
>
> *Victor Hugo*

Determining your own love language, and *understanding the love language of those around you*, will go a long way to communicating the love that is truly there.

3 ASSESSMENT INTERVIEW

Nobody comes into counseling saying they need to feel loved and that they need to belong. Instead, *not receiving love and belonging will exhibit itself* with the following symptoms: feeling depressed, lacking energy, having no zest for life, having no desire to be social, not feeling fulfilled.

The following questions should be addressed only after some of the aforementioned symptoms have been ascertained:

1. What are your hobbies?
2. Do you share these hobbies with other people?
3. What organizations do you belong to?
4. What is a typical Saturday or day off like for you?
5. Whom do you love in your life?
6. How do you show that love?
7. Of the five love languages (noted above), which is yours?
8. What do you think are the love languages of those closest to you?
9. Who loves you? How do these people show it?
10. Do you think that some people may be showing you love in a different "language," and you're just not understanding it?
11. Do you think that you are showing love to some people but that your "language" is different from theirs, and they aren't understanding it?
12. Do you deserve to be loved by others?
13. Who doesn't love you?
14. Do you think that everyone should love you?

15. How do people get to know you?

16. Do you think that they are getting to know the real you, not the you that you want others to see but the deeper you?

WISE COUNSEL : 4

We love because God first loved us. If you are going to be a change agent in someone's life, love needs to be so given over to them that they feel that you prize and value them like no one else on this earth.

ACTION STEPS : 5

1. Be Realistic

- Everyone needs to feel loved and accepted, but no one will be loved and accepted by everyone.
- It is unreasonable to expect that your friends or family will never be upset or disappointed.

2. Refuse to Be Offended

- It doesn't matter who your friends are or what family you belong to or where you work, the opportunity to be offended will come. Wherever people are together, sparks will fly. Do not take the opportunity to be offended.
- Too many people leave friends, jobs, organizations, or even marriages because they have been offended. This is not the answer to problems in relationships. You must work through these situations if you expect to grow and mature into the person God wants you to be.

> Love is an action, an activity. It is not a feeling.
> *M. Scott Peck*

3. Get Involved

- Find an activity that will force you to associate with other people. It doesn't matter what activity or hobby you choose. The goal is to get into a situation where other people will get to know you better.
- Join a club or organization or ministry that you haven't been a part of before— and be committed for no less than three months of involvement.
- Write in a journal about the social interaction you experience.
- Call someone at least once a week from the ministry or club you join.

4. Pay Attention to the Primary Love Language

- Love in the way others want to be loved.

6 BIBLICAL INSIGHTS

Two are better than one, because they have a good reward for their labor. For if they fall, one will lift up his companion. But woe to him who is alone when he falls, for he has no one to help him up.

Ecclesiastes 4:9–10

The Preacher in Ecclesiastes observed the importance of friendships. God created people to be in relationship with Him and in relationships with one another.

Friends who work on a task can rejoice together in its accomplishment. Friends can help each other—if one should fall, the other is there to "help him up."

Those who have both a strong relationship with God and strong friendships with other believers will have bonds that strengthen life's joys and limit life's sorrows.

Friendships among believers are precious, for they have the bond of Christ and of eternity. We should both find good friends and be good friends.

> Joy is love exalted; peace is love in repose; long-suffering is love enduring; gentleness is love in society; goodness is love in action; faith is love on the battlefield; meekness is love in school; and temperance is love in training.
>
> *D. L. Moody*

This is My commandment, that you love one another as I have loved you. Greater love has no one than this, than to lay down one's life for his friends.

John 15:12–13

Jesus gave two commandments to His followers: "love Me" and "love each other." Jesus said that His followers should love each other as He loved them.

So great was his love that Jesus would give His life for them. We are to love others as Jesus loved us. We probably won't have to die for anyone but we show our great love for others by listening, helping, encouraging, and giving. Christ's humble, sacrificial love is our example.

[Love] bears all things, believes all things, hopes all things, endures all things.

1 Corinthians 13:7

"Bears all things" means that love enables one to assume and absorb some degree of loveless behavior by another.

"Believes all things" means that love never loses faith in others and is willing to think the best of them.

"Hopes all things" means that love looks forward with optimism, knowing that God works all things together for good.

"Endures all things" means that love holds on. In the end, love never fails and it never ends.

When we love, we take part in eternity. We can ask God to perfect our love for Him and for others.

Beloved, let us love one another, for love is of God; and everyone who loves is born of God and knows God.

1 John 4:7

God authored the concept of love. When people become believers, they learn how to "love one another" because the Spirit within shows them how as they yield to His leading.

Christian relationships ought to be the most loving in the world. Christians who meet each other for the first time experience a bond of love that transcends understanding.

The love that binds Christians makes for solid and eternal relationships. The love in our relationships reveals God in us.

PRAYER STARTER : 7

Thank You for the love You have shown us through Your Son, dear Lord. Thank You for the others You have placed in our lives. Your child has come today with a feeling of not belonging, of not being loved. I pray that You will reveal to him [her] the special person You created him [her] to be, and show him [her] that love from others is often the result of showing love . . .

RECOMMENDED RESOURCES : 8

Allender, Dan B., and Tremper Longman III. *Bold Love.* NavPress, 1992.

Chapman, Gary. *The Five Love Languages: How to Express Heartfelt Commitment to Your Mate.* Northfield Publishing, 1995.

Clinton, Tim. *The Bible for Hope: Caring for People God's Way.* Thomas Nelson, 2007.

Clinton, Tim, Archibald D. Hart, and George Ohlschlager. *Caring for People God's Way: Personal and Emotional Issues, Addictions, Grief, and Trauma.* Thomas Nelson, 2006.

Clinton, Tim, and Gary Sibcy. *Why You Do the Things You Do: The Secret to Healthy Relationships.* Thomas Nelson, 2006.

Eggerichs, Emerson. *Love and Respect: The Love She Desires Most; The Respect He Desperately Needs.* Thomas Nelson, 2004.

Hemfelt, Robert, Frank Minirth, and Paul Meier. *Love Is a Choice: Letting Go of Unhealthy Relationships.* Thomas Nelson, 1989.

Parrott, Les and Leslie. *Love Talk: Speak Each Other's Language Like You Never Have Before.* Zondervan, 2004.

Wilson, Sandra. *Freedom in Christ/Abba's Arms.* American Association of Christian Counselors Life Enrich Video Series. See www.aacc.net for more information.

Websites

American Association of Christian Counselors (www.aacc.net)

Ecounseling (www.ecounseling.com)

> Faith, like light, should always be simple, and unbending; while love, like warmth, should beam forth on every side, and bend to every necessity of our brethren.
>
> *Martin Luther*

Mental Disorder

1 PORTRAITS

- Barbara was a vigorous, energetic woman who loved to help at the local shelter. But every so often she'd stop her volunteer work and not leave her house for weeks. At other times, she'd hang out at the shelter for days, often not leaving to sleep, being very gregarious and giving away a lot of cash.

- No one at church knew exactly why Michael seemed so odd. He'd been a star basketball player in high school and college and he'd graduated with honors from law school and joined a good firm. But now he was unemployed, supported by his wife and son. People at church thought he'd damaged his brain with drugs, because he acted so spaced out, but his fall from success was not of his own doing.

- Sandy did everything to extremes. She was dramatic, loving, and enthusiastic some of the time. Then she'd become angry, obnoxious, and belligerent. She was divorced and had held a lot of different jobs and attended a lot of different churches. She was known among the local pastors as a troublemaker.

- Matt was shy and reclusive. He worked with computers and rarely spoke in Sunday school class. When he did speak, he often voiced bizarre opinions about numerological schemes in the Quran and predictions of the exact time of the end of the world.

2 DEFINITIONS AND KEY THOUGHTS

- Thoughts and behaviors that cause individuals to *experience extreme problems in functioning* in significant areas of their lives—relationships, employment, education, financial well-being, even spirituality—are associated with what is often called mental disorder.

- Mental disorder is *not short-term but it is also not necessarily permanent.* By definition, mental problems must endure for a certain minimum period of time before a mental disorder can be diagnosed.

- Most mental disorders *resolve after treatment* with counseling and/or medication, or simply the passing of time.

- Other mental disorders are *lifelong and cause ongoing problems* for those afflicted with them and for their families.

- If someone is mentally ill, he or she is not simply "odd." *Labels of mental disorder ought never to be applied without a professional assessment.* Mental disorders are—by definition—serious disturbances.

- These are some common types of mental disorders:

  - *Psychotic disorders* are those that result in *bizarre, paranoid, or delusional thinking.* The most common one is schizophrenia. Individuals with psychotic illnesses manifest the symptoms *most often thought of as "crazy"*—seeing or hearing things that aren't there, making bizarre connections between unrelated events, or showing grossly inappropriate responses to ordinary occurrences.

  - *Mood disorders* are those that primarily affect a person's *emotional stability.* The most common are depression and bipolar disorder (formerly called manic depression). Individuals afflicted with depression feel discouraged and hopeless almost every day, have lost interest in activities in which they used to take pleasure, and sometimes consider or attempt suicide. Those with bipolar disorder exhibit cycles of wildly changing emotions and behaviors.

  - *Anxiety disorders* are characterized by *extreme nervousness, panic, or phobias.* Persons suffering from anxiety disorders cannot calm down, feel panicky much of the time, and have physical symptoms of constant nervousness. Those with post-traumatic stress may experience flashbacks of trauma and may react to loud noises or other reminders of the precipitating event.

  - *Personality disorders* are disturbances in thinking and behavior that are *a part of a person's basic character.* They result in lifelong patterns of counterproductive behavior. Unlike the above mental disorders, personality disorders do not often respond to medications or short-term therapy.

  - There are many other disorders, some associated only with children, but there is not enough space here to deal with them all.

- There are *huge differences between mental disorder, sin, and demonic influence.* Treatment must take place after a thorough assessment and careful diagnosis.

- In a church, mental disorder most often *becomes apparent in relationships.* Mentally ill people who are active in church may have difficulty tolerating the opinions of others, getting along on committees, or accepting limits. Other mentally ill people may be on the periphery of the church—a churchgoer's spouse or child who is often the subject of prayer requests.

- *Misdiagnosis and improper treatments are common.* Far too many suffer needlessly. The failure to understand the multiple reasons people suffer—including the distinction between sin, mental illness, and demonic influence—has significant consequences.

Four of the ten leading causes of disability in the U.S. and other developed countries are mental disorders—major depression, bipolar disorder, schizophrenia, and obsessive/compulsive disorder. Many people suffer from more than one mental disorder at a given time.[1]

If ADHD is suspected, the diagnosis should be made by a professional with training in ADHD. This includes child psychiatrists, psychologists, developmental/behavioral pediatricians, behavioral neurologists, and clinical social workers.[2]

Some people are only confessing sin when they should be taking medication; others are blaming an illness when they should be confessing their sin.

Demons are being cast out of schizophrenics who need medical treatment; people who need to challenge evil are put into mental hospitals and drugged to complacency.

- The church and mental health professions must *value the contribution each can make and work together* to relieve human suffering.

3 ASSESSMENT INTERVIEW

Keep in mind that much that passes for "insanity" in the general population is simply a brief crisis due to extreme circumstances. *Don't jump to conclusions* or place labels on people.

Some people with mental disorder struggle for *just a short time*. Others are able to live nearly normal lives with regular medication and supportive counseling. Some will *suffer from constant emotional and behavioral chaos*, inability to maintain relationships or jobs, and difficulties with the law and with substance abuse. People's responses to medications vary widely, and some disorders (such as bipolar disorder) cause symptoms that make afflicted individuals unlikely to stay on the medication.

With some forms of mental disorder, *there is the risk of violence* due to severe depression, feelings of hopelessness, or aggression. Ask the rule-out questions below to assess for the potential for violence. All the questions are directed toward the family member or concerned friend of a mentally ill person, but they could also be asked directly to the ill person.

Rule Outs

1. Has your family member ever been violent?
2. Does he [she] have access to weapons?
3. Has he [she] ever expressed feeling threatened? (*If so, turn to Action Steps 1 and 2.*)
4. Does your family member seem despondent or hopeless?
5. Has he [she] ever attempted suicide? (*See Suicide for more information on how to handle this situation.*)
6. [If a woman] Has she recently had a baby?
7. Who could be endangered if this person becomes violent?

General Questions

1. Has anyone in this person's family ever been under the care of a psychiatrist or admitted to a psychiatric hospital?
2. If so, what reason was given?
3. Are you aware of a diagnosis?

4. What makes you think that this person has a mental disorder?

5. Describe the history of this person's most significant relationships. (*Unstable relationships—or lack of any personal relationships—may be an indicator of underlying mental problems.*)

6. Has this individual ever been convicted of a crime? If so, what crime and when?

7. Does this person ever speak in bizarre ways?

8. Does this person express fear that people are "after" him [her]?

9. Does this person describe hearing or seeing things that are not there? (*Questions 7–9 are all symptoms of psychosis.*)

10. Does this person show cycles of emotions or behaviors?

11. Does he [she] ever go for long periods with little sleep?

12. Does he [she] ever spend a lot of money recklessly or act grandiosely and above the law? (*Questions 10–12 are symptoms of bipolar disorder.*)

> Mental disorders are common in the United States and internationally. An estimated 22.1 percent of Americans, ages eighteen and older—about one in five adults—suffer from a diagnosable mental disorder in a given year.[3]

WISE COUNSEL 4

Though only a small percentage of persons with mental disorder become violent, you should still *be vigilant for the risk of violence*.

People who are *paranoid*—believe that others are working against them, perhaps in an elaborate plot—can feel threatened enough to strike out at others. *Mania*—feeling grandiose and on top of the world—can also breed violence when the manic individual is crossed.

Never risk the safety of yourself, your family, or your congregation members by naively thinking that violence will not occur. If a situation is escalating, it is better to *call 911* unnecessarily than to overlook the potential of violence.

Police and paramedics are *trained to assess the situation* and bring to local emergency rooms people who are exhibiting signs of mental problems. At the emergency room, medical professionals should be available to assess the individual and decide on a course of action. You can help by reporting your concerns to the police or paramedics.

ACTION STEPS 5

Encourage the family member or concerned friend of a mentally ill person in the following Action Steps.

1. Lessen the Risks

- If there is any risk of violence, get professionals involved immediately.
- Remove any weapons (guns, knives, anything else sharp) and ropes, scarves, sheets, or belts, as well as drugs from the home. Try to observe the person until help arrives.

2. Watch Yourself

- If you are with the person who is expressing extreme anger or paranoia, you should get out of the way.
- Do not block the individual's exit. Instead, let him or her leave and then call 911.

3. Get Professional Help

You should talk with a professional if your loved one is

- threatening violence
- causing financial hardship
- abusing substances (see also the section on Addictions)
- participating in dangerous or destructive behavior
- disappearing without explanation

4. Get Medical Help

- The answer to the problem may be medication.

5. Join a Support Group

- There are many support groups for those who love persons with mental disorders. The best-known is NAMI, the National Alliance for the Mentally Ill, which sponsors both support and advocacy across the country.
- Other groups can be found by contacting your church or local mental health agencies.

6. Get Practical Help

- Local mental health agencies should have information about financial help, health insurance, supportive counseling, and other interventions that can aid persons with mental disorders and their families.
- Persons with *chronic mental disorder* who need ongoing help may benefit from programs such as day treatment or supportive living facilities.

7. Get Spiritual Help

- God is for those with mental disorders. Be sure to be spiritually sensitive and unbiased in your love for them.
- Help the person with mental disorder understand his or her need for Christ. Is he or she a Christian? Does he or she know the plan of salvation? Does he or she understand what Jesus can do in his or her life? (See John 1:12; Rom. 3:23; 6:23.)

- Pray for wisdom regarding your approach to helping the person with mental disorder. Does he or she need advice, encouragement, education, correction, a support system, insight, confession, verbal reinforcement, modeling, or confrontation?

8. Live in Peace

- Do not blame the person with a mental disorder or get sucked into arguments with him or her.
- The person is, indeed, ill; blaming the person is like blaming a patient for his or her heart attack.

BIBLICAL INSIGHTS 6

But the Spirit of the LORD departed from Saul, and a distressing spirit from the LORD troubled him.

1 Samuel 16:14

King Saul, who reigned in Israel before David, displayed classic characteristics of mental disorder, including wide mood swings and fits of depression and anger. A person can develop such debilitating emotional symptoms for many reasons. In this case, Scripture indicates that "a distressing spirit from the LORD troubled" Saul.

Saul's heart had turned from God, so God permitted affliction by a spirit of distress—possibly a demonic influence—to occur. Not all mental disorders are a result of direct demonic influence, but like any sickness or disease, the battle for our minds is a result of the fall and Satan's presence in this world.

That very hour the word was fulfilled concerning Nebuchadnezzar; he was driven from men and ate grass like oxen; his body was wet with the dew of heaven till his hair had grown like eagles' feathers and his nails like birds' claws.

Daniel 4:33

> More than half of U.S. adults have a mental or physical condition that prevents them from working or conducting their usual duties (for example, role disability) for several days each year, and a large portion of those days can be attributed to mental disorders.[4]

We are spiritual beings, created by God and incomplete without Him. Also we are physical beings, and a physical disease can lead to psychological or spiritual problems, and vice versa. And then too we are psychological beings, meaning that each person has a mind, emotions, and a will. The interrelationships among these three realms in our humanity mean that specific problems may have many symptoms and causes behind them.

If believers face some form of an emotional problem, they should seek counsel from wise, qualified Christians who can treat them with a comprehensive approach. During such a time, other believers must surround the hurting brother or sister in prayer. God promises to help His people through even the most difficult times.

Then they sailed to the country of the Gadarenes, which is opposite Galilee. And when He stepped out on the land, there met Him a certain man from the city who had demons for a long time. And he wore no clothes, nor did he live in a house but in the tombs.

Luke 8:26–27

In this case, the man's situation was caused by demon possession. Usually, however, mental disorder has other causes, such as genetics or hormonal imbalances.

People who are afflicted with a mental disorder need assurance of their worthiness before God, as well as Christian professional help. Jesus has the power to heal but He may not always choose to do so. God's people must trust His wisdom through any difficult time.

7 PRAYER STARTER

Dear Lord, we are concerned about _____. We have good reasons to be concerned. Please lead us to the people who will be able to help us, to offer resources, and to aid this person we love. Give us strength, patience, and rest . . .

8 RECOMMENDED RESOURCES

Clinton, Tim. *The Bible for Hope: Caring for People God's Way*. Thomas Nelson, 2007.

Clinton, Tim, Archibald D. Hart, and George Ohlschlager. *Caring for People God's Way: Personal and Emotional Issues, Addictions, Grief, and Trauma*. Thomas Nelson, 2006.

Clinton, Tim, and Gary Sibcy. *Why You Do the Things You Do: The Secret to Healthy Relationships*. Thomas Nelson, 2006.

Lyles, Michael. *Battling Bi-Polar Disorder*. American Association of Christian Counselors Courageous Living Series. See www.aacc.net for more information.

———. *Psychiatric Medication and the Christian*. American Association of Christian Counselors Courageous Living Series. See www.aacc.net for more information.

Martin, Grant. *Facing ADHD*. American Association of Christian Counselors Courageous Living Series. See www.aacc.net for more information.

Meier, Paul, and Robert L. Wise. *Crazy Makers: Getting Along with the Difficult People in Your Life*. Thomas Nelson, 2001.

Websites

American Association of Christian Counselors (www.aacc.net)

Ecounseling (www.ecounseling.com)

Money Crisis

PORTRAITS 1

- Carl and Laura's credit card debts have run out of control. Carl can't get Laura to stop spending, so they are constantly overwhelmed with bills they cannot pay. Carl wants a counselor to talk some sense into Laura.
- Bill just lost his job due to the downsizing of the company. He is trying to find work, but the job market is tough. He's struggling with believing God's care for him is sufficient in the midst of this crisis.
- Sherry's husband of twenty years ran off with another woman. After all the negotiating between the lawyers, Sherry is left with virtually nothing. She hasn't worked for years—how will she make ends meet?

DEFINITIONS AND KEY THOUGHTS 2

- Money has to be *mastered* or it will master us.
- *Jesus talked more about money* than about any other single topic. Why? "Where your treasure is, there your heart will be also" (Matt. 6:21).
- A person who comes for counsel about money will need advice about handling the difficult financial situation, but he or she also needs something deeper—an understanding that, amid the difficulty, *God still cares and will meet his or her needs.*
- It may be important to help the counselee make some *lifestyle changes* that can help with the crisis. If the crisis is the result of personal irresponsibility, the counselee needs to make changes that will keep this crisis from happening again.

ASSESSMENT INTERVIEW 3

Practical Questions

1. What do you consider to be the cause of the financial crisis you're in today? (*If spouses, do they agree on the source of the problem?*)
2. What do you think needs to happen for you to get out of this crisis?
3. How has this crisis affected you and your family?
4. How are you currently coping with the situation?

5. Who usually handles the bills in your home?

6. Describe the process for handling your monthly financial commitments.

7. What is the shortfall between what you have and what you need to meet your commitments?

8. In what areas can you pare back and save some money?

9. Do you think you can commit to "tightening your belt" for a while?

10. What lifestyle changes do you need to make to keep this money crisis or problem from happening again?

11. Will you commit to these changes?

Spiritual Questions

1. How are you doing spiritually?

2. Are you tithing?

3. How do you feel about your relationship with God at this point?

4. How do you feel about prayer? Do you think you can pray about this situation?

5. In what ways have you seen God answer your prayers?

6. In what ways do you still want Him to answer?

7. Are you refusing any of His answers because of pride? (*For example, has help been offered but refused? Has a job been offered but considered "beneath" the person?*)

8. Is there any sin that may have led you into this situation? Do you wish to repent of that sin?

9. What do you think God wants to teach you through this situation?

4 WISE COUNSEL

Some issues your counselee may be facing:

Perspective: The person may be so completely overwhelmed that he or she cannot function in life and loses perspective on what really matters. You need to help the counselee see that there *is* a way out if he or she takes a breath and begins to think creatively.

Prayer: The person may feel he or she cannot pray because the situation is his or her fault. You need to help the counselee understand that, no matter what the cause of the crisis, God wants him or her to pray about it.

Blame: The person blames the entire problem on someone else and focuses too much on that person. You need to help him or her see that spending all of his or her time thinking about the anger is not helping the financial situation.

Quick Fix: The person is focused on some speedy way to get out of the problem (like winning the lottery or filing for bankruptcy). Help him or her see that financial management is going to be hard work. It will take some belt-tightening and lifestyle changes to solve the problem and assure it doesn't happen again.

Therefore humble yourselves under the mighty hand of God, that He may exalt you in due time, casting all your care upon Him, for He cares for you.

1 Peter 5:6–7

The borrower is servant to the lender.

Proverbs 22:7

ACTION STEPS :5

1. Get Perspective

- *The client needs to get his or her perspective back. Ask him or her to say aloud:* "Money will not solve all my problems." Sure, money is important, but the more important issue is what God wants to do in your life.
- Credit card companies are not staying awake at night worrying about *you.*
- Go do something free and enjoyable. You have today—enjoy it. Keep on living. Walk the dog, hug your kids, listen to a CD, borrow a movie from the library or a friend.
- Set new priorities. Give back to God and God promises to provide (see Mal. 3:10; Acts 20:35).

2. Pray

- Is it okay to pray about money? Yes, of course. In the middle of a financial crisis, as in any crisis or suffering, God wants you to run to Him.
- In addition to praying about your financial crisis, pray for guidance and wisdom.
- If you caused the financial problem, ask God to forgive you and to help you learn so it will not happen again.
- God is concerned about *all* of life. His goal is to make you more like Him. Your financial crisis can be part of that growth.

3. Deal with the Immediate Problems

- Face the problem and decide what sacrifices or changes may be necessary in the short term, such as:
  - Is there sin? Look it in the face and deal with it.
  - Do you need professional help (such as for a gambling addiction)?
  - Communicate with creditors; set up payment plans.
  - Put the credit cards on ice (literally), so you can't get to them. Cut up as many as possible.
  - What other fires need to be put out?

4. Develop a Plan

- Prepare a budget. Start with your income; figure fixed payments (rent or mortgage, tithe, utilities, car payments, insurances), then regular expenses per month (such as food and gas), then other monthly payments (creditors—start with minimum payment amounts).

The Motley Fool's Credit Center features several mind-blowing statistics:

- Total consumer credit: $1.7 trillion.
- Credit card debt carried by the average American: $8,562.
- Total finance charges Americans paid in 2001: $50 billion.
- Percent of U.S. households deemed credit worthy by the lending industry: 78 percent.
- Number of credit card holders who declared bankruptcy last year: 1.3 million.[1]

- List all the creditors you owe, from lowest total to highest total.
- After working your budget, how much money can you put toward the creditors' bills? If only the minimum (such as with credit cards), start there. (If you can't even make minimums, you will consider other options in number 5 below.) List each bill and the monthly amount you will pay beside it.
- Decide how much additional money you can pay toward each creditor's bill. Try to pay off first the bill with the highest interest rate, while paying the minimum on the others. When the first one is paid off, go to the next highest, and so on. Gradually you will be paying larger amounts of money on the larger bills.
- Prepare a worksheet that lists all bills. Organize them according to due dates and which will be paid with which paycheck during the month. Make this reproducible so you can use it each month, checking off payments as you go.

5. Get Help

Wall Street closed out its worst year since the Great Depression, Wednesday, December 31, 2008—wiping out 6.9 trillion dollars in stock market wealth.[2]

- Brainstorm ways to get additional money to help retire debts. (*Be sure the counselee understands that any additional money must go toward the debt, not to raise his or her standard of living.*)
  - Sell something of value.
  - Consider consolidating your debt. Take out a home equity loan or refinance an existing mortgage.
  - Take on a new job (spouse goes to work outside the home, or money is earned at home by babysitting, tutoring, and so on).
  - Get a loan from family or friends (careful with this one).
  - Obtain advice from an accountant or financial advisor who can help keep you on track (see also Recommended Resources below).
  - Get help from the church or the government.

6. Set New Priorities and Parameters

- Do *not* run up any new debt. Leave credit cards for true emergencies only.
- Discuss needs versus wants (see Phil. 4:11).
- Decide on a thirty-day moratorium on any purchases over a certain amount of money. You may find you don't want it so much after thirty days.

7. Be Patient

- Your crisis is not a permanent condition. It's a turning point. It will get better.
- Don't be ashamed. Hold your head high, trust God for guidance, follow that guidance, and remember that somehow God is going to work all these things together for your good (Rom. 8:28; see also Matt. 6:25–26).
- Where is God guiding? What is God teaching? Read Matthew 6:19–21.

- Don't let the crisis turn you from God. Draw nearer. Study His Word. Pray for wisdom, protection, and provision.

BIBLICAL INSIGHTS 6

The sleep of a laboring man is sweet, whether he eats little or much; but the abundance of the rich will not permit him to sleep.

Ecclesiastes 5:12

Many people desire to be rich, thinking that they will have no more worries. This is a paradox, however. Riches give freedom to do many things, but the chains of worry often ruin any true enjoyment.

God would have us be content with our financial status, for all wealth ultimately belongs to Him.

"You have sown much, and bring in little. . . . And he who earns wages, earns wages to put into a bag with holes." Thus says the LORD of hosts: "Consider your ways!"

Haggai 1:6–7

People spend money on what they consider most important. Haggai pointed out that the people in Jerusalem were valuing the comforts of their own homes over God.

We need to reevaluate where we spend our resources. Do our activities and spending habits reflect our dedication to God?

"Bring all the tithes into the storehouse, that there may be food in My house, and try Me now in this," says the LORD of hosts, "if I will not open for you the windows of heaven and pour out for you such blessing that there will not be room enough to receive it."

Malachi 3:10

> In 2008 six years of stock gains disappeared as the economy crumbled and markets crashed around the globe, shaking the confidence of professional and individual investors alike.[3]

God's ways are not our ways. People think that to be secure, they must hoard their money. God says the opposite.

Jesus issued the same challenge: "Give, and it will be given to you: good measure, pressed down, shaken together, and running over" (Luke 6:38). To refuse to give is actually to rob God; to give generously is to know God's abundant blessings.

Be anxious for nothing, but in everything by prayer and supplication, with thanksgiving, let your requests be made known to God; and the peace of God, which surpasses all understanding, will guard your hearts and minds through Christ Jesus.

Philippians 4:6–7

These verses apply to many kinds of worries—and they certainly fit financial pain. If you're in a financial crisis, the first place you need to go is to God, letting "your requests be made known to" him.

For the love of money is a root of all kinds of evil, for which some have strayed from the faith in their greediness, and pierced themselves through with many sorrows.

1 Timothy 6:10

The Bible doesn't say that money is the root of all evil. Money can do good things for God's kingdom. The root of all evil is the *love* of money.

Those who love money never have enough, and they do any number of stupid, illegal, or risky things to obtain more. They are never satisfied.

How do believers stay away from the love of money? "Godliness with contentment" (1 Tim. 6:6) is the answer. When we are content with what we have, we can give the extra back to Him.

7 PRAYER STARTER

Lord, _____ has come today with a difficult situation. We know, Lord, that nothing is too hard for You. We humbly ask that You help him [her] to be wise as he [she] prepares a budget, seeks new income, and tries to pay off these debts, because we know this honors You. Show him [her] what You would have him [her] do, and we ask for provision and protection . . .

8 RECOMMENDED RESOURCES

Alcorn, Randy. *The Treasure Principle.* Multnomah Books, 2005.

Burkett, Larry. *Debt Free Living.* Moody, 2001.

Clinton, Tim. *The Bible for Hope: Caring for People God's Way.* Thomas Nelson, 2007.

Ramsey, Dave. *The Financial Peace Planner: A Step-by-Step Guide to Restoring Your Family's Financial Health.* Penguin, 1998.

———. *The Total Money Makeover: A Proven Plan for Financial Fitness.* Thomas Nelson, 2007.

Organization

Christian Credit Counselors (www.christiancc.org)

Websites

American Association of Christian Counselors (www.aacc.net)

Crown Financial Ministries (www.crown.org)

Ecounseling (www.ecounseling.com)

Pain and Chronic Pain

- Sally had deteriorating arthritis. The pain had become so bad she could no longer help in the nursery with the toddlers as she had loved to do for the past twenty years. "What use am I if I can't even do the simplest thing to serve the Lord?" she asks dejectedly.

- Ben, a construction worker, was in a car accident that left him with several crushed discs and constant pain. "Why me?" he asks. "What did I do to deserve this? I can't work and we can barely get by on my disability check. I feel like I'm hitting a closed door when I try to get answers from God. He doesn't seem to care."

- Kristy was diagnosed with lupus a year ago. "Every day I feel like I have the flu," she sighs wearily. "The fatigue is debilitating. I can't make any plans with the kids because the day we plan to go to the beach or to a movie I always end up too sick to go. I'm so tired of this stupid disease!"

- Josh's leg was amputated below the knee due to bone cancer. Now after months of painful chemotherapy, he has learned the cancer is in the thigh bone and he will have to begin another round of chemo with the chance of losing the rest of his leg. *I don't know what's worse, the pain or the fear,* he wonders. *How much more can I stand? I'm so afraid.*

DEFINITIONS AND KEY THOUGHTS 2

Pain hurts, and chronic pain hurts all the time. Pain refers to unpleasant and unwanted sensory/emotional experience that is associated with body or tissue damage or injury. Acute pain is usually attached to bodily injury, and by its intensity—the level of felt pain—reveals the seriousness of the injury. Chronic pain refers to these unpleasant feelings occurring over a longer time span.

- *God is present* and always working, even in a person's pain. The *physical, emotional, and spiritual are all connected.* When people are in pain, they may feel God is not there. Nothing could be further from the truth. Their brain is not sending the right signals; their feelings are not to be trusted. They must put their faith in God's Word, not their feelings.

- Pain tends to blind the eyes. When a person says, "I'm knocking at God's door, but *He doesn't answer,*" his or her feelings contradict Matthew 7:7 where Jesus says, "Knock, and it will be opened to you." When a person says, "I pray, but *God is not listening*," his or her feelings contradict Isaiah 65:24 where God says, "Before they call, I will answer; and while they are still speaking, I will hear." People need to be challenged with the truth that God's words in the Bible trump their feelings.

- *Illness or chronic pain is not due to a lack of faith.* On the contrary, it is often the suffering itself that drives a person to God, motivates him or her to grow spiritually, and helps a person understand that he or she cannot cope alone. We cannot conclude that the presence of pain (or illness) implies that a person doesn't have a deep and mature faith, hasn't been praying enough, has sinned in some terrible way, or has neglected his or her spiritual growth. We know that a deep religious faith does equip people with a powerful tool to endure and cope with their pain.

- *God allows pain for a reason.* If pain is to have meaning, it must bring us closer to God. We can hear God in our pain. Many who have suffered chronic pain state that if they had to choose between never becoming ill or learning the things they learned through pain, they would choose the pain because of the wisdom it brought.

- *God's grace is sufficient.* Paul's thorn in the flesh gives authority to his claim that God's grace is sufficient (2 Cor. 12:7–10).

- What the world considers blessings—health, family, and riches—can sometimes draw a person away from Christ. *When one has everything, he or she may forget the need for God.* What the world considers curses—tragedy, pain, and heartache—reveal a need for Him. People run to Him because they have nothing left but Him.

- The Center for Spirituality, Theology and Health at Duke University has conducted more than twenty-five research studies exploring the association between religion, mental health, and the need for health services. Hundreds of additional studies around the globe have recently been completed on these issues. This is what was found:

  - Many people turn to religious beliefs and practices to *help them cope when they become sick.* When people are anxious, suffering, and at the end of their rope, they turn to God. Often there is no other place to turn.

  - Religious beliefs and practices are associated with *better mental and physical well-being.* Physical wellness includes lower blood pressure, better immune system functioning, and a longer life span.

  - People actively involved in a religious community, who pray regularly, and who keep religion as an instrumental part of their lives often experience *less depression and anxiety and greater hope, meaning, and purpose.*

  - They also *recover more speedily from hurtful emotions.*

  - Religious persons are *less likely to engage in addictive behavior,* such as alcohol or drug abuse. They are less likely to participate in *risky sexual practices* outside of marriage.

  - It seems that it is during the most difficult and trying circumstances that *religion separates those who can cope* from those who cannot.

I've realized more strongly than ever before that you don't truly discover your roots until you are at the bottom of the pit. From this perspective you are no longer distracted by usual superficialities which disguise themselves in masks of importance.

Tim Hansel

ASSESSMENT QUESTIONS : 3

Rule Outs

1. On a scale of 1 to 10 with 10 being no depression and 1 being extremely depressed, where are you today?
2. Do you abuse alcohol or drugs to escape the pain? (*If you suspect that severe depression or substance abuse is present, you should deal with this problem along with pain management.*)
3. Do you ever have thoughts of suicide? (*If you think the person is suicidal, make out a safety contract in which he or she promises not to hurt self without first calling you. If he or she calls you, take the person to the safe environment of a hospital for medical help. See the section on Suicide.*)

General Questions

1. What brought you to counseling today?
2. When did the pain first start?
3. How long has it been going on?
4. What are its symptoms?
5. How has this changed your life?
6. How are your family and friends responding to your pain?
7. How do you like them to respond?
8. What things have you tried to help manage the pain?
9. How have these been working?
10. Besides the physical pain, have you had any feelings of anger, doubt, or fear?
11. Tell me about these feelings.
12. Where do you think God is in all this?
13. Why do you think God let this happen to you?
14. What are your feelings toward God right now? Be honest.
15. What do you want God to do?
16. If He chooses not to heal you, how do you feel about that?
17. Has anything good come out of your pain?

> Pain is inevitable—misery is optional.
>
> *Tim Hansel*

WISE COUNSEL : 4

Empathize with the client about the pain. He or she needs to know that you understand the difficulty of the situation and that you care.

Explain that the client has experienced a loss that may feel similar to losing a loved one. Make clear to the person that *a loss of health needs to be grieved.*

Validate the struggle and the strength the person has already shown. People in chronic pain get down on themselves because they can't do what they used to and what they see others doing. They may see themselves as weak, pathetic, or useless. It is important to identify their strengths and help them see how strong they are just to cope with the pain each day.

Explain that God understands and cares what the client is going through. Even if the person can't feel His presence, He is still there. Share verses that show this truth and talk about how the suffering person needs to trust God's Word.

Share Paul's story of the thorn in his flesh (2 Cor. 12:7–10). Though Paul prayed to God to remove the thorn, God refused, stating that His grace was sufficient. Ask the suffering person what he or she thinks grace looks like and how it could be sufficient for him or her. Ask questions that require the person to think through what God means in these verses.

5 : ACTION STEPS

1. Live within Your Limits

- Part of acknowledging the lordship of Christ is living within the limits *He* gives. If you need pain medication, take it. If you need a nap, take one.
- There is nothing heroic about going beyond your God-given limits to the point where you are grouchy and nasty to everyone around you. Pace your day so you don't get too tired. Ask for help when you need it.
- Good nutrition, exercise that your doctor approves, and sufficient sleep are essential. Make it a priority to get these three.

2. Do Things That Improve Your Attitude

- It will not be the pain that defeats you; it will be your attitude toward it that will lead to despair or hope.
- Identify what helps lift your spirits and do those things. Some suggestions are:

  – Pray.
  – Read the Bible.
  – Sing and praise.
  – Listen to music that feeds your soul or tickles your fancy.
  – Watch a funny TV show and comedy movies (laughter releases endorphins that improve mood).
  – Try to see the humor in situations.
  – Spend time around cheerful people.
  – Write in a journal or write letters to friends.
  – Start a hobby or pick up a pastime you enjoy.
  – Help someone else.
  – Learn something new.
  – Cultivate a grateful attitude.

You can't change what happens; you can only change how you respond to it.
Tim Hansel

3. Get Support

- The only thing worse than pain is bearing pain alone.
- Read books about people who lived with pain and see what helped them.
- Join a support group. Do not isolate yourself. God made us to be in community with others. People in a support group can comfort you with the same comfort God has given them (2 Cor. 1:3–4).

4. Keep Truth before You

- When self-pitying and negative thoughts come into your mind, replace them with truth.
- Write your negative thoughts in a notebook. Divide the page in half and on one side write LIES and on the other side write TRUTH. Under LIES, write the self-defeating thought that came into your head. Under TRUTH, write the truth that contradicts the negative thought. For example, when you think: *God isn't here for me*, replace it with: *How can you say the Lord does not see your troubles? No one can measure the depths of his understanding* (see Isa. 40:27–28).

5. Comfort Others

- Redeem the pain by comforting others with the same comfort God gave you (2 Cor. 1:3–4).

In answer to Corrie ten Boom's question, "Why is our Lord allowing this to happen?" during their time in the Nazi death camps, her sister Betsy said, "If we know Him, we don't have to know why."[1]

BIBLICAL INSIGHTS 6

For we do not have a High Priest who cannot sympathize with our weaknesses, but was in all points tempted as we are, yet without sin. Let us therefore come boldly to the throne of grace, that we may obtain mercy and find grace to help in time of need.

Hebrews 4:15–16

We have a Savior who can "sympathize with our weaknesses." He understands temptation, because He faced it. He understands weakness, because He experienced it. He understands pain, because He felt it.

People who live with chronic or acute physical or emotional pain have a Savior who truly understands. Far from sitting in the heavens simply feeling sorry for sick and sinful humanity, He clothed Himself with our humanness.

When we come to Christ with our hurts, He reaches out with human arms, truly understanding how we feel. He is able to help us. Christ does not always take away the pain but He does tell us to bring it to Him. Whatever our pain or difficulty, we are encouraged to come to Him.

> *When Jesus saw him lying there, and knew that he already had been in that condition a long time, He said to him, "Do you want to be made well?"*
>
> *John 5:6*

Jesus has the power to heal any pain, but His first priority is to heal people spiritually. He may take away a person's pain, as He did the man's pain in this verse in John. Or He may not take away the pain, as He would not remove Paul's physical difficulty (2 Cor. 12:7–10).

Whatever the Lord does, however, it's because He understands the big picture and knows what He can accomplish either through healing a person's pain or through giving the person grace and peace in spite of the pain.

We can pray for healing, but most of all, we need to pray for spiritual growth and maturity and that God will work through people's lives for His glory.

> *And lest I should be exalted above measure by the abundance of the revelations, a thorn in the flesh was given to me, a messenger of Satan to buffet me, lest I be exalted above measure. Concerning this thing I pleaded with the Lord three times that it might depart from me. And He said to me, "My grace is sufficient for you, for My strength is made perfect in weakness." Therefore most gladly I will rather boast in my infirmities, that the power of Christ may rest upon me. Therefore I take pleasure in infirmities, in reproaches, in needs, in persecutions, in distresses, for Christ's sake. For when I am weak, then I am strong.*
>
> *2 Corinthians 12:7–10*

Those in pain may think that, if God would heal them, they would be much more valuable and effective in ministry.

But God's power is often best revealed when He works through human weaknesses. His "strength is made perfect in weakness."

> God whispers to us in our pleasures, speaks to us in our conscience, but shouts to us in our pain. Pain is God's megaphone to rouse a deaf world.
>
> *C. S. Lewis*

7 PRAYER STARTER

The pain Your child is facing today is acute, dear Lord. He [she] is suffering and doesn't understand why. He [she] wants to feel better, wants to function better, wants to serve You better, but the pain constantly gets in the way. What are You seeking to teach him [her] through this pain, Lord? What wisdom and comfort can You give Your child today? . . .

8 RECOMMENDED RESOURCES

Clinton, Tim. *The Bible for Hope: Caring for People God's Way*. Thomas Nelson, 2007.

Clinton, Tim, Archibald D. Hart, and George Ohlschlager. *Caring for People God's Way: Personal and Emotional Issues, Addictions, Grief, and Trauma*. Thomas Nelson, 2006.

Koenig, Harold G. *Chronic Pain: Biomedical and Spiritual Approaches.* Routledge, 2003.

———. *Medicine, Religion, and Health: Where Science and Spirituality Meet.* Templeton Foundation Press, 2008.

Tan, Siang-Yang, and George Ohlschlager. *Chronic Pain Management.* American Association of Christian Counselors Video Series. See www.aacc.net for more information.

Websites

American Association of Christian Counselors (www.aacc.net)

Ecounseling (www.ecounseling.com)

Today many medical schools teach courses that introduce aspiring doctors to the benefits of religious faith and spirituality. Medical students are now being trained on how to partner with religious belief in clinical practice. The June 16, 2004, issue of the *Journal of the American Medical Association* was entirely devoted to spirituality in medicine.[2]

Parenting

1 PORTRAITS

- "If the principal calls me one more time, I think I'll scream. Why can't that boy just listen?" Martha yells with exasperation.
- Randy and Casey, just one year apart, are constantly fighting with each other. Randy just hit Casey in the face with a soccer ball, which sent Casey running to his mother in tears.
- Little Ruthie was an answer to her parents' prayers for a child. She is so precious but she just won't behave. She just turned three and seems to test her parents at every turn.

2 DEFINITIONS AND KEY THOUGHTS

- God placed certain people in leadership roles over children and named them parents. *God has ordained parents to be the leaders* in the home.
- *Children need both a mother and father*. Unfortunately, fathers are often physically or emotionally absent. It is estimated that 40 percent of American children are being raised in homes where no father is present. These children have more physical, emotional, and behavioral problems than children whose father is present, and it is more likely that they will be incarcerated.
- Raising children is a *high calling* that God has given to parents. We must not take this position lightly.
- We must recognize that as a parent, *we have been given authority* over our children. In other words, we have been handpicked by God Himself to assume the leadership role in the raising of our children.
- Dr. James Dobson says that our role as a parent is to *work ourselves out of a job*. While we never really stop being a parent, our role changes as our children grow and mature. Ultimately our role becomes less and less active and we serve more as an advisor or friend to our adult children.

> Foolishness is bound up in the heart of a child; the rod of correction will drive it far from him.
>
> *Proverbs 22:15*

Ingredients for Good Parenting

Just as bread needs yeast to rise, children need certain ingredients to reach the potential that God has placed in them. Three of these ingredients are love, discipline, and guidance. While the ingredients will be required at all stages of parenting, the actual amount of each required at various stages in the parenting process will depend on the age and maturity level of the child.

1. Love

- Children need hugs, physical contact, words of encouragement and affirmation, and quality time—all of these *communicate love*. Love also helps break down barriers and walls that we can't see with our eyes.

- Keep in mind that adolescent children are very *aware of appearances* and may not want to be hugged in front of peers.

- Sometimes, especially in adolescence, our children can feel like our enemies, but in reality they are simply learning how to think and act on their own. A *certain amount of rebellion is normal*.

- As a parent, you are to love your children even when it is undeserved. That doesn't mean you accept everything they do. Love and acceptance are not synonymous. It does mean that you remind them that you *love them even when you disagree* with or are heartbroken by their actions.

2. Discipline

- The Bible cautions fathers *not to discourage* their children (Col. 3:21), but it also says that those who love their children are careful to discipline them (Prov. 13:24). *Discipline, unlike punishment, always envisions a better future* for the child.

- *Balance is the key.* As a parent, you must discipline and train your children, but you should not discipline as though you are running a boot camp.

- Too many parents try to reason with their youngsters instead of simply delivering on the consequences that were threatened. If you say the child must go to his room if he "does that one more time," and he does it again, *you must follow through* with exactly what you said.

- *Consistency is king.* The actual consequence is less important than the consistency of having consequences when children misbehave.

- There are *three rules* that may help to serve as guides in disciplining your children.

  - *The KFC Rule*: KFC stands for *kind, firm,* and *consistent*.
  - *Granny's Rule*: This simply means that, first, the child does what the parent wants and then the child gets to do what he or she wants. For instance, the parent might say, "If you want to go swimming, then first you must do these chores."
  - *The Millennial Rule*: This simply means that if you allow your child to get away with something, it may take a thousand times of correction to retrain him.

> Do not withhold correction from a child.
> *Proverbs 23:13*

In a study by the *Journal of American Academy of Child and Adolescent Psychiatry* published December 2008, findings concluded that maternal inconsistent discipline was associated with attention deficit hyperactivity disorder combined type, even with child oppositional defiant disorder and conduct disorder diagnosis.[1]

3. Guidance

- As a parent, it is in your job description to *teach your children about life*, guiding them in all areas, especially in God's Word (Deut. 6:4–9).
- Guiding your children may also mean *allowing them to make mistakes*. When a mistake is made and the principal or police officer calls to inform you of the situation, understand that as the parent you are about to walk through a crisis with your child. Be prepared to be disappointed with some of your child's choices and behaviors. Do not make the mistake of too readily helping your child get out of difficulties he or she is experiencing because of his or her choices and behaviors. More growth takes place through a crisis than at any other time.

3 ASSESSMENT INTERVIEW

Parents often *feel that they have failed* if their child needs help. Being a parent is not easy.

Reassure parents that seeking *counseling is proof that they are, in fact, good parents.* Having a family problem does not mean that the child is a "problem child." Avoid labeling anyone with such a title.

If the family is seeking help because the child is unruly or uncontrollable, you may want to consider having them *see their family physician* to rule out a physical problem. Problems like attention deficit disorder seem to be more and more prevalent and a professional evaluation may be warranted.

> Our job as parents is not just to fight the culture, but also to teach our kids to see through its shallowness and the motives of those who shape it.
>
> *Ron Luce*

General Questions

1. What can you tell me about your child's early development?
2. Can you define the problem behavior clearly?
3. When did the problem first begin to surface?
4. How often do you struggle with this issue?
5. How have you addressed the problem in the past?
6. Can you describe a typical scenario in which everything seemed to fall apart?
7. Are you both consistent in how you discipline?
8. Can your children play one of you against the other, or do they know you are united?
9. Do you follow through on threatened consequences?
10. What is each member of the family doing when the problem arises?
11. What does each member of the family do after the problem occurs?
12. Has there been a significant change in your family that may have created additional family stress?
13. What can you tell me about the other children in the family?
14. What would the perfect family look like?
15. What would you want your family to be like?

WISE COUNSEL : 4

Again, convey to the family that *God has placed them together.* God will help them and show them how to journey together as a family.

Changes may need to be made and, while the *changes may be difficult* at first, the parents will be able to accomplish these changes with the Lord's help.

Encourage the parents of *tough or strong-willed children* not to panic when considering their child's future. Some of the most successful adults were the most difficult children.

Encourage parents to *envision through faith a positive future* for the child and sharing that vision lovingly with the child.

Talk about the importance of *spending time together.* In this day and age it can be quite difficult to get the whole family together unless there is a crisis.

ACTION STEPS : 5

Your goal is to help this family develop a plan. This may be a plan regarding the rules to be followed:

- how discipline will be handled for infractions of the rules
- what is negotiable and what is not (for example, curfews are nonnegotiable)
- setting aside family times (a particular night of the week or breakfast or dinner together)
- chores (who does what, what is required, when the chores must be completed)

1. Develop the Plan

- What needs to be in the plan (*this varies depending on the ages of the children and the issues involved*).
- *Have the whole family talk together and share ideas to be incorporated into the plan.*
- Try to incorporate everyone's ideas into the plan. Even the youngest members can have input, but you as parents are responsible for the final plan.

> A wise son heeds his father's instruction, but a scoffer does not listen to rebuke.
>
> *Proverbs 13:1*

2. Adjust the Plan as Needed

- *If you sense that the parents are immature enough that they won't even be able to develop a good plan (or that their kids will run over them), follow up after they have had their family meeting to look over the plan they developed. You may need to help them take on the parental role or be more realistic.*
- *If the parents are capable of making the changes and following through, tell them to work through the plan for a couple weeks and make tweaks as needed—always*

with a family meeting. (For example, if chores are still not getting done, you may need to add consequences that will bring results.)

- The plan should reward desired behavior and specify consequences for undesired behavior.

3. Review the Plan on a Regular Basis

A wise son makes a glad father, but a foolish son is the grief of his mother. . . . He who gathers in summer is a wise son; he who sleeps in harvest is a son who causes shame.

Proverbs 10:1, 5

- Lifestyles change and children grow up, so the plan should be evaluated occasionally for fit. The basics are still the same (certain behaviors are still expected), but consequences will be different for older children.
- Review the plan as part of a family meeting.

4. Be Consistent

- Post the plan where everyone can see it.
- Mom and dad must be 100 percent together on this. The kids must not think that they can get one to overrule the other or that they can pit their parents against each other.

5. Pray Together

- Ask for God's leading in your family as you raise your children to be responsible adults.

6. Spend Time Together

- Try to get at least one meal a day together as a family. Eating breakfast together may be more feasible than eating dinner together, depending on your family's commitments.
- Direct the conversation into positive learning experiences. Do a Bible study or simply talk about the mistakes that others made that day. Take the focus off your family and learn by discussing other situations.
- Use a family meeting time to discuss a family vacation or even a fun weekend activity. Try to choose varied activities so everyone has fun.

6 BIBLICAL INSIGHTS

"For this child I prayed, and the LORD has granted me my petition which I asked of Him. Therefore I also have lent him to the LORD; as long as he lives he shall be lent to the LORD." So they worshiped the LORD there.

1 Samuel 1:27–28

Parenting is demanding and rewarding. Many people prepare and study for years to enter a chosen profession, but for parenting we usually receive on-the-job training.

The goal of parenting is to let the children go eventually.

For I have told him that I will judge his house forever for the iniquity which he knows, because his sons made themselves vile, and he did not restrain them.

1 Samuel 3:13

Eli did not discipline his sons even though they were priests under his supervision. These men were treating the sacrifices of the people with contempt (1 Sam. 2:12–17) and were committing sexual sin with women of the tabernacle.

Eli, as parent and as high priest, certainly had the authority to deal with his sons but he chose not to do anything. Eventually God stepped in.

God gives parents authority over their children. Parents should use their authority wisely to guide their children away from sin.

Then Adonijah the son of Haggith exalted himself, saying, "I will be king"; and he prepared for himself chariots and horsemen, and fifty men to run before him. (And his father had not rebuked him at any time by saying, "Why have you done so?" He was also very good-looking. His mother had borne him after Absalom.)

1 Kings 1:5–6

Adonijah was a son of David, and it is apparent that one of David's weaknesses was the inability to discipline his children.

David's failures as a father led to a number of failures and sins in his children. Parents always influence their children—for good and bad. There is no substitute for invested, caring, loving parents who discipline when necessary.

But the mercy of the LORD is from everlasting to everlasting on those who fear Him, and His righteousness to children's children, to such as keep His covenant, and to those who remember His commandments to do them.

Psalm 103:17–18

One of the great promises of the Bible is that the mercy of the Lord continues from one generation to the next, even to our children's children.

This does not mean that the children of believers will automatically believe in God, but that God's mercy and goodness are available to each generation that follows the good example set by the previous generation.

Parents must set the right example for their children. They are living not merely for themselves; they are setting a precedent that will affect generations to come.

But you must continue in the things which you have learned and been assured of, knowing from whom you have learned them, and that from childhood you

---

Behold, children are a heritage from the LORD, the fruit of the womb is a reward.

Psalm 127:3

Between 1970 and 2006, the number of children living with only their mother rose from 10 percent to 24 percent while the number living with only their father grew from less than 2 percent to 5 percent.[2]

have known the Holy Scriptures, which are able to make you wise for salvation through faith which is in Christ Jesus.

2 Timothy 3:14–15

Timothy had been learning the Holy Scriptures from childhood. Christian parents have the God-given responsibility to raise their children to know and love God and His Word.

Young children can learn the great truths and stories found in the Bible that show God's love and power.

The teaching given to young children will be embedded in their minds, giving them a strong foundation on which to build. That training is able to make them "wise for salvation through faith which is in Christ Jesus."

7 : PRAYER STARTER

Thank You for these parents who have come today, Lord. They want to raise their children well; they want to be good parents. Right now, they feel as if things are going awry at home and they don't quite know which way to turn . . .

8 : RECOMMENDED RESOURCES

And you, fathers, do not provoke your children to wrath, but bring them up in the training and admonition of the Lord.

Ephesians 6:4

Clinton, Tim. *The Bible for Hope: Caring for People God's Way*. Thomas Nelson, 2007.

Clinton, Tim, Archibald D. Hart, and George Ohlschlager. *Caring for People God's Way: Personal and Emotional Issues, Addictions, Grief, and Trauma*. Thomas Nelson, 2006.

Clinton, Tim, and Gary Sibcy. *Loving Your Child Too Much*. Integrity, 2006.

Dobson, James C. *Bringing Up Boys*. Tyndale House, 2005.

———. *Parenting Isn't for Cowards*. Tyndale House, 2007.

Kimmel, Tim. *Grace-Based Parenting*. Thomas Nelson, 2005.

Leman, Kevin. *Have a New Kid by Friday: How to Change Your Child's Attitude, Behavior, and Character in Five Days*. Revell, 2008.

Luce, Ron. *Battle Cry for a Generation*. NexGen, 2005.

———. *Re-Create: Building a Culture in Your Home Stronger than the Culture Destroying Your Kids*. Regal, 2008.

Townsend, John. *Boundaries with Teens*. Zondervan, 2006.

Websites

American Association of Christian Counselors (www.aacc.net)

Ecounseling (www.ecounseling.com)

Perfectionism

PORTRAITS 1

- Genevieve, a young wife, is constantly complaining to her new husband about the way he hangs his clothes in the closet, parks the car in the driveway, and even how he sets his shoes by the bed. Everything has to be perfect for her, and Randall can't seem to do anything right. He is always on pins and needles.
- Matt, the teenage perfectionist, always feels his schoolwork and efforts on the hockey rink are never good enough. Matt studies for hours and practices his hockey in the driveway until dark. When he gets anything less than a 95 on a test, he is crushed and ends up with migraine headaches.
- Danny and his new boss, William, are constantly butting heads. Danny has worked in the same accounting firm for ten years and is fairly set in his ways and how he does things around the office. William has come in with some very perfectionistic and demanding requests.

DEFINITIONS AND KEY THOUGHTS 2

- Perfectionism is a disposition to feel that *anything less than perfect is unacceptable*. It is rooted in the need for control and affirmation.
- Theologically, perfectionism is the *destructive belief* that people can be equal to God. Specifically, perfectionistic people think they should be all-knowing (omniscient), all-powerful (omnipotent), everywhere at once (omnipresent), and generally without human frailty.
- Perfectionistic people *think* they should *know everything* and so beat themselves up for mistakes. They think they should be *totally powerful* and they become upset when things are out of their control. They believe they should *accomplish the work of ten people* in a given day and they become depressed and discouraged over what "little" they can accomplish.
- Perfectionistic people *are idealistic* in that they frequently think about how things "should" be, not how they really are. They are always *setting impossibly high goals,* which lead to discouragement, failure, and ultimately quitting. They are *afraid of failure*, equating failure to achieve their goals with a lack of personal worth. They are *tied up in the "shoulds"* of life and require rigid rules. With such an overemphasis on "shoulds," perfectionists rarely take into account their own wants and desires. They are *product-minded,* believing that contentment, hap-

> Perfectionists need to find their worth not in what they do or how well they do it, but in being God's creation.
>
> *Chris Thurman*

189

piness, and a sense of accomplishment are not permissible until their current project or activity has been completed. The "process" is overlooked because the end result has not been reached, thus there is no "joy in the journey."

- Perfectionistic people *feel* that they *have to be the best* at what they do. To simply do one's best is not good enough. They believe their *worth is determined by their performance.* Since day-to-day performance in various areas of life fluctuates, a perfectionist's sense of worth fluctuates as well.

> Being confident of this very thing, that He who has begun a good work in you will complete it until the day of Jesus Christ.
>
> *Philippians 1:6*

Personality Types

- *Type A people* are usually very *strict and rigid* and are often called perfectionists. They have a certain way for things to be done, and *flexibility is not an option.* They need to be *on time* and have problems with people who are more relaxed with time. They are often described as *workaholics* and are driven. They were probably given *conditional love* at some time in their lives; that is, only if a standard was met were they rewarded and accepted. They are more likely to *suffer heart attacks* at an earlier age than other personality types.
- *Type B people* are usually more *laid back*, more carefree with their time. They are not so rigid and are considered *more flexible* in their relationships. They tend to *cope with daily stress* in a more positive way than Type A people.
- Many references in the Bible use the word *perfect*; for example, "Therefore you shall be perfect, just as your Father in heaven is perfect" (Matt. 5:48). We need to help people understand that *perfection is not something God demands* from them. God knows we cannot do it or He would not have had to send His Son.
- As Christians, we need to be *more concerned with our relationship with God—* allowing Him to make us perfect—than with being perfectionists. A perfect heart will do more to insure a life of healthy relationships and a good self-worth than any perfectionist's rigid schedule or ways will.

3 : ASSESSMENT INTERVIEW

1. Describe perfectionism for me.
2. Do you feel that you have to be the best at everything?
3. Do you feel that you need to be in control?
4. What kinds of goals do you set for yourself?
5. Are those goals pretty much across the board in every area of life; that is, are your expectations as high at home as they are at work?
6. Do you see life as "all or nothing," "black or white"?
7. Do you find it difficult to be flexible?
8. Tell me about your growing-up years. When did you feel most loved by your friends and family?
9. Did you ever feel that you were loved based on your performance?
10. Have you always felt this way?

11. How do you feel when you don't get things done to perfection?

12. How do you feel about someone who is not a perfectionist?

13. Would you define yourself as a Type A or Type B personality? *(See descriptions above.)*

14. Do you think one personality type is better than the other?

15. Does God say we are to be perfect?

WISE COUNSEL : 4

Your job is *not to overhaul totally an individual's personality or makeup.* Wouldn't you prefer to have a perfectionist performing heart surgery on you than someone who is willing to be just "good enough"? We need to celebrate what perfectionists bring to their work while helping them manage their personality in a manner that minimizes damage to themselves and others.

Perfectionism is a problem if it is *adversely affecting the person's health or self-esteem* or if it is *dripping over onto others* at work or at home and causing stress. Remind the person that *God is all-powerful*; He can help the perfectionist relax with who he or she is and become more flexible in what he or she demands of other people.

If your counselee is *struggling with someone* who is a perfectionist, there is a good chance that the counselee is a Type B personality dealing with a Type A. He or she needs to understand how the Type A individual thinks, that a Type A person is more likely harder on self than he or she is on the counselee.

ACTION STEPS : 5

1. Determine Your Personality

- Do some self-exploration by taking a personality inventory, such as the Myers-Briggs or other similar test that is available online. This is a great way to discover what makes you tick. Seeing yourself on paper and realizing that you have personality tendencies that are similar to those of others can be part of your life journey in discovering the *you* God made.

2. Change Is Not the Issue

- You do not need to change as much as begin to understand your God-given nature and how to use it when appropriate and rein it in when not appropriate.

3. Learn Flexibility and Acceptance

- Realizing, for example, that "I am more rigid with my time and you are more flexible," is okay and doesn't mean that I am better than you.

- Ask, "What's the worst that can happen?" The answer (for example, that the report goes through with one typographical error) probably isn't worth losing sleep over.
- God's love is unconditional. You don't have to earn His love by being a perfectionist or by setting unrealistic standards for yourself or others.
- God sets no conditions that we have to meet to be His children. We, in turn, need to be unconditional in how we accept and love others.

4. Laugh a Little

- Don't be so judgmental of yourself and others. Find humor in who you are.
- Laugh at yourself when you do something foolish or funny. Be prepared to laugh with others who are laughing with/at you.

5. Be Realistic

- You're not going to be God, so stop trying.
- Look at life as it *is*, not as you think it *should be*.
- Meet people halfway.
- Don't expect the impossible—of yourself or others. Set attainable goals and reasonable time limits.
- In your life, determine when perfectionism is appropriate and when it is not. Learn to accept "good enough" on certain tasks.
- Realize that many positive things can be learned from making mistakes.

6. Be Perfect in Heart

- Concentrate on having a perfect heart with God. This will release you to a less stressful life. You'll live for God and not for your perfectionist tendencies.
- Being perfect in heart (not being a perfectionist) and having one will with the Father enables you to overcome perfectionist tendencies that disconnect you from your loved ones, and inhibit your relationships in general.

And He said to me, "My grace is sufficient for you, for My strength is made perfect in weakness." Therefore most gladly I will rather boast in my infirmities, that the power of Christ may rest upon me.

2 Corinthians 12:9

6 BIBLICAL INSIGHTS

Therefore you shall be perfect, just as your Father in heaven is perfect.

Matthew 5:48

Jesus was not commanding His people to be perfectionists.

One day Christ will make us perfect; during our time on earth, we should be striving for Christlikeness, always realizing that we have much room to grow.

I am indeed a Jew, born in Tarsus of Cilicia, but brought up in this city at the feet of Gamaliel, taught according to the strictness of our fathers' law, and was zealous toward God as you all are today.

Acts 22:3

Paul could have been considered a "perfect" Jew. He had the right pedigree, the right training, the right desires, the right enthusiasm. But being "perfect" in one's own eyes doesn't make a person saved before God.

No one's pedigree, training, background, wealth, abilities, gifts, appearance, or anything else can be perfect enough to earn salvation. We must not be enslaved to the "perfectionism" of this world that is ultimately worthless.

Only when we cast ourselves before God and allow *Him* to use our backgrounds, training, and gifts for His glory will we find complete fulfillment.

> Nearly 11.7 million cosmetic surgical and nonsurgical procedures were performed in the United States in 2007, according to statistics released by the American Society for Aesthetic Plastic Surgery.[1]

For by grace you have been saved through faith, and that not of yourselves; it is the gift of God, not of works, lest anyone should boast.

Ephesians 2:8–9

God is perfect; people are sinful. Fortunately, God does not require people to reach a certain level of perfection before He will accept them. Otherwise, no one could ever be saved!

God provided a perfect way of salvation—grace.

For by one offering He has perfected forever those who are being sanctified.

Hebrews 10:14

Believers have been made perfect in God's eyes because of the death and resurrection of Jesus Christ. At the same time, however, we are "being sanctified," being made perfect and holy progressively through our walk with Him.

We are considered perfect, even though we have a long way to go. As we let God work in us, He perfects us.

Instead of measuring perfection by worldly standards, we should seek to obey God, looking forward to the day when He will finally make us perfect for life with Him in our perfect eternal home.

PRAYER STARTER 7

Lord, we know that You call us to be perfect, but Your child needs to understand better what that means. He [She] wants to do well at everything he [she] does, and that's a good quality. Unfortunately, his [her] drive for perfection is ruining his [her] life and his [her] relationships . . .

8 RECOMMENDED RESOURCES

Antony, Martin, and Richard Swinson. *When Perfect Isn't Good Enough: Strategies for Coping with Perfectionism.* New Harbinger Publications, 2009.

Clinton, Tim. *The Bible for Hope: Caring for People God's Way.* Thomas Nelson, 2007.

Clinton, Tim, Archibald D. Hart, and George Ohlschlager. *Caring for People God's Way: Personal and Emotional Issues, Addictions, Grief, and Trauma.* Thomas Nelson, 2006.

Thurman, Chris. "Perfectionism" in *The Soul Care Bible*, ed. Tim Clinton. Nashville, 2001.

Parrott, Les. *The Control Freak.* Tyndale House, 2000.

Winter, Richard. *Perfecting Ourselves to Death: The Pursuit of Excellence and the Perils of Perfectionism.* InterVarsity Press, 2005.

Websites

American Association of Christian Counselors (www.aacc.net)

Ecounseling (www.ecounseling.com)

Americans spent just under 13.2 billion dollars on cosmetic procedures last year.[2]

Pornography

PORTRAITS : 1

- Sharon couldn't shake the nagging feeling she had. Finally she asked Paul if he has ever been involved in pornography. He replied in a defensive manner: "I have but I have it under control now. You have nothing to worry about." Sharon wept as she described her horror in finding obscene pictures on their computer that he had downloaded from the Internet. "I trusted him," she said.

- Fifteen-year-old Andrew remembers the first time he viewed sexually arousing material. He was at his friend's house and was checking his email. He got a message from someone he didn't recognize with a file attachment. He opened the file and saw a photo of a man and woman engaged in sexual activity. Andrew felt flush with excitement and guilt. Soon he was going online when no one was home to view similar sites because he liked the feeling it gave him.

DEFINITIONS AND KEY THOUGHTS : 2

- Pornography is *sexually explicit material* that dehumanizes, objectifies, and degrades men and women for the purpose of sexual arousal. Often it is photos; sometimes it takes the form of stories or comic book drawings and stories.

- Pornography *promotes "sex without consequences"* and serves as an aid to self-gratification.

- Generally, a *man will come* to counseling because he has *been found out* by someone at work or by a loved one. Or sometimes a man will seek counseling because he is weary of his feelings of guilt and shame.

- A *woman may come* for counseling because she either *suspects or has found evidence* that her husband has been involved in pornography and she does not know what to do.

- A *teenager may come* in for counseling at the insistence of *his or her parents.*

- Many *rationalize their behavior as "harmless"* because they think they are not actually committing adultery or sexual sin.

- Eventually, use of pornography *loses its power to stimulate,* and the user is enticed to involve others (usually strangers).

> In 2006, the revenue of the pornography industry in the United States equaled 13.33 billion dollars. Every second 3,075.64 dollars is being spent on pornography. And every second 28,258 Internet users are viewing pornography.[1]

- Pornography is used by many as a *stress reliever* that gives *escape* from life's perceived hardships.
- Pornography use may be a *symptom of a deeper issue* (low self-esteem, loneliness, past sexual abuse).
- Many use pornography *to avoid emotional or sexual intimacy with their spouse.*
- Consistent use of pornography promotes the notion that *women are to be viewed as objects* and that *sex is unrelated to love*, commitment, and marriage.
- Viewing pornography *increases the likelihood of sexual addiction* and sexual pathology.
- Use of pornography can create *unrealistic sexual expectations* of one's spouse.
- The user of pornography will *struggle consistently* with anger, guilt, shame, increasing anxiety, and oppressive memories.
- It is not uncommon for many people to have their *first exposure* to pornographic material during the *junior high school years.*
- Many adolescents begin viewing pornography because of *curiosity* and as a release for hormonal tension.

> But each one is tempted when he is drawn away by his own desires and enticed. Then, when desire has conceived, it gives birth to sin; and sin, when it is full-grown, brings forth death.
>
> *James 1:14–15*

3 : ASSESSMENT INTERVIEW

Interviewing the Person Viewing Pornography

Recognize that the person who is struggling with this issue will feel a *great deal of shame* and will be reluctant to speak about it.

It is important to *communicate acceptance* and a willingness to understand the struggle that has been occurring.

Approach the person with grace rather than judgment. Cite Romans 3:23: "For all have sinned and fall short of the glory of God."

Be patient in encouraging the person to relate how the struggle began, how it progressed, and what is currently happening.

In the assessment process you need *to evaluate the length of time* the person has been involved in this activity and *the extent of the involvement*. (Is it daily or sporadic? Is it reaching an addiction? Is it affecting his or her work or home life?) In addition, it is important to evaluate the degree to which the person feels *sorrow and regret* and to test his *willingness to change*.

1. How long has this pattern been going on?
2. What prompted you to start?
3. When do you find you most often engage in viewing pornography (at night; when stressed; when you are on the computer and no one is around)?
4. What is it like to admit to this? (*Listen for the degree of defensiveness.*)
5. How do you think this is affecting your relationship with your spouse/friends/family?
6. When do you find yourself most tempted?

7. Have you made any attempts to stop? If so, how?

8. What are you willing to do about this?

9. How do you see God in your life right now?

Interviewing the Spouse Seeking Counsel

If the counselee is a wife of someone suspected of using pornography, she will probably be *expressing a variety of emotions* from anger to shame to guilt (feeling as if she is somehow at fault).

In the initial interview you will need to show a willingness to *listen and provide hope* that God will show a way through this difficult experience.

It will be important to *evaluate what specifically she wants to do*. She may be dealing with fear of confronting her husband. She may be struggling with thinking clearly about this situation and needs to talk it through with you.

1. When did you find out about this?

2. How did you discover this information?

3. Have you made any attempts to talk with your husband about this?

4. If not, why not? Are you afraid of his reaction?

5. If so, what happened? How did you approach it and what did you say?

6. How did he respond?

7. Have you seen any unusual changes in his behavior lately?

8. How are you feeling in regard to finding this out?

9. How specifically can I help you?

10. Would you like me to talk to your husband? Do you think he will be willing to talk to me?

> There are 4.2 million pornographic websites (12 percent of total web sites). 100,000 websites offer illegal child pornography specifically.[2]

WISE COUNSEL 4

For the Person Viewing Pornography

Evaluate how *honest* the person is being with himself/herself and you. *Repenting is a crucial spiritual component* in the healing of sexual sin. You may wish to investigate with the person David's confession of sin in Psalm 51.

Determine how *willing the person is to take steps to change*. Honest confession and repentance are pivotal to begin the process of change.

It is important to *identify the triggers* that are involved in tempting the person. Alcoholics Anonymous narrowed down most of the moods associated with triggers to a simple acronym: HALT, standing for:

Hungry

Angry

Lonely

Tired

Provide hope that the counselee will be able to realize victory over this. Let the person know that there will be times of temptation and possible setbacks, yet God is faithful to forgive and restore.

Assure the person of your continued support through this process. Instruct the person to structure a system of accountability through the help of a trusted friend.

5 ACTION STEPS

For the Person Viewing Pornography

1. Flee Temptation

Help the person identify all the locations and activities that provide temptation.

- Avoid bookstores that sell pornographic magazines.
- Use the computer when someone else is in the room.
- Purchase software that blocks the access to undesirable Internet sites.

2. Identify Emotional Triggers

- Are there work associates, times of the day, or particular stressful situations that trigger the temptation?
- Which part of HALT (hungry, angry, lonely, tired) is the strongest trigger for you?
- *Encourage the person to take specific steps to minimize the triggers.*

3. See It as Sin

- It is important to see the behavior as sin and no longer to justify it.
- *Discuss how God views the sin, the nature of forgiveness, and God's unconditional love. Evaluate with the counselee how he sees himself in relationship to how God sees him.*

4. Refocus on Christ

- You will need to develop a plan to strengthen and deepen your relationship with Jesus Christ.
- You will be accountable for daily Scripture reading and prayer.
- Memorize Scripture so that you can bring "every thought into captivity to the obedience of Christ" (2 Cor. 10:5).

5. Get Support and Accountability

- Get involved in a local Christian ministry that supports men who are experiencing this struggle.

> There are 68 million daily pornographic search requests (25 percent of total search requests), with the largest consumer base of Internet pornography being the 30–40 age group.[3]

6. Check In on the Marriage

- *Evaluate his relationship with his spouse (if married) and provide an invitation to meet with both to explore the effects of this behavior on their relationship and to find healing for wounds.*

7. Seek Further Help

- Pornography use can cause long-term problems.
- If this has been a *long-standing pattern* with a high degree of involvement, it is important to *enlist the support of a professional* trained in the arena of sexual addiction and/or a local 12-step group.

For the Spouse Seeking Counsel

If the husband will not come in and talk with you, or if the wife doesn't want him to know about her conversation with you, then you will need simply to offer encouragement to the wife.

1. Watch for Triggers

- Identify the locations and activities that provide temptation.
- You can help your husband avoid bookstores that sell pornographic magazines (for example, you should not send him late at night to the local 7-Eleven on an errand).
- Move the computer out of isolation. If your husband is willing to be helped, he should go along with this. If not, you can explain that you don't want the kids finding pornography on the computer.
- Purchase software that blocks the access to undesirable Internet sites.

2. Identify Emotional Triggers

- Do you sense that there are work associates, times of the day, or particular stressful situations that trigger the temptation? What can you do to help?
- Which part of HALT (hungry, angry, lonely, tired) is the strongest trigger for your husband? What can you do to offset this?
- If your husband is willing to be helped, you can talk to him about these triggers and how you can be his ally in minimizing them.

3. Continue to Love Him/Her

- Nagging, anger, or humiliation will not work. Continue to love your husband. It will be difficult because you will feel "cheated on" but ask God to help you choose to love him through this.
- Let him know that you want him back from the darkness and you want your marriage unhindered by these "other women."
- Tell him how you feel when he views pornography.

> Let us walk properly, as in the day, not in revelry and drunkenness, not in lewdness and lust, not in strife and envy.
> *Romans 13:13*

> Among Christians, 47 percent said that pornography was a major problem in their home. Ten percent of American adults admit to an Internet sexual addiction.[4]

- Ask him if he wants his children similarly enslaved when they are older.
- Explain to him that eventually pornography will not satisfy and he will need more, other types, or will be led into an affair.

4. Pray for Him/Her

- Your husband is making bad choices; fortunately, God gives us the ability to make good choices.
- Pray that your husband will be sickened by what he sees and will choose to turn away.
- Let God go to work in your husband's life.

5. Encourage Support

- Encourage your husband to join a support group or men's Bible study that will provide accountability.
- Do whatever it takes to free him up to attend such a group.

> Beloved, I beg you as sojourners and pilgrims, abstain from fleshly lusts which war against the soul.
> *1 Peter 2:11*

6 BIBLICAL INSIGHTS

Now Israel remained in Acacia Grove, and the people began to commit harlotry with the women of Moab.

Numbers 25:1

Sexual sin always progresses, drawing people farther and farther from God. What may start as an "innocent" flirtation with sin can lead to deadly consequences.

Dabbling around the edges of sexual sin can take hold and consume a person, leading to pain and brokenness.

For this is the will of God, your sanctification: that you should abstain from sexual immorality; that each of you should know how to possess his own vessel in sanctification and honor, not in passion of lust.

1 Thessalonians 4:3–5

The Bible is very clear about sexual sin. God created sex as a beautiful expression of love in marriage. Satan took that beauty and distorted it.

Sexual sin encompasses a wide range of activities forbidden by God. No matter what society allows, believers must look to God for instruction in this serious matter.

Christians need to avoid activities or thoughts that warp what God intended for building oneness in marriage.

Believers must have no part in sexual sin. God knows its power to destroy people. His commands are for our good.

I am He who searches the minds and hearts. And I will give to each one of you according to your works.

Revelation 2:23

Sometimes people think they can hide portions of their lives from everyone.

Christ searches minds and hearts. Nothing is hidden from Him. No sexual sin can escape His notice. People may think they are getting away with it, but God knows.

Everywhere we go, everything we say, think, or do is seen by God. That understanding alone should help us steer clear of sexual sin.

PRAYER STARTER 7

Oh, Lord, this family is being devastated by Satan's abomination of something You created to be good and wholesome. Help this family deal with the pain that pornography is causing. We ask that You strengthen Your child to stand firm in his commitment to be free from the addictive power of pornography . . .

RECOMMENDED RESOURCES 8

Arterburn, Stephen, Fred Stoeker, and Mike Yorkey. *Every Man's Battle: Winning the War on Sexual Temptation.* WaterBrook, 2000.

Clinton, Tim, Archibald D. Hart, and George Ohlschlager. *Caring for People God's Way: Personal and Emotional Issues, Addictions, Grief, and Trauma.* Thomas Nelson, 2006.

Crosse, Clay and Renee. *I Surrender All: Rebuilding a Marriage Broken by Pornography.* NavPress, 2005.

Ethridge, Shannon, and Stephen Arterburn. *Every Woman's Battle: Discovering God's Plan for Sexual and Emotional Fulfillment.* WaterBrook, 2003.

Laaser, Mark. *Healing the Wounds of Sexual Addiction.* Zondervan, 2004.

Rogers, Henry J. *The Silent War: Ministering to Those Trapped in the Deception of Pornography.* New Leaf Press, 2000.

Websites

American Association of Christian Counselors (www.aacc.net)

Ecounseling (www.ecounseling.com)

Familysafemedia (www.familysafemedia.com)

Prejudice

1 PORTRAITS

- Joey, president of his church youth group, struggles with accepting Ellie, a new member. Ellie and her family have just moved to Joey's town. Even though Ellie claims to be a Christian, Joey is suspicious of her and feels she is faking, just to get accepted. He likes his youth group just the way it is and resents this foreigner (even though Ellie is a citizen) who eats different foods and talks with an accent.
- Janna is a young adult who is serious about her career in Human Resources. She has risen to a position to where she is hiring personnel. Janna struggles with prejudices she has against people of different races.
- Matt grew up in a small town where there were "two sides of the tracks" and he was always taught that he was on the "right" side. The summer after his high school graduation, he became a Christian. On arriving at college in a large cosmopolitan city, he encountered teammates on his ball team who were from "the wrong side of the tracks." He struggles with this and how it fits with his newfound Christianity.

2 DEFINITIONS AND KEY THOUGHTS

- Prejudice is *an emotional response* based on fear, mistrust, and ignorance. It is usually directed at a racial, religious, national, or other cultural group, although it can also focus on other differences, such as financial.
- Prejudice is also a superiority mindset that often is *passed on from one generation to the next*. Children having lived in an environment where one or both parents have shown prejudice toward others' religion or ethnicity (for example) will often become adults with those same prejudices.
- The prejudiced person will *refuse involvement* in situations and with groups of people simply because of who is involved. The fellowship that God intends for His children to share is therefore short-circuited.
- Prejudice causes the whole body of Christ to suffer: "For as the body is one and has many members, but all the members of that one body, being many, are one body, so also is Christ" (1 Cor. 12:12).
- Some argue that prejudice is a matter of personal opinion, and say, "I can't help the way I feel." However, Christians are instructed to *exercise personal choices* based on what they see in the character of God. (See Acts 10:9–48.)

- Second Chronicles 19:7 states: "Now therefore, let the fear of the LORD be upon you . . . for there is no iniquity with the LORD our God, no partiality." Romans 2:11 says that God does not show favoritism: "There is no partiality with God."

- God's unbiased disposition toward the world is the basis for John 3:16: "For God so loved the world that He gave His only begotten Son, that whoever believes in Him should not perish but have everlasting life."

- The prejudiced person:

  – needs to address deep issues of anger and/or attitude

  – has issues that stem from *parental attitudes or from an event* in his or her past

  – is *negatively affected* by prejudice in the way he or she can relate to others and the way he or she perceives situations

  – has a *false view of self*—seeing self as uniquely separate and better than others

  – has an *incorrect understanding of God* and His creation of and love for all people

- This type of individual will eventually *alienate himself or herself* in this now global, multicultural world.

- Prejudice can lead to *discrimination*—putting prejudicial attitudes, thoughts, and opinions into action.

- If the person had a negative experience with someone from another culture that led to prejudice, he or she needs *to be realistic* about his or her assessment. For example, if the person had a bad experience with a doctor, would he never go to see another doctor?

> He who oppresses the poor reproaches his Maker, but he who honors Him has mercy on the needy.
>
> *Proverbs 14:31*

ASSESSMENT INTERVIEW 3

1. Have you ever thought about why you have prejudices?

2. Did you learn this attitude toward this group of people from your parents? Explain what your parents taught you about them.

3. Did you ever have a negative experience with a person from this culture?

4. Does one negative experience make all of these people bad?

5. How have you expressed your prejudice? Have you been discriminatory?

6. Why do you feel this person deserves this kind of treatment?

7. Have you ever been misunderstood?

8. Has someone ever shown a prejudice toward you for being a Christian? How did that make you feel?

9. Has someone ever made fun of you or where you are from? How did that make you feel?

10. When you feel prejudice toward someone, how does that make you feel?

11. What does it mean to you when you hear: "Walk a mile in someone's shoes"?

12. How did Jesus treat those who were different from Him?

4 WISE COUNSEL

Don't assume that the client has any *knowledge of life outside* his or her own cultural boundaries. As a society, we are becoming more globally minded but many are still very narrow-minded in their understanding of differences in cultures.

Share some *examples of how other cultures live or think*. For example, the Japanese make decisions very quickly—unlike Americans who frequently utilize long board meetings. This does not mean that we are right or that they are right; we are just different.

Help the person understand that he or she must learn to *celebrate the differences* instead of judging the differences.

As the love of God flows through Christians, we are drawn together as one body; our relationships with one another are rooted in biblical teachings like:

> If a stranger dwells with you in your land, you shall not mistreat him.
>
> *Leviticus 19:33*

"Be kindly affectionate to one another" (Rom. 12:10).

"Be of the same mind toward one another" (Rom. 12:16).

"Love one another" (Rom. 13:8).

"Pursue the things which make for peace and the things by which one may edify another" (Rom. 14:19).

"The members should have the same care for one another" (1 Cor. 12:25).

"Through love serve one another" (Gal. 5:13).

"Be kind to one another, tenderhearted, forgiving one another" (Eph. 4:32).

"Bearing with one another, and forgiving one another" (Col. 3:13).

5 ACTION STEPS

1. Grow in Cross-Cultural Appreciation

- Examine your own cultural roots and become more personally aware of who you are and where your ancestors came from (we are a nation of immigrants—everyone came from somewhere else, unless you're Native American).

- Look up information about the culture in question—the one causing the prejudice. (*Give one specific item to look up, for example, meals or special celebrations. The client may find something like brides wear white in the United States, but in India they prefer red or yellow.*) This item of information should be brought to the next session.

2. Get Personal

- Think of a time when you were made fun of (perhaps for your curly hair or your "Irish temper"). Remember how it made you feel.

- How is that any different from the prejudice you are showing someone? (*Encourage the individual to answer this—it may really stretch his or her thinking and bring the client to a point of realization.*)

3. Avoid Stereotypes

- Would you want to be generalized as a "dumb blonde" or a "tough German" or a "loud Italian"? Then don't do that to others.
- Generalizations are made about people without regard to their uniqueness.
- Usually when you make generalizations, it is a way of avoiding the need to deal with the person as an individual.

4. Practice Empathy

- Walk a mile in someone else's shoes before you make a judgment about that person. Get into his or her head, think about what life must be like for this individual. This is called empathy.
- Consider how you would feel landing in another country where you don't know the customs or the language.

5. Do What Jesus Would Do

- Remember your common bond in Christ with fellow believers. This common bond tears down any walls of prejudice (see Col. 3:11).
- For those who aren't believers (or you don't know if they are), develop sensitivity with God's help. This along with empathy will help you begin living outside the box.
- Changing your deeply rooted attitudes and beliefs will not come overnight. This is a process that will take time. As you continue to examine your own beliefs and talk to others about them, change will occur.
- People who wish to overcome prejudice need to have renewed minds (Eph. 4:23). By studying God's Word, we can acquire the mind of Christ (Phil. 2:5). Christ will then empower you through the Holy Spirit to remove the prejudice that can do harm to your ability to relate to all persons and fellow image-bearers.

Always remember that children model adult behavior. What parents say and how they act concerning others will influence impressionable minds. Racist jokes, generalized statements or hateful expressions plant unwanted seeds—in the victim and in the offender. Instead, plant healthy seeds in the tender soil of your child's heart, building respect toward others.[1]

BIBLICAL INSIGHTS 6

Gilead's wife bore sons; and when his wife's sons grew up, they drove Jephthah out, and said to him, "You shall have no inheritance in our father's house, for you are the son of another woman."

Judges 11:2

Jephthah was rejected by the rest of his family because his mother was a harlot (prostitute). His half brothers' prejudice against him was so intense that they drove him out of their home.

Prejudice can cause people to turn away from what could otherwise be a good friendship or working relationship.

The Bible teaches that we should not be prejudiced against anyone, for all people are created by God and all are one in Christ (Gal. 3:26–28).

> It shall be that I will gather all nations and tongues; and they shall come and see My glory.
>
> *Isaiah 66:18*

But he disdained to lay hands on Mordecai alone, for they had told him of the people of Mordecai. Instead, Haman sought to destroy all the Jews who were throughout the whole kingdom of Ahasuerus—the people of Mordecai.

Esther 3:6

Haman's prejudice was focused against one Jewish man and then was extended to the Jewish race and religion.

Prejudice is a powerful tool of Satan, making one person feel that he or she is superior to another. That should never be the attitude of the followers of Christ.

Believers ought to see all people as created in the image of God and should accept all other believers as part of God's family. In love, they should also readily share Christ with lost people of all races and nations.

Then he said to them, "You know how unlawful it is for a Jewish man to keep company with or go to one of another nation. But God has shown me that I should not call any man common or unclean."

Acts 10:28

At this point in the early church, it was hard for Jewish believers to comprehend that Gentiles might also become Christians.

At this critical time in the growth of the early church, God made it clear that the Good News would be for everyone.

Today we must not allow any prejudice to keep us from sharing the message of salvation with the world.

> But in every nation whoever fears Him and works righteousness is accepted by Him.
>
> *Acts 10:35*

There is neither Jew nor Greek, there is neither slave nor free, there is neither male nor female; for you are all one in Christ Jesus.

Galatians 3:28

This verse describes how Christ breaks down all barriers.

All believers have personal identities, which provide rich variety in the church. But all have also been made "one in Christ Jesus." This oneness provides deep unity. As part of a huge, diverse family, we should not allow anything to separate us from other believers.

If you really fulfill the royal law according to the Scripture, "You shall love your neighbor as yourself," you do well; but if you show partiality, you commit sin, and are convicted by the law as transgressors.

James 2:8–9

James warned the believers against showing prejudice. They were not to fawn over a rich person while ignoring a poor one.

People often want to be associated with those who are successful, popular, and powerful. God demands impartiality, however, for all people are equally valuable in His eyes.

Favoritism goes against God's command to love one's neighbor as oneself. He wants us to respect all people and treat them equally, regardless of their background or economic status. Each person is God's creation.

PRAYER STARTER 7

Thank You, Lord, that Your child has come today to deal with this issue of prejudice. The reasons run deep, but not so deep that You cannot heal, Lord. Help him [her] see that You created all people in Your image and because of that all people have dignity and value . . .

RECOMMENDED RESOURCES 8

Clinton, Tim. *The Bible for Hope: Caring for People God's Way*. Thomas Nelson, 2007.

Clinton, Tim, Archibald D. Hart, and George Ohlschlager. *Caring for People God's Way: Personal and Emotional Issues, Addictions, Grief, and Trauma*. Thomas Nelson, 2006.

Clinton, Tim, and Gary Sibcy. *Why You Do the Things You Do: The Secret to Healthy Relationships*. Thomas Nelson, 2006.

Sharp, Douglas. *No Partiality*. InterVarsity Press, 2002.

Woodley, Randy. *Living in Color: Embracing God's Passion for Ethnic Diversity*. InterVarsity Press, 2004.

Websites

American Association of Christian Counselors (www.aacc.net)

Ecounseling (www.ecounseling.com)

Premarital Sex

1 PORTRAITS

- Laurie was in high school and was devastated when she broke up with her boyfriend. Only her best friend knew that her emotional pain was heightened by the knowledge that she'd surrendered her virginity to this boy.
- Jake is a good Christian kid who attends youth group. His parents are very surprised to discover that he has contracted a sexually transmitted disease.
- Kim is twenty years old and in college and has just discovered that she's pregnant. The young man who got her pregnant has shown himself to be immature and possibly addicted to drugs.
- Dave has been having sex with his girlfriends since middle school. He really doesn't understand what all the fuss is about.

2 DEFINITIONS AND KEY THOUGHTS

- Sex is a *God-given appetite* that needs to be controlled.
- According to the whole counsel of the Bible, *sex outside of marriage is wrong*—no matter how old you are or how much you love your partner.
- *Sex* can be defined in a few different ways. Typically, it refers to intercourse between a man and a woman, but a more accurate definition might be *any activity that intends or causes at least one partner to become sexually aroused*. This broader definition dispenses with the distinctions that allow people to have sex without calling it sin and is more consistent with Jesus's revelation that sin is already done when one harbors lustful thoughts.
- Many teens think that "it's not really sex" if it's *oral sex*. The Bible teaches that any sexual engagement with another outside of the covenant of marriage is sin. (See Exod. 20:14; Prov. 5:1-6, 15–20; 1 Cor. 6:12–20.) Additionally, most teens do not understand that *STDs (sexually transmitted diseases) can be transferred* during oral sex.
- Our society has been sexualized by media that *use sex to sell and to entertain*. The situation for teenagers is very different from what their parents experienced. Now they regularly view homosexual and extramarital sex on TV, and they virtually never are reminded of the negative aftereffects of sex or of the fact that God labels these behaviors sin.

> I say then: Walk in the Spirit, and you shall not fulfill the lust of the flesh.
>
> *Galatians 5:16*

- *Divorce may contribute* to early sexual activity as teens seek attention because parental guidance is spread thin.

- Divorced or widowed parents present *mixed messages* to their children if they tell their teens to wait to have sex but are sexually active themselves.

- Kids who are *not allowed to go on dates* by themselves may be less likely to indulge in risky sexual behavior.

- Teens whose parents *speak to them openly* about sexual ethics will be more informed and more thoughtful about their behavior than those whose parents don't talk with them about sex. Ignorance can lead to recklessness.

- More than anything else, *drugs and alcohol* contribute to risky sexual behavior and impulsive decision making.

- Often *teen girls who mature early* struggle to accept their sexuality. They are frequently treated as sex objects by boys whose sexuality is just awakening, and they may be rejected by other girls who are envious of the attention they get.

- Girls who *strive for acceptance* and rarely assert themselves may be susceptible to boys who tell them they must have sex or they will no longer date them.

- Whether true or not, the statement *"everybody is doing it"* is frequently cited by teens to justify sexual acting out.

- *Rape and date rape* may be far more common than we think, especially on college campuses where reporting a rape may carry a stigma.

> Keep your heart with all diligence, for out of it spring the issues of life.
>
> *Proverbs 4:23*

ASSESSMENT INTERVIEW 3

Most people who seek counseling for a sexual indiscretion will be hyperattuned to criticism. This may be particularly true if the encounter involved a person of the same sex. You will have to make every effort to *appear nonjudgmental*. If you feel repulsed or angered by the individual's behavior, you need to refer the person to another counselor.

Teens may *seek counseling for an unrelated problem* and then slowly—if trust develops—admit to premarital sex, pregnancy, or abortion. The following questions will help you assess the situation once it becomes clear that sexual misbehavior has occurred.

Rule Outs

1. Were you forced to have sex? If so, when did this take place? (*If it has just occurred, the rape should be reported to the police so that evidence can be gathered.*)

2. Is there any possibility that you are pregnant? If so, what are your thoughts? (*If she is considering abortion, see the section on Abortion.*)

3. Sexually transmitted diseases can be caught through oral sex as well as intercourse. Have you engaged in unprotected oral sex or intercourse? (*If so, the person needs a medical exam immediately. If infected, the counselee should*

contact every person he or she has been with, at least within a particular window of time, so those people can be tested.)

4. Has your sexual experience caused you to feel depressed? Have you considered harming yourself? (*If yes, see the section on Suicide.*)

5. Have all of your sexual encounters been heterosexual? If not, how long have you been having sex with someone of the same gender?

6. If you have engaged in homosexual activity, has this been continual or just experimental? (*If homosexuality/lesbianism is an issue, see the section on Homosexuality.*)

General Questions

1. Do you have sexual boundaries between you and your partner?

2. Have you violated them? If so, how?

3. Do you enjoy having sex? If not, why do you do it?

4. With how many partners have you had sex?

5. Do you use protection when you have sex?

6. Do you plan your sexual activity ahead of time, or does it just happen?

7. Do you believe that your behavior is right and healthy, or do you want to change it?

8. If you want to change, what strategies have you tried? How well have they worked?

9. Have you ever been pressured into having sex? What would you do if it happened again?

10. Is there any relationship between love and sex? If so, what is the relationship?

11. Are you feeling guilty? What do you plan to do with your feelings?

12. Do you think that God can forgive you?

13. What do you think you should do now?

4 WISE COUNSEL

If you allow the person to talk *without judging him or her*, the person will be more open.

Through processing the behavior, the client will probably come to the clear conclusion that the act was wrong and that the *behavior needs to change*. If that does not happen, you at least will have built a strong relationship and can begin gently teaching the person biblical values.

To repeat, *if you are repulsed or angered* by the person's behavior, you must *refer him or her* to another counselor.

ACTION STEPS : 5

1. Talk It Out

- *If the client is a young person, help him or her feel comfortable. Simply listen and encourage the person to talk.*
- *The client may not have come in with issues about premarital sex, but you may discover that it underlies presenting issues such as self-esteem, depression, and so on.*

2. See a Crisis Pregnancy Counselor if Needed

- *If you discover that the counselee is pregnant or has gotten a girl pregnant, encourage her or him to reveal this information to family members.*
- *Refer the person to a crisis pregnancy center to discuss the options for raising the child or giving the baby up for adoption.*

3. Confess Sin

- You must be willing to admit and confess the sin. Confession, repentance, and forgiveness are crucial elements in the healing process.

4. Accept God's Forgiveness

- *The person may be suffering from intense feelings of guilt. Help him or her process these feelings, confess the sin(s), and experience forgiveness.*
- Sometimes using a guided visual meditation to teach a biblical truth helps us feel forgiven. Imagine placing all the sins into a trash bag and turning it over to Jesus. He deals with it by destroying it and then covers you with a clean, perfect coat. *It is important to help some people feel God's presence and experience His leading as parts of their healing journey.*
- Focus on God's love and forgiveness. Passages like Psalm 51 remind us that God forgives even the worst of sinners and heals their pain.
- Even though you have lost your virginity, you can, in a sense, start over with God. You can determine from now until marriage to remain pure.
- Having sex is a mistake that is permanent. Once gone, virginity cannot be restored. However, there are ceremonies that have been established to reaffirm purity, to achieve "renewed virginity," after a person has sinned and to encourage continued purity. Such a ritual can provide a healing way of getting beyond a past sin and setting a commitment to purity for the future. (See secondaryvirginity.com or lovematters.com.)

> Nationwide in 2007, 47.8 percent of high school students had had sexual intercourse during their life. Overall the prevalence of having had sexual intercourse was higher among male than female students, higher among black and Hispanic than white students, and higher among black than Hispanic students.[1]

> Nationwide in 2007, 7.1 percent of high school students had sexual intercourse for the first time before age thirteen.[2]

5. Discover the Reasons

Help the counselee understand the reasons he or she engages in sex. Is it:

- a search for intimacy?
- a desire to prove manhood or womanhood?
- a need to be accepted or popular with others who are having sex?
- a need to hold on to a particular boyfriend or girlfriend?
- a good physical sensation?

6. Remain Pure

Having sex is like many other life-dominating, impulsive behaviors. Brainstorm ways to avoid having sex outside of the biblical covenantal context in the future. This might include:

- ending the dating relationship if the other person does not share the conviction that sex should stop
- seeking out new friends who believe in preserving sex until covenantal marriage
- searching for activities that will help to refocus sexual drives
- being physically active on a daily basis
- asking every day for God to take over and sanctify your sexual drive

6 BIBLICAL INSIGHTS

But it happened about this time, when Joseph went into the house to do his work, and none of the men of the house was inside, that she caught him by his garment, saying, "Lie with me." But he left his garment in her hand, and fled and ran outside.

Genesis 39:11–12

Nationwide in 2007, 14.9 percent of high school students had sexual intercourse with four or more persons during their life.[3]

Lust has no logic. Sometimes you can't talk someone out of doing wrong—you just have to get out of the way.

Joseph knew only one answer to this moral challenge: view it from God's perspective. Thus he concluded that violating his sexual integrity would be a "great wickedness" and "sin against God" (v. 9).

Sexual sin hurts one's relationship with God and can destroy relationships with others. Joseph realized that he had no choice but to run!

I am my beloved's, and his desire is toward me.

Song of Solomon 7:10

Throughout the Song of Solomon, the husband and wife exult in each other's physical attractiveness. These explicit descriptions of their love underscore the importance of the soul relationship and deep commitment of the couple to one another.

When a man and a woman become one in marriage, the bond of intimacy will strengthen their relationship. Within the bonds of marriage, God approves of and encourages sexual pleasure.

Do you not know that your bodies are members of Christ? Shall I then take the members of Christ and make them members of a harlot? Certainly not!

1 Corinthians 6:15

Sex is more than a physical act. When God created sex, He said that in that moment, the two people "become one flesh" (Gen. 2:24). Sex is meant by God to be a holy union in which a man and a woman share a deep bond.

Sex itself is not evil, for God created it. However, people pervert it. Believers must practice sexual integrity.

God's people must abstain from sex outside of marriage; but within the bonds of marriage, a husband and wife should be faithful, always seeking to lovingly meet each other's needs.

PRAYER STARTER : 7

Dear Lord, thank You that _____ is seeking help. Please aid _____ to see Your plan for sexuality. Help _____ learn new strategies to handle temptation. We know that once we ask for Your forgiveness, we have it. And once we are forgiven, we are pure. This is a reality. We praise You for this reality and thank You for Your forgiveness. Please be with us every step of the way as we seek to preserve purity in the days to come . . .

RECOMMENDED RESOURCES : 8

Anderson, Neil, and Dave Park. *Purity under Pressure.* Harvest House, 1995.

Arterburn, Stephen, Fred Stoeker, and Mike Yorkey. *Every Man's Battle: Winning the War on Sexual Temptation.* WaterBrook, 2000.

Clinton, Tim. *The Bible for Hope: Caring for People God's Way.* Thomas Nelson, 2007.

Clinton, Tim, Archibald D. Hart, and George Ohlschlager. *Caring for People God's Way: Personal and Emotional Issues, Addictions, Grief, and Trauma.* Thomas Nelson, 2006.

Ethridge, Shannon, and Stephen Arterburn. *Every Woman's Battle: Discovering God's Plan for Sexual and Emotional Fulfillment.* WaterBrook, 2003.

Smalley, Michael and Amy. *Don't Date Naked.* Tyndale House, 2008.

Websites

American Association of Christian Counselors (www.aacc.net)

Ecounseling (www.ecounseling.com)

Self-Esteem

1 PORTRAITS

- Jennifer believes her marriage has no hope. She feels that apart from her husband and children she has no purpose in life. Her husband keeps reminding her that without him she is nothing.

- Henry has lived his entire life trying to please his parents. At forty he still sees every decision he makes as an opportunity to win the favor of his father. He is sad and discouraged and he can't seem to hold a job or a long-term relationship.

- From the time she was a young child, Sandy has been told that she is ugly and stupid. At eighteen she is frightened to enter college for fear of failure in relationships.

- Jill has had multiple boyfriends during her adult life. She feels frustrated and pressured to give in to their sexual advances to escape rejection.

2 DEFINITIONS AND KEY THOUGHTS

- Self-esteem refers to an *inner sense of worthiness* that gives a person resilience and resistance to attack or criticism.

- Generally speaking, each person has a *concept about his or her self-worth* (which may or may not be accurate), and self-esteem is how the person *feels about (or evaluates) that concept*.

- Having healthy self-esteem *does not mean being proud* or having an overblown view of one's own importance. Paul encourages us to "think soberly" when it comes to evaluating ourselves (Rom. 12:3). This means assessing ourselves with honesty and fairness.

- *Low self-esteem* can manifest itself in many ways:

  - feelings of self-hate, believing that one is unworthy or incompetent
  - refusal to get close to people, believing one doesn't deserve strong or supportive relationships
  - refusal to trust others
  - inability to accept oneself as special and unique
  - rejection of what God intended the person to be in Him
  - depression

- suicidal thoughts

- a need for lots of attention

- a competitive spirit

- poor decisions made that are based on fears and not reality

- People's self-esteem is in trouble when they *allow others to assess and convince them of their value or significance* instead of relying on the assessment of the One who created them.

- Poor self-esteem is often the result of *prolonged periods of negative feedback* in a person's life, resulting in deep wounds and pain. As counselor, you need to apply active listening skills to determine *how far back the negative influence has gone.*

- Society is *constantly assessing our value*. At work, we have performance evaluations. We are graded in schools. We are evaluated for loans. Assessment of our value begins early in life and continues even after we are dead.

- Often the imposition of value is *a means to an end*. A negative example of this is the young lady who finds herself in the backseat of a car with a boy who says: "If you want me to value you, you will have sex with me." This is the worst form of value imposition.

- God has determined our value based on *His purpose for creating us* in the first place and on the *price He has paid* to redeem us for all eternity.

- Many Christians feel that self-esteem doesn't even belong in a Christian's vocabulary—that any assessment of our own value is vanity and therefore sinful. This, of course, is true when a person has an overinflated sense of his or her worth, resembling conceit powered by pride. However, as counselors we must deal with those who come with a *damaged or painful sense of their worth*. Searching for God's perspective on our worth or significance is worthy of our time and spiritual energy.

- Most who struggle with low self-esteem are believing lies about their significance to God.

- The goals of counseling should be to:

  - correct false or erroneous beliefs about the individual's worth and significance

  - make an accurate, genuine assessment of the person's strengths, gifts, significance, and potential

  - bring healing from deep relationship wounds

  - help the person get over the distortions and be able to admit honestly his or her strengths as well as weaknesses

  - help the person on the journey to adopting God's perspective on his or her worth

And because you are sons, God has sent forth the Spirit of His Son into your hearts, crying out, "Abba, Father!" Therefore you are no longer a slave but a son, and if a son, then an heir of God through Christ.

Galatians 4:6–7

3 ASSESSMENT INTERVIEW

Most clients tend to feel bad about themselves *without having ever identified the problem* as related to self-esteem. They may feel like a failure or have strong feelings of inadequacy that can result in periods of depression and anxiety.

Some people with poor self-image have been *sexually abused and still feel dirty and worthless* as a result. If your counseling session uncovers sexual abuse, you will need to deal with this issue or refer the person to someone else. (See the section on Sexual Abuse in Childhood.)

Many individuals with poor self-esteem have come from families where a *divorce* made them insecure or where they might have even been *blamed* (or just assumed responsibility) for the divorce.

Some may simply have *overly sensitive personalities* that make them vulnerable to slights or criticism.

Use "normalization" to help build rapport and *make it clear that the person's feelings are normal.*

> See, I have inscribed you on the palms of My hands; Your walls are continually before Me.
>
> *Isaiah 49:16*

1. Have you ever been told that you have low self-esteem? If so, by whom and when? Do you agree?

2. Do you ever think that you cannot feel good about yourself unless you meet some standard in your life that someone else has set for you?

3. Do you consider failures or mistakes as direct reflections of your worth?

4. Has your need for approval from others ever caused you to make decisions that you knew were not beneficial?

5. Do you ever avoid taking risks because you are afraid you will fail?

6. Do you ever hear yourself saying that you are stupid and can't do anything right?

7. Do you ever hold your family or loved ones to unreasonable or unrealistic expectations? Or do your loved ones complain to you that you do this?

8. Is it difficult for you to forgive?

9. Have you been told that you are unforgiving?

10. Do you obsess about your weight and appearance?

11. Do you consider yourself competitive?

12. Do you often find yourself wishing you were another person—or that you had the talent or looks of another person?

13. What sorts of supportive friendships do you have?

14. In what sorts of situations do you feel most self-conscious? Least self-conscious?

15. What does it mean to you to be a child of God?

16. Do you believe that God loves you? Can you "feel" God's love or is it more of an intellectual understanding that God loves you?

17. How many siblings do you have? Where are you in the birth order?

18. Tell me about life in your family.

19. How were you treated as a child when you did something wrong or failed at something?

20. Did your parents have high expectations or low expectations of you? Or neither?

21. Did anyone in your family play favorites? Who was the favorite and how did that feel?

22. Have you ever been sexually abused or raped? Did you report it? How was it handled and what happened?

23. Describe the people in your life who made you feel good about yourself. Where are they now? Are any still in your life?

24. What makes you feel good about yourself?

WISE COUNSEL 4

Helping a person with low self-esteem *does not mean telling him or her untruths.* Instead, help the person develop a *realistic assessment of his or her unique set of skills, abilities, and character traits.* Further, help this individual develop a *strong sense of God's love and forgiveness.*

Remind your client of the story in John 5 where Jesus heals the crippled man who had lived for thirty-eight years with brokenness and pain. Jesus asked him if he *wanted* to be healed. Why would Jesus ask that? It seems that a person can live for so long with brokenness that he or she may not want to do the work that it takes to receive healing. Is your client willing to *do the work to receive healing?*

ACTION STEPS 5

1. Recognize Your Value

- There is a difference between having an inflated ego and simply understanding your significance based on your God-given gifts and value to Him.

- Make a list of ten talents, character traits, physical traits, abilities, accomplishments, and so on that set you apart. (*You can give this as homework. The person must come back to another session with the list in hand and be ready to share it with you.*)

- On the list, include five traits that you perceive are negative. Write down some ideas for how you can turn these negatives into positives.

- You mentioned a few people who made you feel good about yourself (*Assessment Interview question 23*). Are these people still in your life? If not, is there a way you can get them back into your life?

- Identify other positive people and spend more time with them.

2. Stop Harmful Thought Patterns

- Consider some of the thought patterns and other factors that are leading you to believe lies about your worth.
- Rent and watch the movie *It's a Wonderful Life*. George Bailey felt like a failure until the angel showed him how much different—and worse—the world would have been without him. Everyone influences others, and chances are that you have had a positive influence on some people.
- Think back on things you've done, such as taught a Sunday school class, helped with Boy Scouts, given a perfect gift to a relative, taught a child to shoot a basketball, taken a bag of groceries to a food pantry, invited a new co-worker to lunch. List all of the big and little things you've done for others. Then consider the impact your actions may have had on these people.

> I have been crucified with Christ; it is no longer I who live, but Christ lives in me; and the life which I now live in the flesh I live by faith in the Son of God, who loved me and gave Himself for me.
>
> *Galatians 2:20*

3. Begin New Thought Patterns

- Each negative thought can be countered with God's assessment of your value. For example, if you feel your self-worth sizzle when a co-worker with less experience is promoted over you, stop the negative thoughts before they take hold of you. Ask yourself if there might be any good reason this person received the promotion over you. If not, remind yourself that life isn't always fair.
- Remember that God has your life in His hands. Not receiving that promotion may end up being a blessing in disguise.

4. Be Patient

- It has taken years of bad habits to get to where you are with your self-esteem. Healing will not happen overnight and will require replacing the bad thought patterns with good ones.
- It may take a while until your reflex action is quick to respond in a proactive way to negative thinking.

5. Read God's Word

- Study what the Bible says about your worth to God. Explore what God says about His love for you and His purpose for your life. (*Give the client the verses from Biblical Insights below for starters.*)
- Keep a journal to record significant breakthroughs.

6 BIBLICAL INSIGHTS

But Moses said to God, "Who am I that I should go to Pharaoh, and that I should bring the children of Israel out of Egypt?"

Exodus 3:11

Moses was certain God was making a mistake by choosing him to lead the Israelites. His five excuses indicated a lack of confidence in his ability to get the job done. He had: a crisis of identity ("Who am I?" v. 11); a crisis of authority ("what is His name?" v. 13); a crisis of faith ("they will not believe me," 4:1); a crisis of ability ("I am not eloquent," v. 10); and a crisis of obedience ("send . . . whomever else," v. 13).

Yet as God was with him, Moses led the nation to freedom. With God's help and guidance, great things are possible.

What is man that You are mindful of him, and the son of man that You visit him? For You have made him a little lower than the angels, and You have crowned him with glory and honor.

Psalm 8:4–5

Insignificant, sinful human beings don't seem worthy of God's care. Yet God does care, for He created people "a little lower than the angels" and crowned them "with glory and honor."

He loves us so much that He sent His Son to die for us so that we could one day have the glory and honor for which He created us. We are important to God.

But now, thus says the LORD, who created you, O Jacob, and He who formed you, O Israel: "Fear not, for I have redeemed you; I have called you by your name; you are Mine."

Isaiah 43:1

Society determines people's importance based on what they do or what they know. God chose Israel to be His covenant people and to display His glory to the nations. As a nation, Israel failed to recognize their Messiah, and God established His new covenant with all who would trust Jesus Christ as Savior.

God's people know that Christ is their God, Savior, and King. Our self-esteem is not based on what we do, but on who we are in Christ.

Are not two sparrows sold for a copper coin? And not one of them falls to the ground apart from your Father's will. But the very hairs of your head are all numbered.

Matthew 10:29–30

Jesus described God's loving concern for every person, explaining that "the very hairs of your head are all numbered." He added that because God cares even for small birds—"not one of them falls to the ground apart from your Father's will"—imagine how much more He cares for His people!

What a boost to personal encouragement! We are important to God—created in His image and loved. He loves us so much, in fact, that "He gave His only begotten Son, that whoever believes in Him should not perish but have everlasting life" (John 3:16).

Your eyes saw my substance, being yet unformed. And in Your book they all were written, the days fashioned for me, when as yet there were none of them. How precious also are Your thoughts to me, O God! How great is the sum of them! If I should count them, they would be more in number than the sand.

Psalm 139:16–18

Behold what manner of love the Father has bestowed on us, that we should be called children of God!

1 John 3:1

No one can love more than God. The thought of God's astounding love bestowed on sinful humanity is beyond understanding. It's incomprehensible that, while we were still sinners in rebellion against God, Christ died for us (Rom. 5:8).

Through that sacrifice, God brought His own people to Himself, bestowing on them the title and relationship of "children." He allows us to call Him Father. No believer should ever feel alone, worthless, or unimportant. Everyone who has faith in Christ is a beloved child of God!

7 PRAYER STARTER

Thank You that Your precious child is here today, Lord, to talk about how he [she] feels of so little value. Lord, help him [her] see that he [she] is of great value to You. Help him [her] see the gifts You have given him [her] and the special "package" that he [she] is—his [her] background, interests, abilities, and ideas make him [her] Your special creation . . .

8 RECOMMENDED RESOURCES

Clinton, Tim. *The Bible for Hope: Caring for People God's Way*. Thomas Nelson, 2007.

Clinton, Tim, Archibald D. Hart, and George Ohlschlager. *Caring for People God's Way: Personal and Emotional Issues, Addictions, Grief, and Trauma*. Thomas Nelson, 2006.

Clinton, Tim, and Gary Sibcy. *Why You Do the Things You Do: The Secret to Healthy Relationships*. Thomas Nelson, 2006.

McGee, Robert S. *The Search for Significance*. Thomas Nelson, 2003.

Rainey, Dennis and Barbara. *Building Your Mate's Self-Esteem*. Thomas Nelson, 1995.

Thurman, Chris. *Finding Truth: Dispelling the Lies That Can Destroy Your Life*. American Association of Christian Counselors Courageous Living Video Series. See www.aacc.net for more information.

Websites

American Association of Christian Counselors (www.aacc.net)

Ecounseling (www.ecounseling.com)

For You formed my inward parts; You covered me in my mother's womb. I will praise You, for I am fearfully and wonderfully made; marvelous are Your works.

Psalm 139:13–14

Sexual Abuse in Childhood

PORTRAITS : 1

- Jean had never told anybody what had happened when she was growing up. She had hoped if she never talked about it, the memory would go away. After all, it had happened only once and it really wasn't that bad. She had never told her parents because she didn't think they would believe her. She had avoided her uncle as often as she could after that. She really didn't think it made sense to talk about it now.

- Betty had tried to tell him no, but he had kept touching her. She had been so excited to have been asked out by an older guy that she had tried to act more sophisticated than she felt. Now she kept having thoughts about what had happened and didn't know what she should do.

DEFINITIONS AND KEY THOUGHTS : 2

- Abuse generally is taking *unfair advantage of a difference of power* to take control of someone else.

- Childhood sexual abuse occurs when a *person exploits another, aged 17 and younger,* to satisfy the abuser's needs. It consists of any sexual activity—verbal, visual, or physical—engaged in with a minor.

- Sexual abuse is most often perpetrated by an adult who has access to a minor by virtue of *real or imagined authority* or kinship.

- When a child is abused, often *the child knows and even loves the abuser*, and this may cause intense confusion and damage.

- Sexual abuse *violates personal boundaries*. The abuser crosses a person's boundaries to take what he or she wants. A key to helping the abused person is to set up boundaries that cannot be crossed.

Trafficking and exploitation plague all nations, and no country, even ours, is immune.

Condoleezza Rice

Physical Consequences

Long-lasting physical symptoms and illnesses have been associated with sexual victimization, including chronic pelvic pain, premenstrual syndrome, gastrointestinal disorders, and a variety of chronic pain disorders, including headache, back pain, and facial pain.

Psychological Consequences

Immediate reactions to sexual abuse include shock, disbelief, denial, fear, confusion, anxiety, and withdrawal.

Victims may experience emotional detachment, sleep disturbances, and flashbacks. Approximately one-third of sexual abuse victims have symptoms that become chronic.

Sexual abuse victims often experience anxiety, guilt, nervousness, phobias, substance abuse, sleep disturbances, depression, alienation, suicidal behavior, and sexual dysfunction. Often they distrust others, replay the assault in their minds, and are at increased risk of revictimization.

Social Consequences

Sexual abuse can strain relationships because of its negative effect on the victim's family, friends, and intimate partners.

Victims of sexual violence are more likely than nonvictims to engage in risky sexual behavior, including having unprotected sex, having sex at an early age, having multiple sex partners, and trading sex for food, money, or other items.

Limits of Confidentiality

As you counsel a person who has been sexually abused, you must know the limits of confidentiality:

Sexual abuse is *illegal and must be reported.* You must *report it to the appropriate agencies,* such as local law enforcement, the Department of Social and Health Services, or Child Protective Services.

You must report sexual abuse *within a period of time,* usually between twenty-four hours and seven days.

Usually you can *report by phone, in writing, or in person.*

Even if the counselee does not admit to abuse, but you highly suspect it, you should *report your suspicions.*

If the person is over eighteen at the time of disclosure, reporting abuse may not be mandatory. However, *if the abuser still has access to children,* you may have an ethical obligation to report the abuse to protect the children.

3 ASSESSMENT INTERVIEW

Rule out any *suicidal risk, depression, or medical concerns* (especially if the abuse was recent).

> To be abused is to be touched by evil. Chronic childhood abuse does damage to the body, the mind, the emotions, and the ability to relate to another person.
>
> *Diane Langberg*

Assess for the *type of abuse* perpetrated—its degree and its history. Sometimes the person is *seeking help for other problems* that actually stem from sexual abuse. You need to get him or her to talk about the core issue. Be careful, however, not to retraumatize the person with your questions. Trust and safety are of vital importance.

Assume Three Things in the Process of Treatment

1. The problem is treatable and your client will be a survivor.
2. The client is not responsible for the abuse; he or she is only responsible for recovery.
3. To heal, your client needs to express, accept, and be prepared to deal with his or her feelings.

General Questions

1. What has happened that has brought you here today?
2. Is this the first time you've sought help?
3. Tell me about your family. How are things going at home?
4. Tell me about your past. Have you had any painful or unusual things happen—even a long time ago?
5. How long did that go on?
6. Can you tell me who was doing this to you? (*If the person seems reticent, explain that you need to know to help him or her, others who might be abused, and the abuser. In addition, if your client is a minor and still in contact with the abuser so that the abuse might recur, immediate action must be taken.*)
7. Do you know if others are being abused?
8. What problems are you currently having as a result of what has happened? (*Listen to how the abuse affected the person. No two people are alike in their experiences or the consequences of the abuse. Be aware that victims tend to minimize the impact of the abuse.*)
9. How do you feel about what has happened to you? (*The client needs to have permission to feel his or her true emotions.*)
10. Do you feel responsible for the abuse? (*Reassure the client that he or she is not alone and that he or she is not responsible for the abuse.*)
11. What do you believe about yourself? (*Dig down for unhealthy beliefs that have developed as a result of abuse. For example, what does the person think about self since he or she allowed this abuse to continue?*)
12. What do you believe about the person who is abusing you? (*Listen for rationalizations. "He couldn't help it; he was drunk." These defenses have helped the client cope, but have also made him or her less capable of seeing self as a true victim of abuse.*)
13. Have you ever tried to stop the abuse? What happened?
14. What would you like to have happen as a result of our meeting today?
15. What kinds of boundaries do you think need to be set up to protect you?

> The FBI estimates that well over 100,000 children and young women are trafficked in America today. They range in age from 9 to 19, with the average age being 11.[1]

> Approximately 1 in 6 boys is sexually abused before age 16.[2]

223

16. Who else have you told about this?

17. How did that person respond?

18. Who can help you maintain the boundaries that you set? Who will be your ally?

19. Where do you think God has been in all of this?

20. To heal from this, what do you need?

4 WISE COUNSEL

People who have been abused have had their boundaries violated in a horrible way. Healing from abuse involves *restoration of healthy boundaries and of trust*. The counseling process must be gentle and not contribute to an unintentional rewounding or shaming of the person.

Follow the client's lead in the telling of his or her story. Reassure the person that the abuse was not his or her fault.

One of the questions often asked by someone who has been sexually abused is "Why me?" Sometimes feelings of lack of value and worthlessness result from sexual abuse. As counselor, you need to keep your own anger in check to provide a safe environment so the client is able to talk freely.

5 ACTION STEPS

1. Be Patient

- Healing from sexual abuse is a process and people will vary in the amount of time required for their healing.
- It takes courage to seek help for healing, to talk about your experience, and to bring what was once in darkness into the light.

2. Grieve Your Loss

- Much has been taken from you, so you are allowed to feel the pain and grieve the loss.
- Allowing yourself to feel the feelings will help you regain some of the power you need.

3. Regain Control

- Being believed and being able to say what happened has been the first step.
- You have permission to stand strong, to say no, to be empowered over the one who has exerted power over you.

4. Find Support

- Attending a group for survivors of sexual abuse can be an excellent next step.

5. Establish Boundaries

- Now you need to learn how to take care of yourself and reestablish healthy boundaries. What are the healthy boundaries you need to establish?
- Be sure trusted people are aware of these boundaries. That's the reason others will need to be let in on what is happening—no matter how painful. You may need their help in dealing with the abuser.
- Establishing boundaries may take the form of (1) speaking the truth to the abuser, (2) having the support of others in the Christian community, and/or (3) informed withdrawal from the abuser.
- If the abuser will not honor the boundaries, then other strategies may need to be put in place.

6. Know That You Will Heal

- You do have a bright future. You're not a victim but a survivor.
- You may have lost a lot but you are not "ruined" for the future. God can heal you.

7. Trust God

- Know that God did not leave you and was not working against you as this abuse occurred.
- Plan on several more visits back to discuss the spiritual concept of God's love even in the midst of such painful circumstances.

8. Get More Intense Guidance

- *As much as you can help with the spiritual aspect, the person may need some professional guidance to truly deal with the depth of the pain that sexual abuse causes.*
- *Refer to a Christian counselor with expertise in this area.*

> The National College Women Sexual Victimization Study estimated that between 1 in 4 and 1 in 5 women experienced completed or attempted rape during their college years.[3]

BIBLICAL INSIGHTS 6

When Shechem the son of Hamor the Hivite, prince of the country, saw [Dinah], he took her and lay with her, and violated her.

Genesis 34:2

Shechem first "lay with" Dinah and "violated her," then claimed to love her and to want to marry her.

A young man may think he is in love, but to force a woman to have sex with him violates and abuses her. This does not show love at all.

The consequences of such abuse, no matter how one tries to justify it, are far-reaching and destructive.

> I waited patiently for the LORD; and He inclined to me, and heard my cry. He also brought me up out of a horrible pit, out of the miry clay, and set my feet upon a rock, and established my steps. He has put a new song in my mouth.
>
> *Psalm 40:1–3*

But as for you, you meant evil against me; but God meant it for good, in order to bring it about as it is this day, to save many people alive.

Genesis 50:20

If anyone had good reason for revenge, it was Joseph. His brothers' jealousy provoked them to horrible abuse—selling him as a common slave to be taken away forever (Gen. 37:11–28). Before being raised to power in Egypt, Joseph had lost thirteen years of personal freedom.

Joseph wisely understood that God had sovereignly overruled his brothers' abuse, making their evil turn out for good.

However, disclosing this may require some time and some healing by the victim. Stating this too close to the event would likely be very difficult for the victim to accept.

Beloved, do not avenge yourselves, but rather give place to wrath; for it is written, "Vengeance is Mine, I will repay," says the Lord. . . . Do not be overcome by evil, but overcome evil with good.

Romans 12:19, 21

God knows all that has occurred in our lives. He was present in the darkness and continues to walk with us. The offenses done to us were done to Him as well.

He promises to repay. Our job is to heal.

Do not let the evil overcome you; do not give the abuser that much power in your life. Overcome the evil by doing good to others and to yourself.

All the churches shall know that I am He who searches the minds and hearts. And I will give to each one of you according to your works.

Revelation 2:23

Sometimes people think they can hide portions of their lives from everyone. They try to hide angry tempers, deep jealousies, or sexual sin.

In His message to the church in Thyatira in the verse above, Christ stated clearly that nothing is hidden from Him.

Your abuse has not escaped His notice. The abuser may have thought he got away with it, but God knows. And God promises to judge appropriately.

PRAYER STARTER : 7

We are facing an extremely difficult situation here today, Lord, a situation that You know about but is now just coming into the light for people whom we know and love. Give us wisdom to handle this situation correctly. Bring healing to this child of Yours who has been used so wrongly . . .

RECOMMENDED RESOURCES : 8

Clinton, Tim. *The Bible for Hope: Caring for People God's Way*. Thomas Nelson, 2007.

Clinton, Tim, Archibald D. Hart, and George Ohlschlager. *Caring for People God's Way: Personal and Emotional Issues, Addictions, Grief, and Trauma*. Thomas Nelson, 2006.

Clinton, Tim, and Gary Sibcy. *Why You Do the Things You Do: The Secret to Healthy Relationships*. Thomas Nelson, 2006.

Langberg, Diane Mandt. *On the Threshold of Hope*. Tyndale House, 1999.

———. *Counseling Survivors of Sexual Abuse*. Xulon Press, 2003.

Maltz, Wendy. *The Sexual Healing Journey: A Guide for Survivors of Sexual Abuse*. Collins Living, 2001.

Morrison, Jan. *A Safe Place: Beyond Sexual Abuse*. Shaw Books, 2002.

Websites

American Association of Christian Counselors (www.aacc.net)

Ecounseling (www.ecounseling.com)

Singleness

1 PORTRAITS

- Janelle uses online dating services and speed dating experiences yet rarely finds anyone who both interests her and is interested in her.
- Bart was divorced within a year of a disastrous marriage. Now he can't seem to succeed in any relationship.
- Single after fifteen years of marriage, Ana struggles to figure out who she is as a single woman.
- Ricardo lives with his mother and rarely dates. He is painfully shy and feels that he will probably never marry.

2 DEFINITIONS AND KEY THOUGHTS

- Singleness means *being without a spouse*. People can be single because they *never married* or because they have *lost a spouse* through death or divorce.
- Some people remain *single by choice*, while others *have not met anyone* who attracts them and who is attracted to them.
- Since *women have not been encouraged to be the initiators* in romantic relationships, singleness may feel like something that is out of their control.
- Those with *mental, emotional, or physical disabilities face particular challenges* in finding a spouse.
- *Widowers often remarry* soon after the wife's death, while *widows often remain single*.
- *Being single and being alone and lonely are two different things*. Many single people would not characterize themselves as lonely at all.
- It is very helpful when churches *make single people feel welcome*. Not every activity should be for families. Seek to use the gifts of the single people in your congregation.

3 ASSESSMENT INTERVIEW

Some churches provide a welcoming atmosphere for singles, while other churches are so family-oriented that singles feel out of place. If your church is one of the former, you may have singles to counsel. If they are seeking aid, they may be uncomfortable with their singleness.

1. In your opinion, what is the reason that you are single?
2. Is your singleness your choice?
3. What is your parents' attitude toward those who aren't married? (*Some parents make children without dates feel inadequate.*)
4. Are family members pressuring you to get married?
5. Have you ever been in a close relationship—something that might have led to marriage? What happened?
6. Describe your support system—friends and family members who are "there for you." Does your support come primarily from other singles or from married people as well?
7. Do you have many opportunities to meet other singles? (*There's a wide range in singles' groups—from the dismal support group for the socially inept to the lively social group for well-adjusted singles.*)
8. What does it mean to be a "well-adjusted single"?
9. Do you think you fit that category?
10. Do you have any leisure pursuits, such as sports, hobbies, or volunteer work?
11. What is your first thought when people tell you they want to "set you up" with a friend or acquaintance of theirs?
12. What, if anything, makes marriage preferable to singleness?
13. What advantages do you think married people have?
14. What, if anything, makes singleness preferable to marriage?
15. What advantages do you think single people have?
16. Choose four terms that best describe what singleness means to you, then explain your choices:

    loneliness
    independence
    self-focus
    freedom
    poverty
    spontaneity
    burden
    outward focus
    isolation
    deprivation
    wealth
    inward focus

17. Does our culture view singleness (especially celibate singleness) as a positive or a negative state?
18. How many TV shows can you name that feature a mature single person who is celibate and happy?

> There is never a place in the Bible where it says that marriage makes you happy. It says over and over again that God makes you happy.
>
> *Dick Purnell*

19. Why are so many Christian singles made to feel "incomplete"?

20. What does the Bible teach?

4 WISE COUNSEL

Encourage the person to closely *examine his or her own beliefs about singleness.* Investigate the messages that the person received from his or her family of origin. (Some parents communicated to their children that girls without dates must be unworthy and boys without girlfriends must be gay. These destructive messages can leave an adult bereft of feelings of self-worth and independence.)

Our culture pictures those who marry as "victors" who have won "conquests" and "prizes." So what does that mean for the single person? Help the person understand the *unbiblical values exhibited by those who put down singles.*

Paul made it clear that *singleness is a high calling* that allows the single person to *focus more intensely on God.*

The single person must *come to terms with being single*—knowing that he or she is *complete and whole* as an individual in his or her relationship with Christ.

Single parents may be particularly needy, as parenting keeps them from pursuing many social engagements. They may also worry—rightly—about the effect of dating relationships on their children.

> In 2007 the average age for a first-time marriage was 27 for men and 26 for women.[1]

5 ACTION STEPS

1. Accept Your Singleness

- Live life to its fullest as you seek God's purpose and direction. Accept your singleness as a high calling with the ability, like Paul, to do things for Christ that you might not have the opportunity to do if you were married.

- Seek God in all you do. Never rush to get married.

- Realize that you are a complete and whole person in your relationship with Christ.

2. Remain Celibate

- You may be frustrated by your singleness because you are not sexually fulfilled.

- *Discuss reasons for remaining celibate (if needed, see the section on Premarital Sex).* To be celibate is the spiritual ability to have complete control over your sexual desires. This doesn't necessarily mean you have the *gift* of celibacy—just that you have a biblical mandate to live a chaste life.

- *Discuss sexual temptations and drives. Help the person discover methods for coping with these in positive ways.* Remaining chaste involves more than refraining from sexual activity; it also means bringing all sexual desires under submission to God.

- This is not easy, but if you wish to honor God with your life, you must allow God to be at the center, helping you handle your fears, desires, hopes, and dreams.

3. Get Involved

- Pursue hobbies, sports, or volunteer work so you can meet new people.
- Find a church that has a strong singles program. Lacking that, find a church that provides opportunities for all church members to mix and have fun together. The same activities will both encourage fellowship and sharing and help you get to know new people, including other singles.
- You need a community of friends whom you can trust and with whom you can share activities and interests.
- You need a balance of male and female friends.

4. Learn to Love the Quiet

- Learning contemplation and solitude may help you feel more comfortable with being alone. This teaches that *alone* is not a synonym for *lonely*.
- Learn to listen to God in the undistracted quiet.

> Chastity is a requisite of Christian singleness. Furthermore, chastity is possible. There will always be somebody to suggest that such thinking is legalistic, unreasonable, and unlikely to succeed. My reply can only be: "When it's bigger than I am, so is God."
>
> *Rosalie de Rosset*

BIBLICAL INSIGHTS 6

And the LORD God said, "It is not good that man should be alone; I will make him a helper comparable to him."

Genesis 2:18

God's provision of a "helper" for Adam was not a condescending comment on singleness but an approval of marriage. God was concerned for Adam's loneliness, for He created people to have relationships—with Him and with others.

Though issues may differ, each one faces the potential problems of aloneness, such as isolation, insecurity, and feelings of rejection. Being "unattached" can foster destructive responses, or it can encourage the development of a deeper relationship with God. There's nothing wrong with being single—just don't go it alone!

Then Miriam the prophetess, the sister of Aaron, took the timbrel in her hand; and all the women went out after her with timbrels and with dances.

Exodus 15:20

Miriam, most likely a single woman, played a significant role in the spiritual life of Israel, and she is the first woman to be called a prophetess.

Singleness never denotes inferiority—God has special work for all of His people, whether they are single or married.

In the United States, in 2005, there were 103 women for every 100 men.[2]

Now there was one, Anna, a prophetess, the daughter of Phanuel, of the tribe of Asher. She was of a great age, and had lived with a husband seven years from her virginity; and this woman was a widow of about eighty-four years, who did not depart from the temple, but served God with fastings and prayers night and day.

Luke 2:36–37

Anna was very young when her husband died and then she was a widow for eighty-four years. Anna remained single, choosing to give her life to serving God through fasting and prayer.

People are single for a number of reasons, and they respond to singleness in different ways. Some single people, like Anna, seek to serve God without concern about marriage; others dearly long for a spouse.

It is important to remember that the key to a fulfilled single life is contentment in God. He has places of service for all people—married or single.

But I say to the unmarried and to the widows: It is good for them if they remain even as I am.

1 Corinthians 7:8

Single people must not let family or friends put undue pressure on them to get married. If they feel like they have to be in a relationship in order to be accepted by others, then they are susceptible to being used and hurt by others, or they will use and hurt others in order to be in a relationship of convenience.

Alan Corry

Some have understood this passage to mean that all single people should remain that way. But Paul's words must be understood with his analysis of his cultural context and his mission.

As a single man, Paul understood the need for people to be able to do whatever it took to share the gospel with unbelievers. He knew that persecution could come at any time. His words reveal his total commitment to his call.

He encouraged single people not to apologize for their singleness. They should not seek to be married as if that were all that mattered. God has an important calling for single people, since they can "serve the Lord without distraction" (1 Cor. 7:35).

A married person has many responsibilities, while a single person can be freer to work for the gospel. Neither state is better than the other; different circumstances create different opportunities.

Singleness can be used for God's glory. Whether a person has never been married or has become single by way of divorce or bereavement, a single person is not set aside by God. He has great things for single people to accomplish for His kingdom.

Single people must get their own priorities straight—seeking God and His will above all. Single believers are never alone, because God is always with them.

PRAYER STARTER 7

Dear Lord, _____ is feeling uncomfortable with being single. Please reveal to him [her] Your special purpose for his [her] life as a single person. Encourage him [her]; bring friends and family around him [her] who can help him [her] achieve a new appreciation for his [her] singleness. Give him [her] the wisdom to see his [her] opportunities for service and enable him [her] to serve You with joy . . .

RECOMMENDED RESOURCES 8

Clinton, Tim. *The Bible for Hope: Caring for People God's Way*. Thomas Nelson, 2007.

Clinton, Tim, Archibald D. Hart, and George Ohlschlager. *Caring for People God's Way: Personal and Emotional Issues, Addictions, Grief, and Trauma*. Thomas Nelson, 2006.

Hammond, Michelle McKinney. *Sassy, Single, and Satisfied: Secrets to Loving the Life You're Living*. Harvest House, 2003.

Leutwiler, Carolyn. *Singleness Redefined: Living Life to the Fullest*. P & R Publishing, 2008.

Martin, Cheryl. *First Class Single*. Salem Communications, 2003.

Stedman, Rick. *Your Single Treasure: Good News about Singles and Sexuality*. Moody, 2000.

Websites

American Association of Christian Counselors (www.aacc.net)

Ecounseling (www.ecounseling.com)

Spiritual Warfare

1 PORTRAITS

- Nothing's ever easy for Jenny. No matter what she does, it ends in heartache and failure. She's beginning to think that she shouldn't try anything new.
- Jim is in the hospital again. Just when he thought he was on the mend, he began to have those recurring symptoms.
- Pastor Scott's first year in the ministry was harder than he ever imagined possible. He had to combat against one obstacle after another. Now he's added depression to his list of barriers.

2 DEFINITIONS AND KEY THOUGHTS

- "Spiritual warfare" can conjure up all sorts of images of demonic possession and exorcisms. Other images might include people speaking in an unknown voice or having convulsions or not having control of their own actions. For the purposes of this guide, we must understand *the definition* to be much *broader and simpler* than those images may imply.
- *Spiritual warfare, simply put, is a struggle between light and darkness.* God has secured the victory, but Satan still attempts to wage war against God and His people. *Light* is sourced in God and infuses all that is good; *darkness* is sourced in Satan and permeates all that is evil.

  Psalm 18:28—For You will light my lamp; the Lord my God will enlighten my darkness.

  Isaiah 9:2—The people who walked in darkness have seen a great light.

  John 1:5—The light shines in the darkness, and the darkness did not comprehend it.

  John 3:19—This is the condemnation, that the light has come into the world, and men loved darkness rather than light, because their deeds were evil.

  John 8:12—Then Jesus spoke to them again, saying, "I am the light of the world. He who follows Me shall not walk in darkness, but have the light of life."

  John 12:46—I have come *as* a light into the world, that whoever believes in Me should not abide in darkness.

Acts 26:18—to open their eyes, in order to turn them from darkness to light, and from the power of Satan to God, that they may receive forgiveness of sins and an inheritance among those who are sanctified by faith in Me.

2 Corinthians 4:6—For it is the God who commanded light to shine out of darkness, who has shone in our hearts to give the light of the knowledge of the glory of God in the face of Jesus Christ.

2 Corinthians 6:14—Do not be unequally yoked together with unbelievers. For what fellowship has righteousness with lawlessness? And what communion has light with darkness?

Ephesians 5:11—Have no fellowship with the unfruitful works of darkness, but rather expose them.

Colossians 1:13—He has delivered us from the power of darkness and conveyed us into the kingdom of the Son of His love.

- All believers face spiritual warfare. If you belong to Jesus, then you will engage in a war against the darkness. Sometimes it is very *clear and evident* and at other times it is more *subtle and elusive.* But regardless of our awareness, we all engage in the battle.

- The victory is in direct proportion to our willingness to surrender to Jesus Christ. We don't win by our own strength or by our own intelligence or strategies. *We win by submitting to Jesus and resting in His authority over Satan.*

- Romans 6:16 says, "Do you not know that to whom you present yourselves slaves to obey, you are that one's slaves whom you obey, whether of sin leading to death, or of obedience leading to righteousness?" We will submit to something. Submitting to darkness leads to death and submitting to the Lord leads to righteousness.

- Putting on the full armor of God is key in battling against evil.

    Ephesians 6:11–17—Put on the whole armor of God, that you may be able to stand against the wiles of the devil. For we do not wrestle against flesh and blood, but against principalities, against powers, against the rulers of the darkness of this age, against spiritual hosts of wickedness in the heavenly places. Therefore take up the whole armor of God, that you may be able to withstand in the evil day, and having done all, to stand. Stand therefore, having girded your waist with truth, having put on the breastplate of righteousness, and having shod your feet with the preparation of the gospel of peace; above all, taking the shield of faith with which you will be able to quench all the fiery darts of the wicked one. And take the helmet of salvation, and the sword of the Spirit, which is the word of God.

- These verses found in Ephesians are *not a magical formula* that defeats the enemy when recited like a mantra. It is a biblical truth conveyed in a word picture. For example, putting on the belt of truth simply means that we are to know and to adhere to the truth as spelled out for us in God's Word.

- It is important *not to overemphasize* demonic influences in our lives; at the same time, it is important *not to underemphasize* the fact that we do have an enemy

> You are but a poor soldier of Christ if you think you can overcome without fighting and suppose you can have the crown without the conflict.
>
> *St. John Chrysostom*

235

who leads an army of demons. Their job description is to steal, kill, and destroy (see John 10:10).

- The enemy wants to harm us, yet God promises to protect us. When we step *outside of God's will,* we automatically open up the door for the enemy to sow seeds of destruction. This doesn't mean that all struggles involve demons, but consistently opening ourselves up to evil will bring us into contact with the evil one and his messengers. Discernment becomes important when determining demonic involvement in a person's life.

- Sometimes spiritual warfare occurs because a person is right *in the middle of God's will.* Bible giants such as Daniel, David, Paul, and even Jesus himself fought against the schemes of the devil.

3 : ASSESSMENT INTERVIEW

People don't often come in for counseling complaining about the struggles of spiritual warfare. It takes *discernment* to be able to ascertain when and why people are engaging in spiritual warfare.

What the counselor should look for are:

Doors that were opened or places in the person's life that were repeatedly exposed to sin. (For example, pornography opens the door for sexual problems and dissatisfaction, which if left untreated can lead to sexual abuse.) The person has stepped outside of God's will and needs to get back in by way of repentance.

Projects, persons, or victories in the person's life that could shed light on why Satan is after him or her. The person may be in God's will and needs to put on all the armor, stay strong, and continue to resist the devil.

1. Tell me what brings you here today.
2. When did you first begin to experience these problems?
3. Can you tell me about your life when these problems first began?
4. What was your relationship with the Lord like during that time period?
5. Was anything happening in your life that brought conviction from the Lord?
6. Is there anything in your life that has an addictive quality about it? If so, explain.
7. Do you ever feel like you do things that you shouldn't?
8. Are there thoughts that seem to plague you?
9. What temptations have you faced recently?
10. Do you feel that there is anything you don't have control over?
11. What solutions have you tried?

> In heaven we shall appear, not in armor, but in robes of glory. But here these are to be worn night and day; we must walk, work, and sleep in them, or else we are not true soldiers of Christ.
>
> *William Gurnall*

WISE COUNSEL : 4

"Therefore submit to God. *Resist the devil* and he will flee from you" (James 4:7). *This is the promise* that we can lean on.

The issue may be *the length of time one has to resist*. Too often *people don't resist long enough*. Many times we short-circuit our own efforts by giving up too quickly. Meditate on the promise and resist until you see victory; be assured that victory will come.

ACTION STEPS : 5

Exposure to Sin

If it is determined that resisting the devil is needed because of sin that has come into the counselee's life, then a vital issue within the counseling process is *how the person should go about resisting*. Dean Sherman writes in his book *Spiritual Warfare* that there are three battlefields that need to be fortified against an attack. These battlefields are the mind, the heart, and the mouth. If the person fortifies his life in these three areas, he or she will be waging war from a point of strength. The person will be closing any of those "open doors" that began the battle in the first place. The enemy will not have a way into his or her life and therefore will not be able to influence the person. God will have free access.

1. Confess Any Known Sin

- The only way to get free from Satan's grip is to know where he's holding on.
- Honestly determine the source, then confess and willingly give up your sin.

2. Fortify Your Mind

- How do you fortify the mind? Take every thought captive (see 2 Cor. 10:5).
- Think about pure and godly things (see Phil. 4:8).
- A person cannot think of two things simultaneously. He or she can have two different thoughts in rapid succession, but not at exactly the same time. So you can combat impure thoughts by purposely thinking pure thoughts.

3. Purify Your Heart

- When the Bible uses the word *heart*, it refers to our innermost being. It is more than just thoughts; it is also our emotions and attitudes.
- Stand guard against any bitterness (see Heb. 12:15). Too often people open up the door to strife because they have been treated unfairly and think they have a right to retaliate. Let God retaliate for you (Rom. 12:19).
- If you hold onto it, that bitter root will blossom into pain for both you and the other person. Remember that your own emotions must be filtered through God's Word. If you are not careful, unchecked emotions may lead to sin (see James 1:14–27).

> The Christian life is not a playground; it is a battleground.
> *Warren W. Wiersbe*

4. Guard Your Mouth

- Proverbs 18:21 says, "Death and life are in the power of the tongue." The tongue is small but can do great damage (James 3:2–12).
- Be careful to speak godly things.

Victories in the Christian Life

If it is determined that resisting the devil is needed because of victories in the faith—big projects that Satan wants to hinder, ministries Satan doesn't want to happen, and so on—encourage the person to put on daily the whole armor of God.

1. Pray for Insight

- Be sensitive to God's leading if indeed there is sin in your life. Never assume there isn't!
- Be sensitive to what might be happening in the spiritual realm regarding the situation at hand. Ask God for discernment.

2. Get Dressed!

- *Gird your waist with truth.* The belt was the foundation for the Roman soldier's armor. The truth of the gospel is the foundation of the Christian life, the standard by which we measure everything else. When Satan speaks lies, you must counter with the truth from God's Word.
- *Put on the breastplate of righteousness.* The breastplate protected a soldier's vital organs, covering his body from neck to thighs. The righteousness you put on is not your own, but Christ's, bought for you by His precious blood. Because you are God's child, when Satan attacks with doubts and strikes at the vital parts of your faith and life, counter with the righteousness you have because of Jesus. You are protected because you are His child.
- *Put on shoes of the preparation of the gospel of peace.* You have peace with God because of what Christ has done, and peace to carry you through life because of Christ's promise: "Peace I leave with you, My peace I give to you; not as the world gives do I give to you. Let not your heart be troubled, neither let it be afraid" (John 14:27). When Satan wants to make you worry or keep you up at night, remember your shoes.
- *Take the shield of faith.* A soldier's shield protected him in hand-to-hand combat and against "fiery darts" being shot from a city's walls. Your faith is your total dependence on God. When you hold your shield of faith, nothing Satan sends your way can hurt you.
- *Take the helmet of salvation.* Every soldier must protect his head. You were saved when you trusted Christ as Savior and were rescued from sin's bondage. The helmet of salvation can protect your mind from the doubts that creep in. When you know, beyond a doubt, that you are saved, Satan can do nothing to affect you.

> Spiritual warfare is part of every Christian's daily life. We triumph as we walk by faith in Christ, who turns us from darkness to light, from the power of Satan to God, forgiving sin, and giving us a place among those who are sanctified by faith.
>
> *David Powlison*

- *Take the sword of the Spirit, which is the Word of God.* Your offensive weapon is your knowledge of God's Word. With it, you will be prepared to answer all of Satan's attacks.

BIBLICAL INSIGHTS : 6

How you are fallen from heaven, O Lucifer, son of the morning! . . . For you have said in your heart: "I will ascend into heaven, I will exalt my throne above the stars of God." . . . Yet you shall be brought down to Sheol, to the lowest depths of the Pit.

Isaiah 14:12–15

Although Isaiah's message was directed against the king of Babylon, many believe the imagery parallels the fall of Satan. The evil one may have power on earth for a brief time, but God's judgment on him has already been determined.

As we fight battles against evil, we must remember that the war has already been won.

And He said to them, "I saw Satan fall like lightning from heaven. Behold, I give you the authority to trample on serpents and scorpions, and over all the power of the enemy, and nothing shall by any means hurt you."

Luke 10:18–19

All believers face the constant struggle between good and evil as Satan tries to rule our lives.

Jesus has already defeated Satan and has won this battle through His death and resurrection. Even though the battle continues, we can be assured that, with Jesus's help, the important victory—eternal life—is already ours.

For we do not wrestle against flesh and blood, but against principalities, against powers, against the rulers of the darkness of this age, against spiritual hosts of wickedness in the heavenly places.

Ephesians 6:12

> No soldiers of Christ are ever lost, missing, or left dead on the battlefield.
>
> *John Charles Ryle*

The spiritual realm has two sides—God's side and Satan's side. Those who have accepted Christ as Savior are on God's side; this automatically makes them enemies of Satan.

Our battle is against forces that are real and powerful, and they should not be underestimated. Their goal is to make believers ineffective for God's kingdom and to keep unbelievers away from God.

The battle rages constantly, usually beyond our earthly vision. At times, however, we see it clearly when we face temptation, difficulty, and trials.

Evil knows our weaknesses; Satan knows where to attack. Our strength for the battle is in God.

Be sober, be vigilant; because your adversary the devil walks about like a roaring lion, seeking whom he may devour.

1 Peter 5:8

The moment a person becomes a Christian, Satan tries to make him or her ineffective through sin or through struggles with discouragement or suffering. Believers must be sober and vigilant, resisting Satan by remaining "steadfast in the faith" (1 Peter 5:9). This is a strong defensive action.

Satan is a defeated enemy, so believers need not fear him. When we resist Satan, he will flee (James 4:7).

We resist Satan through maintaining our steadfast faith in Christ, wearing the armor that God provides, and remembering that we are not alone in our suffering.

7 PRAYER STARTER

Lord, we pray about the spiritual battle being faced today. The enemy wants to defeat our friend, and we want to claim the promises that You make in Your Word of victory over Satan and all of his schemes . . .

8 RECOMMENDED RESOURCES

Clinton, Tim. *The Bible for Hope: Caring for People God's Way.* Thomas Nelson, 2007.

Clinton, Tim, Archibald D. Hart, and George Ohlschlager. *Caring for People God's Way: Personal and Emotional Issues, Addictions, Grief, and Trauma.* Thomas Nelson, 2006.

Ingram, Chip. *The Invisible War.* Baker, 2008.

Murphy, Ed. *The Handbook for Spiritual Warfare.* Thomas Nelson, 2003.

Sherman, Dean. *Spiritual Warfare for Every Christian: How to Live in Victory and Retake the Land.* YWAM Publishing, 1989.

Websites
American Association of Christian Counselors (www.aacc.net)

Ecounseling (www.ecounseling.com)

Stress

PORTRAITS | 1

- John sat on the side of the hospital bed and buttoned his shirt. Yesterday he had been sure he was having a heart attack. His chest had been tight and he had struggled to breathe. But today, after many tests, his doctor told him that his heart was fine. Nothing was physically wrong. "I think you're under a lot of stress," his doctor had told him and had recommended seeing a counselor.

- Kailey has been through a lot lately. Her husband lost his job and the bill collectors are beginning to call. In addition, her mom has been sick, her kids have been having difficulty in school, and the water heater just died. Kailey doesn't think she can handle one more crisis.

- Micah is trying to be a good student, but lately things have been tough. His mom and dad are getting a divorce, his grades are slipping, he lost his place on the basketball team for missing too many practices, and he has finals next week. Micah feels completely overwhelmed.

DEFINITIONS AND KEY THOUGHTS | 2

- Stress is defined as the "normal, internal, physiological mechanism that *adapts us to change.*"

- Stress is a normal part of life and *can be positive*, alerting us to a problem area needing attention and helping us respond to it.

- Stress *can also be negative* when a person is constantly stressed without relief or relaxation between challenges.

- Sometimes stress comes from a *difficult life situation*, but sometimes stress results from *perceptions* about life situations, such as worries about failure and perfectionistic tendencies.

- Stress without relief can lead to *physical symptoms,* such as headaches, upset stomach, elevated blood pressure, chest pain, and problems sleeping.

> In 2008, 53 percent of Americans report feeling more fatigued, up from 51 percent in 2007.[1]

- *Some personalities cause stress* in themselves and in others. Some people may have extremely driven or perfectionistic personalities or may live or work with someone who does, thereby feeling the stress of the other person's drivenness.

- Stress can be harmful if it *affects a person's relationships adversely.*

- Stress can *affect the body, mind, and spirit.* Pay attention to each area to reduce the effects of stress on overall well-being.
- If we do not learn to control stress, it will eventually *control us.* We need not be overwhelmed by stress. Philippians 4:6–7 says, "Be anxious for nothing, but in everything by prayer and supplication, with thanksgiving, let your requests be made known to God; and the peace of God, which surpasses all understanding, will guard your hearts and minds through Christ Jesus."

3　ASSESSMENT INTERVIEW

Fifty-two percent of Americans say they are lying awake at night.[2]

1. What brings you here today?
2. What would you say are the stressors in your life right now?
3. Are you being caused stress by someone else (for example, a stressful spouse or boss)?
4. Are you causing your own stress by being a perfectionist or trying to control situations over which you have no control?
5. What percentage of your total stress is being caused by each of these stressors?
6. How long has each of those stressors been present?
7. Tell me about each stressor. (*Get as many details as you can so you can begin to assess how the person views these stressors.*)
8. How realistic is it that the things you're worried about will happen? (*For example, if the person is experiencing persistent fears of job loss, is this fear based in current reality?*)
9. With whom do you talk about your stressors? (*The impact of stress is greater if an individual feels that he or she is alone in handling it.*)
10. Are those people helpful to you?

Twenty-six percent of workers report that they are "often or very often" burned out or stressed by their work.[3]

11. Are you using other things to handle the stress (for example, sports, drugs—either OTC or prescription—alcohol, excessive television or computer use)?
12. Where do you experience the least stress in your life?
13. Is there any place where you do *not* experience stress?
14. Is change possible? Is there any way you can think of to reduce your stress level?
15. If not, what are some healthy ways you can think of to handle the stress you're currently under?

4　WISE COUNSEL

If the person is experiencing physical effects of the stress and hasn't seen a physician, encourage him or her to *schedule a physical.*

Are there *immediate situational stressors* that need attention, such as resolving a concern in the workplace or finding help for a problem with a child?

Assess ways to *provide a break* from the stress. Suggest exercise, frequent breaks throughout the day to pray and meditate on a Bible verse, sharing burdens with a trusted friend, taking a vacation.

Because stress affects the mind, body, and spirit, the person needs to protect all three:

To protect the mind, think truthfully, refuse to make mountains out of molehills, and set priorities.

To protect the body, get enough sleep, eat well, and learn to breathe deeply.

To protect the spirit, meditate on God and His Word, learn to trust God, and pray without ceasing.

ACTION STEPS 5

1. Gain Perspective

- Gain some perspective on what is causing the stress.
- "Break apart" the stress overload into manageable pieces.
- Begin to address each component.

2. Consider What God Is Doing

- One of the best antidotes to stress is seeing God's purposes in the difficulties.
- God may use certain situations to develop one of the fruits of the Spirit in you. Knowing that God uses every situation, even the petty, irritating situations of life, to teach you to become more like Jesus can help you feel less stressed by things you cannot control.

> Do not anticipate trouble, or worry about what may never happen. Keep in the sunlight.
>
> *Benjamin Franklin*

3. Get Alone with God

- Planned times of quiet and solitude are a good balance to a busy life. Cultivating a heart of prayer helps you see God's perspective and to more fully experience His presence throughout the day (Ps. 16:8–11).
- Many use prayer as a way to change a stressful situation. Although this is not a bad idea, prayer often does not change the situation as much as it changes you.
- As you purposely quiet your heart each day, the Holy Spirit has a chance to change the way you see your stressful situation.

4. Share Your Burden with Others

- This can be done literally or figuratively. In other words, talking about your stressors can bring relief and prayer support.

- Perhaps some of the stress is because you're doing too much. Even Moses had to delegate when he got overwhelmed (Exod. 18:13–26). Maybe you can do the same.

5. Guard Your Heart

Stress not only dampens our spirits and frazzles our nerves, but the constant rush of adrenaline overstimulates the heart and can weaken the immune system, leaving us prone to more illnesses and stress related problems.

Leslie Vernick

- Stress has a way of orienting us toward the things that are wrong in our lives.
- Guard your heart and mind against negativity and pessimism. Take time each day to check your thinking and take every thought captive to the obedience of Christ (2 Cor. 10:5).

6. Live Intentionally

- Stop majoring in minor things. At the end of life, many will realize that they spent most of their time on what mattered least, and the least time on what mattered most.
- Decide what is really important, choose your priorities, and live for them. Become more intentional about the way you spend your time and energy. Learn to say no to things that are just not that important.

7. Remember Your Limits

- Often our lives become filled with stress because we refuse to accept our limits.
- Feeling overwhelmed may be a reminder that you are not living within the limits and boundaries that God has created for you. It may be time to reevaluate, cut back, say no, or slow down.

8. Laugh a Little

- Allow for some levity in your life. A comic strip, a favorite saying, a joke. Keep these within sight.

6 BIBLICAL INSIGHTS

You will keep him in perfect peace, whose mind is stayed on You, because he trusts in You.

Isaiah 26:3

Jesus reminded His followers: "In the world you will have tribulation" (John 16:33). The prophet Isaiah wrote that God gives peace in spite of conflict and turmoil.

Peace is so basic to God's nature that it is part of His name. God the Father is the "God of peace" (Phil. 4:9; Heb. 13:20). God the Son is the Prince of Peace (Isa. 9:6).

The Holy Spirit produces peace in our lives (Gal. 5:22). To have "perfect peace," wrote Isaiah, we must focus our minds on God and trust in Him.

Let not your heart be troubled; you believe in God, believe also in Me.

John 14:1

The disciples were bewildered and discouraged. Jesus had said He was going away, that He would die, that one of the disciples was a traitor, and that Peter would deny Him.

"Let not your heart be troubled," Jesus told them. Believers can rest their troubled hearts, knowing that Jesus is in control regardless of the circumstances.

Persecuted, but not forsaken; struck down, but not destroyed . . .

2 Corinthians 4:9

For us, each day is filled with different levels of stress. Regardless of occupation, age, social status, or lifestyle, we experience stress.

Some stress we bring on ourselves—because of poor planning, saying yes too often, or being disorganized. Hopefully we learn our lesson so it won't happen again.

Stress also arises from factors outside our control—the weather, a broken computer, an unexpected difficulty or sorrow. At those times, we can control only our reactions to the stress. Our reactions reveal our character and our trust in God.

Be anxious for nothing, but in everything by prayer and supplication, with thanksgiving, let your requests be made known to God; and the peace of God, which surpasses all understanding, will guard your hearts and minds through Christ Jesus.

Philippians 4:6–7

Stress and its companion, worry, do their best to immobilize believers. People are anxious about the future; they are anxious about events that haven't happened but *could* happen.

So what can believers do about their stresses? When we give our stress to God, He replaces it with His peace that "surpasses all understanding."

When we feel stress rising, we should turn to God in prayer. He will give us the peace He promised.

My brethren, count it all joy when you fall into various trials, knowing that the testing of your faith produces patience.

James 1:2–3

> Of all doctor's office visits, 75–90 percent are for stress-related ailments and complaints.[4]

> Many of us crucify ourselves between two thieves—regret for the past and fear of the future.
>
> *Unknown*

245

Everyone faces trials in one form or another. We cannot control what we will encounter but we can control the stress level that situations cause. Instead of being stressed, we can try being joyful.

This is not a natural reaction, but one that the Holy Spirit can provide. It means choosing an attitude that looks expectantly to the lessons God will teach and the wisdom He will provide. There's no better prescription for dealing with stress.

7 PRAYER STARTER

Thank You, Lord, that _____ has come today for help in relieving this burden of stress. You never intended for Your children to live overwhelmed and unhealthy lives by carrying undue amounts of stress all by ourselves. Give us wisdom to handle what we can, Lord, and we ask for Your hand in the situations that are beyond our control . . .

8 RECOMMENDED RESOURCES

Clinton, Tim. *The Bible for Hope: Caring for People God's Way.* Thomas Nelson, 2007.

Clinton, Tim, Archibald D. Hart, and George Ohlschlager. *Caring for People God's Way: Personal and Emotional Issues, Addictions, Grief, and Trauma.* Thomas Nelson, 2006.

Hager, W. David, and Linda Carruth. *Stress and the Woman's Body.* Revell, 1998.

Hart, Archibald D. *Adrenaline and Stress: The Exciting New Breakthrough That Helps You Overcome Stress Damage.* W Publishing Group, 1995.

Swenson, Richard A. *Margin: Restoring Emotional, Physical, Financial and Time Reserves to Overloaded Lives.* NavPress, 2004.

Websites

American Association of Christian Counselors (www.aacc.net)

Ecounseling (www.ecounseling.com)

When you're laughing, your attention is focused. You can't do anything else. Everything else, whether it's depression or stress, stops.

Robert Leone

Suffering

PORTRAITS | 1

- Janet bit the inside of her cheek to fight back tears. Her friend chatted blithely on about their family going to the church picnic next week, and Janet nodded woodenly and smiled. Inside she was in such pain. She knew her family wouldn't be going to the picnic. No one could understand what it was like for her to continue to live in the marriage that she had committed to ten years ago. Her husband wasn't a believer, and the day-to-day pain of loving and respecting her husband when he did not return her love and commitment was so very difficult.

- Bob just couldn't get through the pain. The death of his eldest son in a car accident had caused a hole in his heart that no one could fill. He couldn't even seem to function with his other children or his wife because the pain was so fresh every morning and the suffering so intense. If only their last conversation had not been an argument.

- Mark and Jill lost everything in the recent flooding on the Mississippi River. Their house was destroyed, and few of the objects inside were even salvageable. They have the clothes on their backs, a few books, a family Bible, and two cots at the local Salvation Army.

> Never judge God by suffering, but judge suffering by the Cross.
>
> *Father Andrew*

DEFINITIONS AND KEY THOUGHTS | 2

- Suffering comes for *many reasons*:

  - Suffering may come as a result of *personal sin and failure*. For example, some people may suffer financially by not carefully budgeting their money or by being wasteful. Some people may suffer the loss of friendship through their hurtful words or gossip.

  - Suffering may also arise due to *other people's sin and failure*, such as the drunk driver who causes an accident and creates suffering for others.

  - Suffering can arise from *forces outside of our control*. For example, a tornado or hurricane can create great suffering for many people.

  - Suffering can come as a *result of a person's faith*—standing for Jesus in some parts of the world is an invitation to persecution.

- The Bible is replete with passages that describe why suffering is a part of life:

– Deserved suffering occurs when we sin or act foolishly—1 Peter 4:15.

– Undeserved suffering is part of following in Jesus's footsteps—1 Peter 2:21.

– Suffering encourages growth—2 Corinthians 12:9–10.

– Suffering may be for testing and to demonstrate God's glory—John 9:1–3.

– We may suffer to help others—2 Corinthians 1:3–5.

- Helping others in pain requires a *"theology" of suffering.* How do you see God using suffering in the lives of those with whom you work? How do you see God using suffering in your own life?

- Suffering is common to all people and is not removed by the presence of the Holy Spirit. Being a Christian is not a "get out of suffering free" card. *Christians experience suffering* like everyone else.

- Sometimes *God sends suffering* into our lives and we do not know why. His promise to us is not to make our suffering understandable but to be present with us in it.

- Needless suffering, such as refusing to take medication, is not taught in Scripture. There is *no merit to simply enduring pain for suffering's sake.*

- Suffering is easier to deal with when it is *purposeful* (2 Tim. 4:6–8) and when there is an *end in sight.* Romans 8:22–23 says, "For we know that the whole creation groans and labors with birth pangs together until now. Not only that, but we also who have the firstfruits of the Spirit, even we ourselves groan within ourselves, eagerly waiting for the adoption, the redemption of our body."

- Suffering *produces character* in us. By contrast our culture views suffering as evidence that we are failing in some way or that we are doing something wrong.

- Guard against wanting to "fix things" or give answers too quickly. It is much more important to *listen.*

> I consider that the sufferings of this present time are not worthy to be compared with the glory which shall be revealed in us.
>
> *Romans 8:18*

3 ASSESSMENT INTERVIEW

Rule Outs

1. Are you suffering physically? Is there pain that needs to be handled? (*If the person is suffering physically, be sure that he or she has gotten adequate medical treatment and if not, encourage him or her to do so.*)

2. On a scale of 1 to 10, with 1 being "feeling terrific" and 10 being "feeling suicidal," where would you place yourself on most days? (*If you sense that the person is suicidal, deal with that issue first. See the section on Suicide and get outside help.*)

General Questions

1. What is going on in your life right now? (*When someone is in pain, it is important not to move too quickly to answers. Begin by trying to understand the situation and empathize with the person in it.*)
2. How can I be of the most help to you?
3. How do you understand your situation?
4. How long have you been facing this pain?
5. Can you give it a definite starting point (a certain event) or is it more vague?
6. Who is walking with you through the pain?
7. What is your support system?
8. With whom are you the most honest?
9. How is this suffering affecting the other parts of your life?
10. Do you see an end to the suffering or of the intensity you're currently experiencing?
11. How is your relationship with God right now?
12. Do you see God's hand at work in any way in your suffering?

> A Christian is someone who shares the sufferings of God in the world.
> *Dietrich Bonhoeffer*

WISE COUNSEL : 4

God promises that "a bruised reed He will not break" (Isa. 42:3). As a Christian counselor, you should endeavor to model your caring after His and *not burden a person who is already suffering.*

If the person is suffering for the *consequences of his or her own sin,* he or she may also be dealing with guilt and shame. You will need to help the individual confess sin, assess the lessons learned, and come up with an action plan to move forward.

If the person's suffering is because *of someone else's sin or failure,* listen to the story and gently guide the person to ways that he or she can walk through the pain and get to the other side.

If the person's suffering is due to *circumstances beyond his or her control* (an illness, a natural disaster, such as a fire or tornado), begin to assess steps to take that will help him or her handle the situation. Taken in one big chunk, the situation is way too big to handle, but taken one step at a time, the person can get through it.

Remind the individual that suffering can do three things in his or her life, if the person lets it:

Despite its painfulness, suffering can be very valuable. Suffering *clarifies what the heart truly worships,* especially when the pain is unexplained and unabated. Does the client worship the idea of deliverance or the Deliverer?

Suffering also *purifies the heart* by deepening the desire for the day when all tears will be wiped away. The client's growing discontent with the sin and evil in this world increases his or her hopefulness for heaven.

Suffering not only clarifies and purifies, but it also *motivates the heart to action.* If we see a child cry, we offer tenderness. If we see the wounds of a victim, we offer solace. Human suffering arouses anger, invigorates action, and as a result, enables us to push back some of the darkness of the fall. Suffering humanizes the heart and increases hunger for God.

Offer *comfort* and *encouragement. Name any strengths* that you see in the one who is suffering. Silently *pray for the discernment* to understand what God is doing in this person's life.

5 ACTION STEPS

1. Trust God

- Sometimes God allows suffering to come into believers' lives to strengthen their faith.
- Rejoice because of what God will do in your life and what He promises for your future.
- Cast your cares on Christ because His faithfulness never changes (Ps. 46; 2 Cor. 12:7–10; Heb. 13:8).
- Allow God to help you endure (Rom. 8:18; 2 Cor. 4:7–10; 2 Tim. 2:12; 1 Peter 4:12–13).

2. Seek His Lessons

- What do you think God is teaching you in this situation?
- What would you like to learn? How would you like to come out of it at the other end?

3. Seek His Actions

- What could God possibly be doing in your situation? Where do you see His hand at work?
- Which of the lessons above (how suffering clarifies, purifies, and motivates the heart) do you think God is teaching you right now?

4. Take Small Steps Forward

- What small step can you take today to move through the pain?
- What do you need to do to function effectively at home, at work, and other places?
- What small step can you take today to begin the process of rebuilding your life?

> Suffering doesn't happen just to people. The Bible teaches that creation itself is suffering until a day when it will be redeemed. God Himself suffers, and looks forward to the day when He will bring His people to be with Him.
>
> *Dan Allender*

5. Get Support

- You should be in a small group that will help walk you through the pain, follow up with you, and help you take some of the needed action steps.
- In addition, find a support group of people who have faced similar pain. This can be a huge help as they will have advice that has been tested "in the trenches."

BIBLICAL INSIGHTS 6

Then Job arose, tore his robe, and shaved his head; and he fell to the ground and worshiped. And he said: "Naked I came from my mother's womb, and naked shall I return there. The LORD gave, and the LORD has taken away; blessed be the name of the LORD."

Job 1:20–21

God never explained Job's suffering or helped him make sense of his loss. Instead, God underlined the reality of His sovereignty and the fact that He acts on His own without human advice or explanation. He expects people to trust Him and His goodness regardless of what happens.

Although Job's health and wealth were eventually restored, that is not the central message of the story. The book of Job shows us that our love for God must not be conditioned on how we think He is treating us. Great suffering well borne is an indication of unshakable trust in God.

Faith in God must be maintained through times of trial as well as times of blessing. Such faith reflects God's nature in us, His redeeming power in Christ, and His unconditional love toward us.

No matter what we face in life, we can trust that God is in control. We must rely on Him and His goodness.

> One sees great things from the valley; only small things from the peak.
> *G. K. Chesterton*

Now when Job's three friends heard of all this adversity that had come upon him, each one came from his own place.

Job 2:11

Job's friends attempted to help him with their advice. Had they listened more and talked less, however, they would have been more helpful. They were convinced that Job was being disciplined by God for his sins. They were sincere but wrong.

People must be very careful about making assumptions regarding others' circumstances. Things are not always what they seem. Often it is more helpful to empathize with a suffering friend than to try to rush in and explain his or her suffering.

> We could never learn to be brave and patient if there were only joy in the world.
> *Helen Keller*

For You, O God, have tested us; You have refined us as silver is refined.

Psalm 66:10

Silver ore must be refined by fire to remove its impurities. Every time the silver is heated and the dross is removed, the metal becomes more and more purified.

In like manner, the fire of trials purges sin, burning away the lusts and impurities that pollute people's lives. Although unpleasant, suffering often removes the impurities from our lives and helps us grow toward perfection. God refines us "as silver is refined" so that we can reflect His glory.

Beloved, do not think it strange concerning the fiery trial which is to try you, as though some strange thing happened to you; but rejoice to the extent that you partake of Christ's sufferings, that when His glory is revealed, you may also be glad with exceeding joy. . . . Therefore let those who suffer according to the will of God commit their souls to Him in doing good, as to a faithful Creator.

1 Peter 4:12–13, 19

Nothing happens to believers that surprises God. He may allow suffering for a time, knowing that it will strengthen His people's faith.

Suffering provides the opportunity to trust God.

We can commit our lives to Him, knowing that He is completely faithful and trustworthy. He will remain with us through our suffering, and in the end bring us to glory.

7 PRAYER STARTER

Lord, _____ has come in today feeling overwhelmed with suffering. The pain is intense and is affecting his [her] daily life. He [She] needs Your strengthening presence in a powerful and personal way today. Put Your arms around him [her] and be a God of comfort and encouragement. Give us wisdom Father, as we seek the best path forward. Our hope is in You, Lord, and the knowledge that You are always with us and always at work in our lives . . .

8 RECOMMENDED RESOURCES

Clinton, Tim. *The Bible for Hope: Caring for People God's Way.* Thomas Nelson, 2007.

Clinton, Tim, Archibald D. Hart, and George Ohlschlager. *Caring for People God's Way: Personal and Emotional Issues, Addictions, Grief, and Trauma.* Thomas Nelson, 2006.

Clinton, Tim, and Gary Sibcy. *Why You Do the Things You Do: The Secret to Healthy Relationships.* Thomas Nelson, 2006.

Elliot, Elisabeth. *The Path through Suffering.* Vine, 1992.

Hegstrom, Paul. *Broken Children, Grown-Up Pain: Understanding the Effects of Your Wounded Past.* Beacon Hill Press, 2006.

Jeremiah, David. *A Bend in the Road: Experiencing God When Your World Caves In*. Thomas Nelson, 2002.

Websites

American Association of Christian Counselors (www.aacc.net)

Ecounseling (www.ecounseling.com)

Suicide

1 PORTRAITS

- Ida had diabetes and was facing amputation of her foot. The day before surgery, she wrote notes to her grandkids and overdosed on her pain medications.
- Aaron had been unable to work due to complications from the hazardous chemicals he used at his job. He was now running out of money. He'd been turned down for Medicaid, Medicare, and disability payments, despite his chronic illness. He did not want to be a burden to his family, so the month that he ran out of money, he gave away his valuables and cleaned up his apartment. He found a home for his cat and put a gun to his head.
- Victor drove off a bridge the night before his graduation from college. Afterward his parents found out that he had been failing all his classes—because he wasn't attending them—and he had been told that he would not be allowed to graduate.
- Raysha got very drunk at a high school drinking party and made a fool of herself. Humiliated, she left the party, focusing on all the other stupid things she'd done lately. When she came to the railroad tracks, she decided to wait for a train.

2 DEFINITIONS AND KEY THOUGHTS

Suicide is the third leading cause of death for adolescents 15 to 19 years old. In 2003 there were 3,988 suicides among people 15 to 24 years old.[1]

- Suicide is the tragic and lethal culmination of a psychological process that results from *unresolved events* that create *depression and hopelessness*.
- Someone who is considering suicide *cannot see any hope* that the future will be different from the painful past or present.
- The risk of suicide is *greatest within the first year after a failed attempt*.
- *Males tend to use more violent means* for suicide (guns, cars) and are *more often successful* than women.
- *Females* tend to attempt suicide *more often than men* but are *less often successful* at the attempt because they use *less lethal means* (pills, cutting).
- *Often suicide and substance abuse* go hand in hand. Substances are involved in 20 to 50 percent of suicides.
- Depressed people are more at risk of suicide *after depression starts to abate*. A person who was inert with depression may become decisive with new energy—enough energy to commit suicide.

- Those who have *recently begun taking antidepressants* may be more at risk because their energy level may rise before their mood does.
- Suicidal individuals suffer from *tunnel vision*. They do not see any option except death. To them, suicide is a "logical" thing to do. That's the reason suicidal individuals sometimes end up taking the lives of others as they kill themselves—they are *not* seeing the big picture.
- Always *take seriously the threat* of suicide.

ASSESSMENT INTERVIEW 3

If you think that the person you are interviewing is suicidal, *do not panic*. Stay calm and know that by coming to you this person has already taken a step away from the decision to harm himself or herself.

Don't contradict the suicidal person. Empathy is more helpful. You won't argue him or her out of the way he or she feels.

Rule Outs

Questions for the suicidal person.

1. Are you feeling as if you want to harm yourself?
2. If so, how would you do this?
3. Do you ever wish you were dead?
4. When was the last time you felt that way?
5. Have you thought about how you would try to kill yourself?
6. Are there weapons at home?
7. If so, are they locked up? Who can get to them?
8. Have you ever attempted to hurt yourself in the past? If so, when? (*A recent, nearly lethal attempt may indicate that this person is very serious in his or her desire to die. Numerous unsuccessful suicide attempts could indicate that the individual uses suicide attempts to gain attention. However, either way, you must take the suicide talk seriously.*)

General Questions for the Suicidal Person

1. How old are you?
2. Have you recently had a baby? (*This checks for postpartum depression.*)
3. Have you suffered a recent loss?
4. What has happened recently to make you feel so hopeless?
5. Do you ever abuse drugs or alcohol?
6. If so, when did you last use?
7. How often and how much do you use?
8. Has anyone in your family committed suicide?

> The problem is not that such despairing people want to die; it is that they do not know how to live.
>
> *Gary P. Stewart*

9. If so, who was it?

10. How old were you when it happened?

11. What happened?

12. Do you know why it occurred?

13. How did it make you feel?

14. Is there someone you'd like to get revenge on? Is there anyone you are very angry at? Have you ever thought of death as the ultimate revenge?

15. What is most distressing to you when you think about the future?

16. Can you think of any reasons to go on living?

17. What would make life worth living for you? See if you can list ten things. Are any of them within reach?

18. Where are you spiritually?

19. Do you think that God cares if you live or die?

General Questions for the Friend or Family Member

1. How old is your loved one?

2. Does he [she] suffer from any painful or debilitating medical conditions?

3. Has this person suffered a recent loss or recently had a baby?

4. If not, are there any other recent distressing circumstances?

5. Is there a family history of suicide?

6. Does this person abuse alcohol or drugs?

7. If so, has he [she] ever tried to stop?

8. Has your loved one's behavior changed recently?

9. If so, in what ways?

10. Has this person been taking care of himself [herself] physically?

11. Is he [she] sleeping regularly (that is, not sleeping too much or too little)?

12. Has your loved one been giving away prized possessions?

13. Has he [she] seemed uninterested in plans for the future?

14. Has he [she] made jokes about death or disappearing?

15. Is this person extremely angry?

16. Would he [she] like to get revenge on someone?

17. Could suicide be a form of revenge for him [her]?

The rate of suicide in 15 to 24 year olds has tripled since 1960. However, people over 60 commit suicide more often than people of any other age group.[2]

4 WISE COUNSEL

Protecting the suicidal person must take priority. Don't worry about embarrassing the person by calling paramedics—better embarrassed than dead.

While some Christians will resist suicide because of a belief that it is a sin, such rules are often meaningless to those with tunnel vision.

Although it may comfort discouraged or sad people to know that God loves them, suicidal people are often too depressed to believe it. Avoid trite spiritual platitudes.

ACTION STEPS 5

1. Get Help Immediately

- *Call police or paramedics if this person has a plan and the means to commit suicide. He or she must be protected.*
- *Inpatient psychiatric units are locked because of the need to protect people from their desire to harm themselves. Every attempt is made to remove from the unit the means of causing harm.*
- *Do not try to transport a suicidal person to the hospital by yourself. It is too dangerous.*
- *If the suicidal person is under the influence of drugs or alcohol, arrange for him or her to be supervised constantly while detoxing or becoming sober. Then the suicidal ideation should be reassessed. If no longer suicidal, this person should be strongly encouraged to seek treatment for substance abuse.*

2. Follow Up

- *See if the suicidal person will sign a contract stating that he or she will not attempt suicide for twenty-four hours. Of course, this contract is only as good as the suicidal person's word. It is not a legal document.*
- *If willing to sign a contract, send the person home with supervision.*
- *Reconnect with the suicidal person the next day. (Don't forget!) See if the suicidal thoughts have decreased.*
- *If the person is still suicidal, seek help immediately.*

In 2006 the number of emergency department visits for self-inflicted injury was 594,000.[3]

3. Investigate the Tunnel Vision

- *Sometimes the problem can actually be solved rather simply.*
- *Ask a person with tunnel vision to sign a contract not to harm himself or herself while you investigate the circumstances for three days. In that time, work to find the beginning of some solutions.*
- *During those three days, the person should be supervised. If you cannot make substantive progress in three days, then refer the counselee to a professional therapist or a hospital.*

6 BIBLICAL INSIGHTS

Then Saul said to his armorbearer, "Draw your sword, and thrust me through with it, lest these uncircumcised men come and thrust me through and abuse me." But his armorbearer would not, for he was greatly afraid. Therefore Saul took a sword and fell on it.

1 Samuel 31:4

Because Saul had turned away from God, he was left completely to his own devices. He had great potential in his position as the chosen king of Israel but he squandered it with jealousy, anger, and disobedience. In the end, when all was lost, he believed he had nowhere to turn but to death.

Suicide is attractive to a desperate person. Such people need to be shown God's gracious love and forgiveness. There is always hope with God.

Then [Judas] threw down the pieces of silver in the temple and departed, and went and hanged himself.

Matthew 27:5

Judas was a complex and deluded man, and his relationship to Christ was complicated. While he acknowledged that he had sinned, Judas did not repent and seek reconciliation.

Suicides are not always spur of the moment, conscious, willful decisions. For example, suicide often results from a prolonged, severe, deep depression. Because we can only guess at his motivation for betraying Jesus, we must be cautious in our conclusions about Judas's life. Judas may have become angry and indignant, nursing his resentments whenever Christ failed to fulfill his expectations of what a Messiah should be and do.

A genuine Christian wouldn't lose his salvation by killing himself, but in the case of Judas, the Bible indicates that even though he regretted the consequences of his betrayal, he died lost, alienated from Christ (John 6:70; 17:12; Acts 1:25).

Faced with the result of one horrible act that he couldn't undo, he made the mistake of committing another such act. We don't know what his final thoughts were, but by his self-destructive act, Judas eliminated the possibility of ever getting right with Christ the way he needed to.

> Four times more men than women complete suicide, but three times more women than men attempt suicide.[4]

7 PRAYER STARTER

Dear Lord, _____ is feeling right now as if there is no reason to live. And even though he [she] feels that way, we know that is not the case. Please take away these feelings. Please protect _____ from himself [herself]. Help him [her] to know and to feel how much You love him [her]. Show him [her] hope for the future . . .

RECOMMENDED RESOURCES : 8

Clinton, Tim. *The Bible for Hope: Caring for People God's Way.* Thomas Nelson, 2007.

Clinton, Tim, Archibald D. Hart, and George Ohlschlager. *Caring for People God's Way: Personal and Emotional Issues, Addictions, Grief, and Trauma.* Thomas Nelson, 2006.

Cox, David, and Candy Arrington. *Aftershock: Help, Hope, and Healing in the Wake of Suicide.* B&H Publishing, 2003.

Fine, Carla. *No Time to Say Goodbye: Surviving the Suicide of a Loved One.* Main Street Books, 1999.

Websites

American Association of Christian Counselors (www.aacc.net)

Ecounseling (www.ecounseling.com)

In 2005 the number of deaths by suicide totaled 32,637 (approximately 89 suicides per day; 1 suicide every 16 minutes).[5]

Trauma

1 PORTRAITS

- Janet startled awake. Her heart was pounding and the sheets were tangled around her. For a few moments she wondered where she was. The nightmare had been so vivid and the screams had been real. *What is happening to me?* she wondered. The accident was three years ago. But lately the dreams were more frequent.
- Mindy has been in a cycle of bad relationships over the course of her college years—often with older men. Only now is she beginning to understand that her desperate need comes from the time when her father walked out on her mom. That moment is forever etched in her brain and the pain is as fresh as ever.

2 DEFINITIONS AND KEY THOUGHTS

- Some events in life cause pain that *goes deep and lasts a long time.* These are "traumas."
- A *trauma* would be considered a situation beyond control, one that *shakes a person to the core.* A trauma can lead to mental disorders or to suicide. Recovery is often slow; flashbacks are common.
- Traumas may not even be remembered but can *still influence people* in certain unhealthy ways or cause them to make unhealthy decisions.
- Those whose traumas don't get healed may grow up to *damage others,* even their own families.
- Traumatic events *overwhelm the person's ordinary adapting or coping mechanisms* to life.
- With trauma, each component of the ordinary response to danger continues to persist in an altered state long after the actual danger is over. There are *profound and lasting changes* in psychological arousal, emotion, cognition, and memory.
- Symptoms of trauma include anxiety and panic disorders, depression, intense fear, anger, loneliness, attachment disorders, flashbacks, helplessness, loss of control, and threat of annihilation. Panic, anxiety, flashbacks, and anger sometimes are labeled under the diagnosis of post-traumatic stress disorder (PTSD).
- Traumatic reactions occur when the person is exposed to an intense emotional situation that threatens the life or well-being of self or others. When neither

The Lord gets his best soldiers out of the highlands of affliction.

C. H. Spurgeon

resistance nor escape is possible, the human system of self-defense becomes *overwhelmed and disorganized*. Traumatized people act as if their nervous systems have been disconnected from the present. They become hypervigilant.

- Traumatic memory becomes encoded in an *abnormal form of memory,* which breaks spontaneously into consciousness, both as flashbacks and as nightmares.
- Traumatic memory is not a verbal linear narrative but can *have a frozen, wordless quality.* When high levels of adrenaline and other stress hormones are circulating, the memories are deeply imprinted.
- Traumatic memory may also *be suppressed.* The intrusion of the memory and the constriction form a dynamic that does not provide a way to resolve the experience of the event and achieve balance.

Invasion Trauma

- In invasion trauma, *something happened* to a person that creates damage.
- *Emotional invasion* occurs when people feel criticized, shamed, or blamed, either verbally or nonverbally.
- *Physical invasion* occurs when a person is physically abused. This form of trauma may create permanent physical damage. The emotional effect of this can also be experienced if a person lives in a home in which someone else is being physically harmed.
- *Sexual invasion* happens when a person is penetrated or touched in sexual areas in a manner that disrespects his or her personal boundaries and leaves him or her feeling confused and violated.
- *Spiritual invasion* takes place when people are led to believe that they are unworthy of God's love and grace. Often rigid, fear-based religious teaching, even if it is well intended, can have this effect. This results in shame that people can't seem to shake.

Abandonment Trauma

- In abandonment trauma, *something did* not *happen* to a person (such as not feeling loved, protected, or nurtured) that creates damage.
- Abandonment trauma can be *harder to recognize* because the person doesn't know what he or she is missing, never having had it.
- *Emotional abandonment* occurs when love, attention, care, nurture, and affirmation are not given. This results in profound loneliness.
- *Physical abandonment* happens when people's basic needs for food, shelter, and clothing aren't met. People who aren't touched enough—with hugs or cuddles—will experience a form of this called "touch deprivation." Another form occurs

The U.S. Department of Veterans Affairs estimates between 12 and 20 percent of the 1.6 million U.S. troops who have served in Iraq or Afghanistan suffer from depression or post-traumatic stress disorder, which can be marked by irritability, anxiety, and flashbacks.[1]

when people aren't getting enough information or modeling on physical self-care.

- *Sexual abandonment* occurs when parents and other responsible adults don't educate children about and model healthy sexuality. Lack of correct information can have devastating results.
- *Spiritual abandonment* happens when healthy spiritual teaching and modeling are not available.
- The above *categories can overlap*. Damage in one aspect of a person's life can have an effect in another. For example, any form of trauma that happens at the hands of a religious authority figure can create profound spiritual damage.

3 ASSESSMENT INTERVIEW

Rule Outs

1. Are you having physical symptoms? Are you able to eat and sleep? (*If the person is dealing with physical issues as a result of the trauma, encourage a medical checkup.*)
2. On a scale of 1 to 10, with 1 being "feeling terrific" and 10 being "feeling suicidal," where would you place yourself on most days? (*If you sense that the person is suicidal, deal with that issue first. See the section on Suicide and get outside help.*)

General Questions

1. What is currently causing your distress?
2. Do you recall a particular event in your life that was traumatic?
3. If you don't recall anything in particular, what can you tell me about your childhood, other past relationships, and other situations in your life?
4. How do you feel about that situation? (*Help in expressing grief or anger is important to survivors of trauma.*)
5. Have you ever sought help for this problem before?
6. Did you receive help at that time?
7. What is daily life like for you currently?
8. Do you feel safe?
9. Whom do you talk to about this?
10. Do you have a support group or network with whom you feel safe?

God will never permit any troubles to come upon us unless he has a specific plan by which great blessing can come out of the difficulty.

Peter Marshall

WISE COUNSEL :4

If the person is exhibiting behavior that reveals some past trauma that *cannot be remembered or attached to any event*, you may want to refer the person to a Christian professional counselor for more lengthy treatment.

While the traumatic event or events can be horrific and the resultant emotional damage overwhelming to the person who is traumatized, *healing from the effects of trauma is possible.*

Often people who are traumatized wonder if they are losing their mind or even losing their self. It can be very reassuring to encourage the survivor that *what he or she is experiencing is a normal reaction to the trauma.*

From you the person needs *comfort, acceptance, and a nonjudgmental listening ear.* He or she wants to know that *there is hope.*

Losses will need to be grieved and anger experienced to move forward. This can be *long-term work* and may involve individual or group counseling.

ACTION STEPS :5

1. Understand the Nature of the Trauma

- *Discuss what happened—if it can all be remembered. Do this gently, as the memories are probably very painful.*
- *Don't allow for any denials of what happened or of the feelings about what happened. Honesty is key.*
- *This can begin with you as the counselor but may be better continued in a support group of survivors of similar trauma.*
- Understand that you did not deserve the hurts that happened to you and that you didn't cause them.
- Depending on the nature of the trauma, understand that you may need to erect some boundaries with particular people so that you will not be hurt again.

> The LORD is near to those who have a broken heart, and saves such as have a contrite spirit.
>
> *Psalm 34:18*

2. Express Your Feelings

- Express your real feelings. If you have anger at the perpetrators of your trauma, express it.
- This does not necessarily mean confronting them. There are symbolic ways, such as writing letters to perpetrators that won't necessarily be sent, which can be just as powerful.
- If you're angry with God, express that as well. He can handle it.
- If you have grief over a loss experienced through the trauma, express that grief. (*If the client is experiencing grief, see the section on Grief and Loss.*)

3. Know That You Will Heal

- Healing will come with God's help.
- It is important that you engage in a process through which this will be possible, either in further individual counseling or group counseling.

4. Know That You Will Have Victory

- Beyond just healing, you will have victory over the trauma. Begin to consider some of the positive strengths you will have in your life as a result of healing from this trauma.
- Know that you will eventually be able to forgive to set yourself free. This is the ultimate spiritual victory. (*To help the client with forgiveness, see the section on Forgiveness.*)
- Know that you will be able to be of great comfort to others who experience similar traumas.

6 BIBLICAL INSIGHTS

Is it nothing to you, all you who pass by? Behold and see if there is any sorrow like my sorrow, which has been brought on me, which the LORD has inflicted in the day of His fierce anger.

Lamentations 1:12

> The Lord does not measure out our afflictions according to our faults, but according to our strength, and looks not at what we have deserved, but what we are able to bear.
>
> *George Downame*

God does not leave our side when we suffer.

When we trust in God, we can change our perspective on life's traumas from "Why me?" to "How can I grow from this?"

And [Jonah] said to them, "Pick me up and throw me into the sea; then the sea will become calm for you. For I know that this great tempest is because of me."

Jonah 1:12

Eventually, trauma upon trauma caused Jonah to pray. God rescued Jonah and gave him the opportunity to fulfill his promise.

Traumatic experiences can drive people away from God or to Him. In both cases, a person may ask, "Why would God do this to me?" Those who turn *from* God ask the question in anger and accusation. Those who turn *toward* God ask the question to learn His lesson for their lives.

When traumatic experiences come, turn to God not away. As Jonah learned: "When my soul fainted within me, I remembered the LORD; and my prayer went up to You, into Your holy temple" (Jonah 2:7).

"Arise, go to Nineveh, that great city, and preach to it the message that I tell you." So Jonah arose and went to Nineveh, according to the word of the Lord.

Jonah 3:2–3

Trauma changes people. Jonah had nearly died in the ocean—he couldn't help but be changed. Jonah recognized the hand of God in his circumstances. And when all hope was lost, God was there.

When Jonah found himself alive on a beach, he praised God who had given him another chance. This time when God called, Jonah obeyed. Trauma changes us. Whether the change is good or bad often depends on how we respond. God uses our troubles as tools to shape our souls.

PRAYER STARTER 7

Your child is in a lot of pain today, Lord, remembering a situation of the past that is still looming large across the landscape of his [her] life even today. We don't yet understand why You allowed this to happen—what purpose it could possibly have—but we want to trust that You are forging a stronger person through this difficult time . . .

RECOMMENDED RESOURCES 8

Clinton, Tim. *The Bible for Hope: Caring for People God's Way*. Thomas Nelson, 2007.

Clinton, Tim, Archibald D. Hart, and George Ohlschlager. *Caring for People God's Way: Personal and Emotional Issues, Addictions, Grief, and Trauma*. Thomas Nelson, 2006.

Floyd, Scott. *Crisis Counseling: A Guide for Pastors and Professionals*. Kregel Academic and Professional, 2008.

Wright, H. Norman. *The New Guide to Crisis and Trauma Counseling*. Regal Books, 2003.

Wright, H. Norman, Matt Woodley, and Julie Woodley. *Surviving the Storms of Life: Finding Hope and Healing When Life Goes Wrong*. Revell, 2008.

Websites

American Association of Christian Counselors (www.aacc.net)

Ecounseling (www.ecounseling.com)

Workaholism

1 PORTRAITS

- "I can't remember the last time I really relaxed," explained Dave. "I think what seems to keep me going is fear, fear that if I do stop, I'll lose everything I have worked so hard to achieve." He continued, "My parents lived through the Depression and instilled in me the notion that what matters most is getting ahead in life. They raised me to never be in a position to depend on anyone for anything. Even when I am with my wife and kids, I can't seem to stop thinking about work. Somehow everything that isn't related to my work seems like a waste of time."

- Pam can't enjoy her home or her children. She is constantly cleaning, picking up after her kids, always attempting to maintain a spotless "Better Homes and Gardens"–type of showplace. The children aren't allowed to play anywhere but in their rooms.

- Bill is climbing the corporate ladder and faces expectations that he feels he must meet to make it to the next rung. The stress is affecting his family.

2 DEFINITIONS AND KEY THOUGHTS

- A workaholic is uncontrollably *addicted to work* to the detriment of self and others.

- "Workaholism" has become an *all-consuming obsession* for too many modern workers, a sleep-depriving, health-robbing, greed-festering monster that may be the most rewarded—and least challenged—addiction in America.

- While God created work as a meaningful part of this life, for some, work becomes the primary avenue by which they find *approval, respect, and success.*

- God calls on humankind to work honestly, heartily, happily, and as though we are working for the Lord (Exod. 23:12; Eccles. 5:19; Col. 3:23).

- This issue is *not limited to men and women in the workplace*. It can also include women at home who are striving to have the "perfect" home and family.

- Workaholism is an *addiction* and needs to be treated like one.

- Work life must be *managed* within the context of a healthy relation to God, marriage, and family life, and commitments to church and community. When this *balance* is not held, work can become an idol, a terrible taskmaster known as "workaholism."

> Don't let Satan let you overwork and then put you out of action for a long time.
>
> *Charles Simeon*

Symptoms of Workaholism

- A *compulsive emphasis on work* because it is perceived as the avenue for achieving control and power over one's life and others.
- Working *sixty to seventy hours a week* or more.
- Work is viewed as the *primary avenue* by which a person finds approval, respect, and success.
- A *chronic sense of urgency* in every activity.
- An *inability to rest*.
- An addictive *need for acceptance and significance* in the eyes of others as a result of one's work.
- *Ignoring the emotional and spiritual demands of family* with the notion that he or she is providing a better lifestyle.
- A workaholic is seen by his or her children as *inattentive, irritable, lacking humor, and always in a hurry*.
- *Valuing performance* over showing love and grace.
- *Family does not feel "safe."* Aside from financial security, the family members know that their feelings or concerns are generally not accepted. Competition is substituted for playful times.
- Struggles with a *poor self-image, rigidity, and problems with intimacy in relationships*.
- *Viewing the stress that work involves as a challenge* to overcome and a way to find significance.

> You can always find reasons to work. There will always be one more thing to do. But when people don't take time out, they stop being productive. They stop being happy, and that affects the morale of everyone around them.
>
> *Carisa Bianchi*

ASSESSMENT INTERVIEW 3

Like all addicts, workaholics must be able to admit their obsessive drivenness and confess its many costs. They must be able to establish and maintain times for rest, play, family, and leisure. Work addicts need to realize that the deeper life with Christ comes only after they are able to be still and know God.

1. Do you work more than forty hours a week?
2. Do you often feel fatigued and stressed?
3. Do you have problems sleeping?
4. Do you have stress-related physical issues, such as back pain, headaches, indigestion, ulcers, or chronic fatigue?
5. Do you take work home daily, on weekends, on vacation, on holidays?
6. Do you feel guilty when you relax or have fun, especially when there is work to be done?
7. Do you sometimes resent others for not working as hard as you do?
8. Do you get impatient with co-workers who have other priorities besides work?

9. Has your family given up expecting you to come home on time?

10. Do you find that it is difficult to schedule time for those you love?

11. Are you able to have fun with your family?

12. Do you feel that the more you work the more pleasing you will be to God?

13. Do you have difficulty saying no?

14. Do you sometimes feel that people who have needs are weak?

15. Do you feel better about yourself when you earn more money or realize achievements in your work?

16. Do you feel that you do things rapidly so as not to waste time?

17. Do you often compare yourself to others?

18. Do you find that free time bores you because you would rather be working?

19. Tell me about your growing-up years. What were your parents like?

20. How did your parents assess your worth? Did you feel that you had to achieve at a certain level to be accepted or loved?

4 : WISE COUNSEL

Generally, people who are addicted to work feel:

- highly self-critical
- a pervading sense of emptiness
- a compulsive need to do things perfectly and be better than others
- pain from the past—their worth can only be found in their achievements
- that unrelenting sacrificial service is honorable before God
- that they must measure up to their own impossible standards
- a constant struggle with pride

Communicate unconditional love and *avoid evaluative remarks.* Initially, affirm the person's inner qualities and the courage to address this issue.

Express empathy about the stress the person is experiencing. Give hope that you will help him or her find a way through the pressure.

The person may be completely unaware as to what is fueling the stress and find little value in self-reflection. You will need to gently encourage him or her to *explore the factors* that are fueling the addictive behavior.

Move the focus from the person and what he or she feels must *be done* to have God's unconditional acceptance. God is more concerned about *who the person is becoming* than what he or she is doing.

God's invitation to the workaholic is to let Him take the burden of his life and give him or her rest in its place (Matt. 11:29).

ACTION STEPS : 5

1. Assess the Problem

- What is causing the stress you feel at work? (*Help the person perceive the problem and own it.*)
- *Help him or her understand that workaholism is an addiction and needs to be treated as such.*

2. Evaluate the Past

- Identify negative messages you received about self-worth from your parents, siblings, and/or peers.
- Your significance is provided through Christ, not through work.

3. Refocus on God

- Take time for daily prayer, Scripture reading, and meditation.
- Seek God's guidance in deciding on the activities for the day.
- Read and meditate on the Scriptures that address God's unconditional love and your identity as a follower of Jesus Christ. (*Be sure to place this activity in the context of a relationship and not just as another job or task.*)

4. Find Balance

- *Evaluate the activities in his or her weekly schedule and assess which involvements are unnecessary and are contributing to the addiction to activity.*
- There needs to be a balance between time spent at work and time spent in close relationships.
- Work must be maintained in proper relation to God and to family. When this balance is not in place, work can become an idol—a false god that is a terrible taskmaster.
- You will need to "schedule" times for leisure and play. Make sure you treat these times as priorities.
- Remember to honor the Sabbath as a day of rest.

5. Slow Down

- *Help the person establish a slower pace for each day and to seek rest.*
- Be sure to honor the body that God has given you by getting sufficient rest and exercise and by eating a nutritionally balanced diet.
- *Explore ways the counselee can include enjoyable activities in his or her schedule— especially family time.*

The workaholic maintains a frantic schedule. He is consistently preoccupied with performance. He finds it difficult to refuse additional responsibilities. He is unable to relax. If someone you know exhibits these characteristics, he or she is probably a workaholic.

Bill Hybels

- Change takes time, and as you try to slow down, God will take care of the things that concern you (Matt. 6:25–34).

6. Get Support

- Seek help from a counselor, accountability partner, or group where the focus is on coming to terms with the underlying motivations for the addiction to work.

6 : BIBLICAL INSIGHTS

Then he said to them, "This is what the LORD has said: 'Tomorrow is a Sabbath rest, a holy Sabbath to the LORD. Bake what you will bake today, and boil what you will boil; and lay up for yourselves all that remains, to be kept until morning.'"

Exodus 16:23

God gave His people a day of rest, a day when they were not supposed to work. But everyone had to work hard in preparation on the day before, to be able to rest completely on the Sabbath.

To take full advantage of our day of rest and worship, we too need to prepare ahead of time. That way we won't need to run to the store or finish a work project. We need to be organized enough to be ready to rest and focus on God on Sundays.

There can be intemperance in work just as in drink.

C. S. Lewis

Then King Solomon raised up a labor force out of all Israel; and the labor force was thirty thousand men. And he sent them to Lebanon, ten thousand a month in shifts: they were one month in Lebanon and two months at home; Adoniram was in charge of the labor force.

1 Kings 5:13–14

God had given Solomon wisdom to rule the nation. There was peace in the land, so the nation could devote itself and its resources to building a glorious temple for God.

Even as Solomon planned its construction, he used great wisdom. He drew on the nation's labor force, divided it into three groups, and rotated the groups so they would be one month in Jerusalem and then two months at home.

Solomon allowed for continuous work without burning out his workers or hurting their families. No matter how important the work, the workers' families were not to be neglected.

Here is what I have seen: It is good and fitting for one to eat and drink, and to enjoy the good of all his labor in which he toils under the sun all the days of his life which God gives him; for it is his heritage.

Ecclesiastes 5:18

Work is a double-edged sword in Scripture. Transformed into "sweat" as part of the curse after the fall (Gen. 3:19), work is also an honored activity through which God delivers many blessings.

The Bible emphasizes the importance of work as a God-given activity in life, and it says that the ability to enjoy the fruits of one's labor is also something that God provides us.

The ability to work, enjoy that work, make money, and enjoy and share our income with others is a gift from God.

PRAYER STARTER : 7

Lord, we know that it is good that we work honestly and diligently, and that work is part of Your plan for us. We know that You are honored through our sincere labor. Lord, as You help us with our tasks and occupations, help us also to honor You with our rest. Give us, God, the wisdom to achieve much needed balance so that we may be still and know that You are God. Free Your precious child here from the destructive pressures of workaholism . . .

RECOMMENDED RESOURCES : 8

Clinton, Tim. *The Bible for Hope: Caring for People God's Way.* Thomas Nelson, 2007.

Clinton, Tim, Archibald D. Hart, and George Ohlschlager. *Caring for People God's Way: Personal and Emotional Issues, Addictions, Grief, and Trauma.* Thomas Nelson, 2006.

Clinton, Tim, and Gary Sibcy. *Why You Do the Things You Do: The Secret to Healthy Relationships.* Thomas Nelson, 2006.

Fassal, Diane. *Working Ourselves to Death: The High Cost of Workaholism and the Rewards of Recovery.* AuthorHouse, 2000.

Websites

American Association of Christian Counselors (www.aacc.net)

Ecounseling (www.ecounseling.com)

Worry

1 PORTRAITS

- Amy said yes to Don's proposal and now they are engaged. Later that night as Don lies in bed, he wonders how in the world he will be able to support her when he can barely live alone on what he makes.
- Randy is two hours late getting home from being out with his buddies. His parents are angry with him for not calling, but also are worried because all they can think is that he must have had car trouble, or worse, had an accident.
- Phil joined his department of five employees two years ago. Now they are down to three and rumor has it that soon they will be down to two.
- Christine is pregnant again. After losing the last baby during the second trimester, she can't help but wonder if this new little miracle will ever have a chance to see this world.

2 DEFINITIONS AND KEY THOUGHTS

- Worry is defined by Webster as "mental distress or agitation resulting from concern usually for something impending or anticipated." In other words, worry is about *things that have not happened*. Worry is not an emotion; it is a mental exercise.
- It is natural to be worried or anxious when things are tough or unpredictable or when a solution to a particular problem is not clearly evident. This causes us to worry—*replaying possible outcomes* over and over again in our mind. Sometimes, even when we can see a solution in our mind, we continue to worry, refusing to be satisfied until the solution becomes a reality.
- Being concerned can be positive when it propels us to action—such as seeing a doctor when we are ill or a mechanic when the car sounds strange. But *worry is rarely tied to constructive action and is unproductive*.
- Worry rises to an unhealthy level and *takes its toll* when:

  You're not sleeping.
  You're not productive.
  You're worried about two or more topics more days than not.

You're focusing on situations of worry more than on the other business
of life.

Your life feels out of control

- Worrying about many things at once can contribute to the development of an
unhealthy level of stress. Then the stress exhibits itself in an anxiety level that
just won't seem to go away.

- Worry is simply a smaller level of fear and *fear is the opposite of faith*. When we
operate in fear or worry, then we do not have the faith or trust that God has a
plan and is in control.

ASSESSMENT INTERVIEW 3

Sometimes the counselor asks questions not to solicit information but to help the
person see things differently. In dealing with worry and anxiety, this might be an
appropriate time for such a strategy. The person may be instructed to just think
of his or her answers and not necessarily speak them out loud. Of course this depends on what you as the counselor prefer to do based on your expertise or need
to delve deeper to help the client process the reasons for worrying.

1. What has worried you the most in the past that you no longer worry about?
2. Did these previous situations work out the way you thought they would or
did they work out differently than expected?
3. Did the pain of these previous situations help you grow? If so, how?
4. What do you currently worry about the most?
5. Do you think that these problems are too big for God?
6. Do you believe that you are important to God?
7. Will God take care of you in this current situation?
8. There is only one person who can circumvent God's plan for your life. Do you
know who that is? (*You.*)
9. Do you have control over whether you worry or not?
10. The Bible says we are not to worry. How can you follow that instruction?
11. What is the worst thing that can happen in this current situation?
12. How has worrying helped you in the past?
13. Do you think that worrying will help you now?
14. What difference will worrying about the situation make one hundred years
from now?

> Worry is like a
> rocking chair;
> it'll give you
> something
> to do, but it
> won't get you
> anywhere.
>
> *Unknown*

WISE COUNSEL 4

The worrier needs to understand that he or she really *does have control* over whether
he or she worries or not. Some people are more inclined to worry than others. That
isn't a character flaw, it's just a built-in reminder to pray and give it to the Lord.

The counselee *needs a plan* to help keep him or her from unnecessary worry. In the Action Steps, help him or her devise that plan. Pray through a plan; let the counselee allow his or her faith and works to coincide.

While it is easy to simply say, "Don't worry!" it can be difficult to change this pattern of thinking. One approach is to *set limits* so that the worry doesn't continue to rage out of control.

5 ACTION STEPS

The following plan is designed to help aid the person in changing the way he or she thinks about any issue that seems to bring worry into his or her life.

1. Start Each Day with God

- Begin each day with time alone with God. Tell Him the concerns of the day (this is your time to pray about your worries—see step 2).
- Anticipate your day. Pray about what's ahead. Ask God to give you peace.

2. Pray about Your Worries

- Set up a specific time period in which you can pray out a plan for your worries.
- Limit worrying to a "worry list," and take that list to the Lord in your daily Bible and prayer time.
- During the course of the day, when a worry strikes you, repeat the following sentence: "I will take care of that with God at my prayer time tomorrow morning."
- During prayer time, bring the worrisome situation to God. Ask for guidance and direction.

> To say that we are waiting on the Lord, and then to go around with a sense of worry, misery, and dread, is to contradict the truth.
>
> *Rosemarie Scotti Hughes*

3. Keep a Journal

- Write down the prayer requests and the worries that you are bringing to God.
- Write down the answers God gives. Go back and read these answers as constant encouragement that any new requests you bring to God will indeed be answered.
- As you talk to God, write down anything you feel He is telling you about your course of action. Keep in mind that the course of action may be purposefully to do nothing until God gives you further direction.

4. Set Boundaries

- Get facts and expert advice to prevent worrying unrealistically about a situation.
- Set deadlines to make decisions, rather than ruminating forever.

- Realize that you will not please everyone all the time.
- Learn to say no.

5. Think Differently

- Delegate chores and other responsibilities.
- Give yourself permission to relax and to make mistakes.
- Eat, sleep, and exercise properly.
- To keep a sense of perspective, try to see the humor in a situation.
- Declutter and organize, using calendars and to-do lists.
- Mentally put your worries in a box with a lid and put them on the top shelf of your closet. No peeking!

6. Seek Balance

- The goal is to walk in peace, in calm, in trust, and in assurance. This is done by finding the balance between prayer and action and, ultimately, this produces freedom from worry.

> Much that worries us beforehand can afterwards, quite unexpectedly, have a happy and simple solution. Worries just don't matter. Things really are in a better hand than ours.
>
> *Dietrich Bonhoeffer*

BIBLICAL INSIGHTS 6

And when Pharaoh drew near, the children of Israel lifted their eyes, and behold, the Egyptians marched after them. So they were very afraid, and the children of Israel cried out to the LORD.

Exodus 14:10

The Israelites found themselves trapped between Pharaoh's army and the waters of the Red Sea. In panic, they accused Moses of leading them to their deaths. By this time, Moses had seen enough of the power of God to respond in confidence.

What unyielding obstacles are you facing? Don't panic. Instead, turn to God and trust in His power to do what seems impossible.

Therefore do not worry about tomorrow, for tomorrow will worry about its own things. Sufficient for the day is its own trouble.

Matthew 6:34

Worry fills people's minds with useless clutter that leaves no room for God. Worry clouds perspective, causing people to focus on themselves rather than on God. Jesus said that God feeds the birds and clothes the flowers, so He will take care of His children.

Trusting God involves trusting Him to care for us. Jesus tells us to "seek first the kingdom of God and His righteousness" (Matt. 6:33).

As believers we must still work to meet our needs; we don't sit back and expect God to do it all. We work but we don't worry. We know that God will care for us.

> *Then He said to His disciples, "Therefore I say to you, do not worry about your life, what you will eat; nor about the body, what you will put on. Life is more than food, and the body is more than clothing."*
>
> *Luke 12:22–23*

Worry can be a time-consuming, almost obsessive, behavior. After all, every day brings new things to worry about! Worrying about every situation in life—whether big or small—will only drive us to distraction.

Not one problem is ever solved by worrying about it. In fact many problems get worse because worry is immobilizing; thus, no action is being taken to try to work through the dilemma. Worry can thwart the work of the kingdom.

Jesus has the perfect solution for worry. Instead of worrying, He invites us to put our faith and trust in God's provision and care. This can free us from the anxiety that is caused by worry.

This total trust doesn't mean that we should not have goals, plans, investments, and so on. It does mean, however, that for everything we should trust in God, putting Him first in our lives.

> *For God has not given us a spirit of fear, but of power and of love and of a sound mind.*
>
> *2 Timothy 1:7*

Those who worry are not trusting God. Worry can be a natural first reaction to an uncertain situation, but to persist in worry reveals a lack of trust that God is in charge.

Power helps us have strength of character and confidence in any situation. *Love* helps us graciously deal with difficult people. A *sound mind* helps us remain self-controlled and self-disciplined no matter what happens.

We can set aside our worry and replace it with these gifts from God.

Be anxious for nothing, but in everything by prayer and supplication, with thanksgiving, let your requests be made known to God; and the peace of God, which surpasses all understanding, will guard your hearts and minds through Christ Jesus.

Philippians 4:6–7

---

7 PRAYER STARTER

Worry is immobilizing Your child today, Lord. We know that we don't know the future and You do. We know that we need to trust You, so we bring our worries to You today, Lord, like a burden we cannot carry, and we ask that You take them . . .

RECOMMENDED RESOURCES :8

Clinton, Tim. *The Bible for Hope: Caring for People God's Way*. Thomas Nelson, 2007.

Clinton, Tim, Archibald D. Hart, and George Ohlschlager. *Caring for People God's Way: Personal and Emotional Issues, Addictions, Grief, and Trauma*. Thomas Nelson, 2006.

Clinton, Tim, and Gary Sibcy. *Why You Do the Things You Do: The Secret to Healthy Relationships*. Thomas Nelson, 2006.

Hart, Archibald D. *Adrenaline and Stress: The Exciting New Breakthrough That Helps You Overcome Stress Damage*. Thomas Nelson, 1995.

———. *The Anxiety Cure*. Thomas Nelson, 2001.

Leahy, Robert L. *The Worry Cure: Seven Steps to Stop Worry from Stopping You*. Three Rivers Press, 2006.

Websites

American Association of Christian Counselors (www.aacc.net)

Ecounseling (www.ecounseling.com)

Acknowledgments

Dr. Hawkins and I would like to say a special thank you to all involved in helping build a resource that we pray will be used by Christian leaders and people helpers all over the world to foster hope and healing for those who are hurting.

A note of deep appreciation goes to Robert Hosack at Baker Books for believing in the project and to Mary Wenger and Mary Suggs for their time in editing.

Likewise, we extend sincere gratitude to our AACC team who helped in the writing, editing, and research for this project:

Pat Springle, MA

Joshua Straub, PhD

Amy Feigel, MA, LMFT

Anthony Centore, PhD

George Ohlschlager, JD

Laura Faidley

We would also like to thank our wives, Julie and Peggy, and our families, for their love and support through the years. We could not enter into the work we do without you.

And to the entire AACC team and tens of thousands of pastors and Christian counselors who are literally entering into the darkness of the lives of hurting people, may this resource help you bring the light and hope of Jesus in every situation. To you we dedicate this series.

Notes

Abortion

1. B. Finer and S. K. Henshaw, "Disparities in Rates of Unintended Pregnancy in the United States, 1994 and 2001," *Perspectives on Sexual and Reproductive Health* 38, no. 2 (2006): 90–96.

2. R. K. Jones et al., "Abortion in the United States: Incidence and Access to Services, 2005," *Perspectives on Sexual and Reproductive Health* 40, no. 1 (2008): 6–16.

3. Ibid.

4. R. K. Jones, J. E. Darroch, and S. K. Henshaw, "Patterns in the Socioeconomic Characteristics of Women Obtaining Abortions in 2000–2001," *Perspectives on Sexual and Reproductive Health* 34, no. 5 (2002): 226–35.

5. S. Lou and M. Sajatovic, eds., *Encyclopedia of Women's Health* (New York: Springer, 2004), 523.

6. L. T. Stauss et al., *Abortion Surveillance: United States.* National Center for Chronic Disease Prevention and Health Promotion: Division of Reproductive Health, 53 (SS09) November 24, 2004.

Addictions

1. General alcohol information from National Center for Chronic Disease Prevention and Health Promotion; retrieved from http://www.cdc.gov/ncipc.

2. Ibid.

3. Ibid.

4. Traffic safety facts: 2007 data. Alcohol impaired driving. (2008). *National Highway Transportation and Safety Administration.* Retrieved from http://www.nhtsa.dot.gov.

5. Ibid.

6. Ibid.

7. Ibid.

8. H. C. Kung, D. L. Hoyert, J. Xu, and S. L. Murphy, "Deaths: Final Data for 2005," *CDC National Vital Statistics Report* 56, no. 10 (April 24, 2008), 10.

9. www.cdc.gov/alcohol.

10. Ibid.

Adultery

1. T. W. Smith, "American Sexual Behavior: Trends, Socio-Demographic Differences, and Risk Behavior," *General Social Survey (GSS) Topical Report No. 25* (University of Chicago: National Opinion Research Center, March 2006), 8.

2. Ibid.

Aging

1. Kung, Hoyert, Xu, and Murphy, "Deaths: Final Data for 2005," 2.

2. "Statistics," *US Administration on Aging*; retrieved from http://www.aoa.gov/AoARoot/Aging_Statistics/Profile/2008/3.aspx.

3. Ibid.

Anger

1. National Institute of Mental Health Press Office (June 5, 2006). "Intermittent Explosive Disorder Affects Up to 16 Million Americans," http://www.medicalnewstoday.com/articles/44628.php.

Burnout

1. American Psychological Association, "Stress a Major Health Problem in the U.S. Warns APA," APA Press Release: Washington, DC (October 24, 2007).

2. Ibid.

Depression

1. "Statistics," *National Institutes of Health* (2003).

2. Moring, M. "Depression: A Special Report," retrieved from http://www.christianitytoday .com.

3. Retrieved April 2009 from http://www. depression.com.

4. F. G. Slebus et al., "Work Ability in Sick-Listed Patients with Major Depressive Disorder, *Occupational Medicine* 58, no. 7 (2008), 475–79.

Divorce

1. U.S. Census Bureau and National Center for Health Statistics, as referenced in "U.S. Divorce Statistics" at Divorce Magazine.com, 2005; retrieved from http://www.divorcemag.com/sta tistics/statsUS.shtml.

2. Ibid.

3. Ibid.

4. Ibid.

Domestic Violence

1. Retrieved from http://www.abanet.org/ domviol/statistics.html.

2. Centers for Disease Control, "Intimate Partner Violence: Fact Sheet," at *Medicinenet.com*, 2003; retrieved from http://www.medicinenet .com/script/main/art.asp?articlekey=41728.

3. Ibid.

4. American Bar Association Commission on Domestic Violence, "Survey of Recent Statistics, 2005; retrieved from http://www.abanet .org/domviol/statistics.html.

5. "Domestic Violence," *Bureau of Justice Statistics*, 2005; retrieved from http://www.ojp.usdoj .gov/bjs/pub/pdf/ipvus.pdf

6. J. A. Gazmararian et al., "Violence and Reproductive Health: Current Knowledge and Future Research Directions," *Maternal and Child Health Journal* 4, no. 2 (2000): 79–84.

Eating Disorders

1. E. J. Cumella, *Eating Disorders: An Introduction.* Remuda Ranch, 2007; retrieved from http://www.remudaranch.com.

2. Ibid., para. 14.

3. Ibid., para. 15.

4. S. Ice, "Statistics: Eating Disorders," Coalition for Research, Policy, and Action; retrieved from http://www.eatingdisorderscoalition.org/ reports/statistics.html (2006).

5. Ibid.

6. Ibid.

7. National Eating Disorders Association, 1995; retrieved from http://www.nationaleating disorders.org.

Fear and Anxiety

1. S. J. Bishop, "Trait Anxiety and Impoverished Prefrontal Control of Attention," *Nature Neuroscience* 12 (2008), 92–98.

Loneliness

1. S. Vendantam, "Social Isolation Growing in U.S., Study Says," *Washington Post*; retrieved from http://www.washingtonpost.com/wp-dyn/ content/article/2006/06/22/AR2006062201763. html (2006).

Mental Disorder

1. *National Institute of Mental Health,* "Mental Health Topics," retrieved from http://www.nimh .nih.gov/health/topics/index.shtml.

2. Ibid.

3. Ibid.

4. K. R. Merikangas et al., "The Impact of Comorbidity of Mental and Physical Conditions on Role Disability in the U.S. Adult Population," *Archives of General Psychiatry* 64, no. 10 (October 2007), 1180-88.

Money Crisis

1. Motley Fool's Credit Center; retrieved from http://www.fool.com.

2. *USA Today*; retrieved from http://www.usa today.com/money/markets/2008-12-31-stocks-2008_N.htm (Dec. 31, 2008).

3. Ibid.

Pain and Chronic Pain

1. Corrie ten Boom, *The Hiding Place* (Grand Rapids: Chosen, 1971).

2. H. G. Koenig, "Lessons Learned at Duke's Center for Spirituality, Theology, and Health," at Ecounseling.com, 2004; retrieved from http:// www.ecounseling.com/articles/606.

Parenting

1. B. Ellis and J. Nigg, "Parenting Practices and Attention-Deficit/Hperactivity Disorder: New Findings Suggest Partial Specificity of Effects," *The Journal of the American Academy of Child and Adolescent Psychiatry* (2008).

2. T. Grall, *Custodial Mothers and Fathers and Their Child Support: 2005* (U.S. Census Bureau, U.S. Department of Commerce, 2007); retrieved from http://singleparents.about.com/ od/legalissues/p/portrait.htm.

Perfectionism

1. "Cosmetic Plastic Surgery Research: 2001–2006"; retrieved from http://www.cos

meticplastic surgerystatistics.com/statistics.html #2007–NEWS.

2 Ibid.

Pornography

1. Pornography statistics from Family Safe Media, 2006; retrieved from http://familysafeme dia.com/pornography_statistics.html#anchor6.

2. Ibid.

3. Ibid.

4. Ibid.

Prejudice

1. Focus on the Family; retrieved from http://www.focusonyourchild.com.

Premarital Sex

1. Centers for Disease Control; retrieved from www.cdc.gov/HealthyYouth/yrbs/slides/yrbs07_sexual_risk_behaviors.ppt.

2. Ibid.

3. Ibid.

Sexual Abuse in Childhood

1. "Teen Girls Stories of Sex Trafficking in U.S.," *ABC News*; retrieved from http://abcnews .go.com/Primetime/story?id=1596778 (Feb. 9, 2006).

2. J. Hopper, "Statistics"; retrieved from http://www.jimhopper.com/abstats/#boys (Oct. 6, 2008).

3. "Sexual Violence Prevention," Department of Health and Human Services: Centers for Disease Control and Prevention, 2004; retrieved from http://www.cdc.gov/ncipc/dvp/SV/default.htm.

Singleness

1. Census data, retrieved from http://www .census.gov.

2. Ibid.

Stress

1. S. Martin, "Money Is the Top Stressor for Americans," *Monitor on Psychology* 39, no. 11 (2008). American Psychological Association; retrieved from http://www.apa.org/moni tor/2008/12/money.html.

2. Ibid.

3. "Stress at Work," Department of Health and Human Services: Centers for Disease Control and Prevention; retrieved from http://www .cdc.gov/niosh/stresswk.html.

4. Ibid.

Suicide

1. B. Shain and the Committee on Adolescence, "Suicide and Suicide Attempts in Adolescents," *Pediatrics* 120, no. 3 (September 2007): 669–76.

2. Mental Health America; retrieved from http://www.nmha.org/go/get-info.

3. "National Hospital Ambulatory Medical Care Survey: 2006 Emergency Department Summary," National Center for Health Statistics: Self-Inflicted Injury/Suicide; retrieved from http://www.cdc.gov/nchs/fastats/suicide.htm.

4. "Fact Sheets," American Association of Suicidology; retrieved from http://www.suicidology .org.

5. "Deaths: Final Data for 2005," National Center for Health Statistics: Self-Inflicted Injury/Suicide; retrieved from http://www.cdc .gov/nchs/fastats/suicide.htm.

Trauma

1. "Troops Prepare to Readjust to Civilian Life," *Chicago Tribune* (Dec. 7, 2008).

THE QUICK-REFERENCE GUIDES

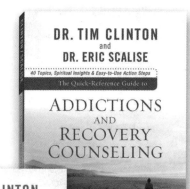

The newest addition to the popular Quick-Reference Guide collection, *The Quick-Reference Guide to Addictions and Recovery Counseling* focuses on the widespread problem of addictions of all kinds. Each of the forty topics covered follows a helpful eight-part outline and identifies (1) typical symptoms and patterns, (2) definitions and key thoughts, (3) questions to ask, (4) directions for the conversation, (5) action steps, (6) biblical insights, (7) prayer starters, and (8) recommended resources.

The Quick-Reference Guide to Counseling on Money, Finances & Relationships focuses on the ever-growing need for sound counsel on financial issues. It is an A–Z guide for assisting people-helpers, pastors, and professional counselors for formal and informal counseling situations.

For pastors, counselors, and everyday believers, *The Quick-Reference Guide to Counseling Women* will be a unique and welcome aid to bring hope, life, and freedom to women in need.

Providing answers on issues such as sexuality, drugs and alcohol, and parent-adolescent relationships, *The-Quick Reference Guide to Counseling Teenagers* prepares those in the position to advise teens to counsel amidst the rapidly changing youth culture.